Student Success with Less Stress

How Students Can Excel
How Parents Can Help

CARLTON R.V. WITTE

BALBOA.PRESS
A DIVISION OF HAY HOUSE

Balboa Press books may be ordered through booksellers or by contacting:

Balboa Press
A Division of Hay House
1663 Liberty Drive
Bloomington, IN 47403
www.balboapress.com
1 (877) 407-4847

Because of the dynamic nature of the Internet, any web addresses or links contained in this book may have changed since publication and may no longer be valid. The views expressed in this work are solely those of the author and do not necessarily reflect the views of the publisher, and the publisher hereby disclaims any responsibility for them.

The author of this book does not dispense medical advice or prescribe the use of any technique as a form of treatment for physical, emotional, or medical problems without the advice of a physician, either directly or indirectly. The intent of the author is only to offer information of a general nature to help you in your quest for emotional and spiritual well-being. In the event you use any of the information in this book for yourself, which is your constitutional right, the author and the publisher assume no responsibility for your actions.

Any people depicted in stock imagery provided by Getty Images are models, and such images are being used for illustrative purposes only. Certain stock imagery © Getty Images.

Scripture quotations marked NKJV are taken from the New King James Version. Copyright © 1982 by Thomas Nelson, Inc. Used by permission. All rights reserved.

Print information available on the last page.

ISBN: 978-1-9822-3960-2 (sc)
ISBN: 978-1-9822-3961-9 (e)

Library of Congress Control Number: 2019920011

Balboa Press rev. date: 12/11/2019

Acknowledgments

With sincere appreciation to my reviewers and editors, my daughter Michelle Lewis; and to my dear wife, Joyce who has patiently supported me through many years of research and writing. I acknowledge my five children, 11 grandchildren, and all my special needs children and their families, who were my inspiration. It is my sincere hope that by bringing the wisdom of others into one book it will help to make many lives joyful and successful.

Contents

PART TWO
Parents' Guide

Preface

"Teens across the U.S.A. are feeling such high levels of stress that it negatively affects every aspect of their lives," states the American Psychological Association (APA). Based on their 2018 study, "Stress in America," one-quarter of the students surveyed say they experience "extreme stress" during the school year. Youth in the age bracket of 13 to 21 (Generation Z) seem to experience more physical and emotional symptoms, such as depression or anxiety triggered by stress than reported by millennials, Generation X, and baby boomers.

Some psychologists, such as Michael Bradley from Feasterville, PA, states that "hard numbers tell us kids are more anxious and depressed than they have ever been." Based on over 40 years of experience as a school psychologist for Delaware County Youth Detention Center in PA, Lew Meltzer would agree. Meltzer reported to me that over the years, he has seen a significant increase in a young person's ability to constructively deal with ordinary life events, both in and out of school.

One high school junior told me, "My friends and I often speak to one another about how stressed out we are. Grades, college entrance examinations, the pressure to win, to meet expectations, combined with a heavy workload, does not leave much time for us to be teenagers."

Negative stress often effects a person's ability to manage time, home and school responsibilities. Stress also adversely affects physical, sleep, eating, and social patterns. Our health, happiness, vitality, and success depend on the proper balance of mental, physical, emotional, and spiritual well-being. When one or more of these is strained, sometimes caused by stress or anxiety, we are thrown off balance.

We can relate stress in children and young adults to society, world events, modern technology, expectations for school and extracurricular performance, and stressful for those seeking admission to colleges and universities. At home, students may experience family discord or violence, divorce, illness, the death of a family member, or a change in living conditions. Socially, youth can experience peer ridicule, bullying, fear of not being accepted, liked or popular, or not being competitive enough in sports or academics. Emotion or physical health issues can also cause stress. Over-extension is a common stressor for today's students in our society. The stress inducers that students experience in school may include assignments, new material, deadlines, fear of poor grades, excessive workload, peer pressure, and finances. High school students worry about what they will do after graduation. "What career field should I go in to?" "How do I prepare for life after high school?" "Do I need a college education, and if so, what college and major should I pursue?" "What do I need to do to prepare for college?" "How do I get accepted, and once there will I be ready for it?"

Many students get discouraged because they think they can't make excellent grades. There are countless examples of bright people who struggled in school. There are also just as many stories of average to below-average students who excelled in their schoolwork and who went on to be successful in their chosen professions. So, if intelligence is not always the key to making top grades (although being smart does not hurt), then what is the secret to doing well in school and doing so with less stress? It doesn't mean just studying harder rather knowing HOW to learn faster and better. It also means learning to use your natural mental capacity more efficiently.

When we refer to "school," we often use the word "education." In reality, "education" involves so much more than what is taught in school. Many schools do not teach or at least spend minimal time on subjects that result in true success and happiness in life. Instead, they focus on course "content." That is, academic subjects that include math formulas, historical places and dates, chemistry equations, the names of the major rivers of the world, and so on. Then they test to see how much has been remembered. As time goes by, we remember little of what was taught. Much of what we are exposed to in school we will never even use. Not that academics are unnecessary.

Basic math principles, writing skills, history, government, sociology, language arts, health, just to name a few, are important. What many schools do not teach are specific "critical skills" essential for success. SECTIONS A, B, and C will help you form the "critical skills" necessary to be successful not just in school, but in life. In other words, to be genuinely "educated."

Colleges and employers report that many high school graduates are lacking skills required to be successful in college and the job market. What is missing? Skills often referred to as "critical or soft skills." Examples include self-management, communication, leadership, time management, teamwork, human relations.

Families and the community play a significant role in the successful education of children. It is not just the teacher's responsibility. According to Anne T. Henderson and Nancy Berla who wrote *A New Generation of Evidence: The Family is Critical to Student Achievement,* "parent involvement produces higher grades and test scores, better attendance and homework completed, more positive attitudes towards school, higher graduation rates, and increased enrollment in post-high school education."

***Student Success with Less Stress* provides many practical tools to help students excel academically and maintain a life balance resulting in increased opportunity for satisfaction, happiness, and success, both in school and out of school. You need not spend years searching for well-proven strategies to form a solid foundation for an education in life. I have done the research and work for you. All you must do is read and apply the principles provided and a path to academic and life success (with less stress) lies ahead.**

Introduction

PART ONE is directed towards the student. To get the most from the guidance provided in the book, look through the Table of Contents (if you have not already done so) and the "Overview" of PARTS ONE and TWO following this part of the Introduction.

Don't feel like you must read all the chapters in a few sittings. In fact, I do not recommend it. When you see a subject that is of interest, turn to that chapter and read through it. Hi-light points that you feel can be of help. Read a few pages at a time. Think about what you read! Ask yourself how you are currently applying the principles described and how you might better use them in your daily life. Older students might discuss topics with parents, adults or friends. Sections A and B should be read in their entirety. I say this because they provide essential tools for building a solid foundation for success in life. I recognize that many young people today prefer to listen to podcasts or watch videos. Unfortunately, this is a book, so it must be read. Sorry about that.

Throughout the chapters, I present many TIPS on the topics presented in each section. When the guidelines are followed conscientiously and consistently, students will significantly increase the odds of academic, social, life, and professional success. Please accept my sincere best wishes for a very successful and enjoyable educational experience.

PART TWO is for parents. When I use the terms "parents" I am referring to any adult who has responsibility for the raising, caring, and influence of a child or children. The guidance can also be of use to adults who can influence a child's psychological and emotional development, even though they may not be the primary caregiver.

Overview of PART ONE
Students' Guide

SECTION A. Chapter 1 defines the concerns and questions that many adolescents have and asks, "Can they be successful and happy and do so with less stress?" Chapters 2 and 3 provide the answer as to why we have difficulty changing the factors that contribute to stress and increase the chances of not achieving what we want out of life.

SECTIONS B and C provide dynamic life strategies that, if conscientiously followed, will virtually guarantee success and happiness.

SECTION D, Chapters 11 through 19, describe established, time-proven study and learning strategies that make honor students. Chapter 20 explains the highly effective study and learning strategies that are not commonly taught in our school system.

SECTION E presents strategies that many students do not use, yet those that do find extremely useful not just in making good grades, but in becoming honor students.

SECTION F addresses potential emotional and social issues that can sabotage a young person's desires for success and happiness in life. Guidance is provided on what can be done to respond to these challenges.

SECTION G addresses options that students must consider after graduation from high school. Included are: "Choosing a Career," "College or Not?" the "Pros and Cons of a Gap Year," and guidance on "The College Search and Admission Process." Chapter 26 provides some final words on what it takes to lead a successful and happy life.

Overview of PART TWO
Parents' Guide

SECTION H provides suggestions for parents/guardians and how they can best help the students in their lives to maximize opportunities for success in and out of school. Subjects include self-discipline, family harmony, and assisting with time management and homework.

SECTION I addresses learning disabilities and differences and offers guidance on how to access school special-needs programs.

SECTION J provides guidance on how parents can help their children make informed decisions, to include making career choices, and considerations whether a college education is in their best interest. For the college search and admission process, Chapter 34C. complements Chapter 25 D. in the "Students' Guide." Chapter 35 describes options on how to help pay for college.

SECTION K examines our current education system and why it is failing our students. Tony Wagner and Ted Dintersmith, who authored *Most Likely to Succeed* (2015), reported that "Despite our enormous investment in education, the majority of our students lack the skills necessary to get a good job, be an informed citizen; or, in some way that defies crisp definition, be a good and happy person." They go on to reference a Gallop poll that found many business leaders think that students are ill-prepared for success in the workplace. This was reported in *American Call for Higher Education*, the Lumina Foundation Study of American Public Opinion on Higher Education (February 2013). Chapter 39 reviews what we can learn from the education systems in other countries, the relationship of academic and social philosophies today and the effects those philosophies are having on a student's achievements, attitudes, and mental health. Alternative programs are also briefly described. Suggestions are provided as to what parents, school officials, and legislatures can do to address our educational challenges.

If what you're doing as a parent/guardian is working for you, then keep doing it! If on the other hand, you are seeking new or additional strategies to help achieve what you want for your student, then read on— and my sincere wishes for a pleasurable experience in mentoring your student.

Four appendices provide many principles for success in summarized form:

Appendix A lists the personal attitudes, interpersonal skills, and work habits that are typical of students who are not only honor students but also successful in other endeavors.

Appendix B is a chart titled "Drive Your Car (and Life) to Success." Many of the analogies presented in this book compare success principles to driving a car. This chart is a summary of the parallels, plus a few more.

Appendix C lists affirmations that supplement the guidance presented in Chapter 20. Affirmations impress upon the subconscious mind positive statements that, when correctly used, can be a powerful tool for achieving success and for improving one's life.

Appendix D lists the success principles from one of the most successful persons that ever lived in America, Benjamin Franklin.

Although I have tried hard to provide the essential components necessary for school and life success, it would be impossible to address everything. When more detail is desired than is presented in this book, readers can consult the References and Resources section.

PART ONE

Students' Guide

Chance favors the prepared mind.
Louis Pasteur

SECTION A
Do You Know Where You Are Going?

Destiny is not a matter of chance; it is a matter of choice.
It is not a thing to be waited for: it is a thing to be achieved.
William Jennings Bryan

Chapter 1
What Do You Want?

What does success mean? What is stress? Let's examine the word "success" first. There are many definitions: accomplishing goals, being knowledgeable in a field, being able to get things done, creating, being an effective leader, service to others. The Oxford Dictionary defines success as, "The accomplishment of an aim or purpose." These are just a few ways that some define "success." Many define success as the attainment of self-satisfaction and happiness. Although this book will provide many tips on how a person can be satisfied and happy, the primary focus is on how you can be a top student. Would this give you satisfaction and happiness? I am sure it would go a long way to doing that.

What is stress and how is it distinguished from anxiety and depression?

Before we get into learning how to deal with stress, let's first look at what stress is. Stress in life is inevitable. In fact, some stress is natural and necessary. Mostly, it is the body's physiological response to real or perceived threats. Most readers have probably heard of the term "burst of adrenaline." When we encounter an emergency or a situation in which we need a spurt of energy, the sympathetic nervous system gives us what we need. Your body reacts to the situation with such symptoms as quickened breathing, tightening of muscles, and rapid heart rate.

What causes stress in one person may not cause stress in another. Symptoms vary from person to person and may include feeling overwhelmed, agitation, difficulty relaxing or sleeping, loss of energy, upset stomach, tense muscles, nervousness, headache, worry, difficulty focusing, forgetfulness, acid reflux, impaired judgment, and procrastination. Feelings of stress are normal when students worry about tests, homework, social/peer relations, or striving to satisfy the expectations of parents, coaches, and teachers. Limited amounts of stress are not severe and do not last long. If they do, self-doubt and fear can result, leading to more severe conditions termed "anxiety disorders."

The American Psychological Association (APA) describes stress as a "feeling of being overwhelmed, worried, or run down," which is caused by minor or major situations. Stress is a completely normal emotional response to life's most difficult and minor situations. Anxiety, on the other hand, is a serious mental health issue that goes beyond feeling stressed. The APA explains that "people with anxiety disorders usually have recurring intrusive thoughts or concerns." In other words, your stress is getting to the point that it is interfering with your daily life, which often becomes evident to others. Anxiety can elicit feelings of fear, worry, unease, frustration, irritability, and anger. Anxiety disorders can have severe psychological and physical responses, which have negative consequences on success in school and in life. If such feelings last for weeks, it may be time to seek professional help.

According to WebMD, half of the people who are depressed exhibit symptoms of anxiety. Symptoms associated with both anxiety and depression are low self-esteem, not being able to sleep, either losing or gaining weight, loss of interest in general activities, and physical symptoms like headaches, or digestion problems that have no apparent explanation or cause. The Anxiety and Depression Association of America states that depression can include those symptoms of anxiety plus extreme sadness, pessimism, hopelessness, and constant fatigue. The risk of suicide is higher for those experiencing prolonged anxiety or depression.

According to the Mayo Clinic, treatment can involve any one or more of several therapies, to include medication, psychotherapy, lifestyle changes, and/or relaxing strategies. Do not try to self-diagnose or treat yourself! Doing so is not productive and can often make things worse.

So, the bottom line is, we want to be happy and successful, and do so with minimal stress. Is this possible? Yes. The following chapters

4

will provide guidelines, if practiced and faithfully followed, that that will ensure a foundation for success (with less stress), not just in school, but in life outside of school as well.

Before one begins a journey, a destination must be determined. If we do not know where we are going, how are we going to get there? People will often plan a vacation yet will not plan their lives. Can you imagine packing your bags, loading up the car, then heading out and not knowing where you are going, much less not knowing what route you will be taking? Maybe not even checking their vehicle to make sure it is tuned up and has fuel? When it comes to our lives, that is often what we do. If you manage school, your personal life, and career without a clear picture in your mind of where you are going, then how can you get "there"? So, to avoid wasted time, failures, and disappointments, ask yourself, "What do I want?" Of course, you may not yet know what you want as a career, but you can identify what grade you want on your next test or paper, grade point average goal, class standing, athletic or extracurricular desires, social wants, family, and peer relations, etc.

Since this book is primarily about school success, start by asking yourself what you want out of school. What do you want to learn? Why? Do you want good grades? How good? Why? Do you have a career goal in mind? School is but a small part of a person's life. Learning, on the other hand, is a lifelong process. To address just classroom strategies would be falling short of a "how to" book on making good grades. Therefore, this book goes beyond helping you answer concerns only about school. After all, young people have other interests besides just school.

What are some questions young people ask themselves that cause them concern and stress or anxiety?

Am I OK?
How do I make friends?
How can I be happy?
How do I overcome problems?
How can I deal with my stress?
What is life all about, and what do I want out of life?

What are my goals, and how do I achieve them?

To the above, add your own questions that you feel contribute to your concerns and stress. Your parents/guardians try to respond to these questions and concerns by providing counsel, comfort, and encouragement. Knowing that we live in a competitive world, they strive to provide their children with the tools to help them not only to cope but also to excel. This is understandable, as the parent's desire is for their children to be successful, and to be successful, they know their child must learn to be competitive. We cannot change the fact that we live in a competitive world. To be competitive is OK, but not to the point that it creates unhealthy stress, that would be counter-productive.

Our education system promotes competition. We pit student against student with class ranks, comparing them with one another through class performance, test scores, and competitive extracurricular activities. Does such competitiveness result in stress? Certainly. But that's not all bad unless it becomes too stressful. Too much tension causes unhappiness and can result in the lack of achievement. Is it possible for young people to deal with the expectations placed on them, yet do well in school and with minimal stress and ultimately maximize the opportunity for happiness? This book strives to put things in perspective. It will not only answer questions students have for improved learning and better grades, it will also provide guidance that can increase happiness and success with reduced chances of unhealthy stress. As stated in the Introduction, the book is divided in to two parts. Part I is directed to students and Part II for parents and guardians. This does not mean you cannot read, or at least skim through both parts focusing on the sections that most pertain to you at the time. I encourage you to discuss with your parent's subjects that you may have questions or concern. Open, trusting dialogue with parents, guardians, and other adults in your life can greatly help you navigate the challenges of school and life.

Chapter 2
Why Aren't You Getting What You Want?

No matter what grade in school you are in, our education system places much emphasis on passing tests and making good grades. Test scores and good grades seem to be paramount as indicators of past and future success. Although this may right for some, it is not so for all. Some students can make good grades or work up to their potential with little effort. Others make good grades, but with much effort. Many cannot make good grades regardless of how hard they work. Then there are those who make poor grades, or at least not work to their potential because they just cannot motivate themselves to study or know how to study effectively. I seriously doubt that many wish to make poor grades, and if they do, then there are underlying emotional or psychological issues that must be resolved before he/she will be able to move on, both in school and in life. Because school grades are used as a measure for academic progress, and because how well they do in school often affects the self-esteem of children, then adults have a responsibility to help children to achieve academic (and life) success. To do this, adults can help set the foundation for children when they are young. Then, as they get older, children can continue to improve with encouragement, coaching, and support.

When it comes to school, many students often ask.
Why can't I do better in school?
Why can't I motivate myself?
Why can't I understand the material?
Why can't I remember the information during the exam?
Why do I procrastinate?
Aren't I smart?
Why do I have to take subjects that I am not interested in or may apply to my future?
Is there a more natural way for me to learn?

Why do I hate school?

Will I be a success in life?

Will I be happy?

How can I meet the expectations of parents, school, and society without being stressed?

Countless publications provide advice on how to make good grades. Although much of the guidance is sound, the authors often miss a crucial ingredient—motivation. Many concerned parents offer their children "how-to" books, pamphlets, papers, or online study and learning techniques—only to have them ignored. Why? Because the children's motivation is just not strong enough. This is not to suggest that students do not want to make good grades. It just means that their motivation is not strong enough to want to change the way they approach studying.

James Prochaska, PhD, professor of psychiatry at the University of Rhode Island, identified four stages that people go through to make changes in their lives. He, together with Carlos Di Climents and John Narcross in their book Changing for Good, refers to these stages as "pre-contemplation," or resisting change; "contemplation," or weighing the pros and cons; "action," or exercising the willpower to make the change, and "maintenance," or using willpower to sustain the change. "Some people," explains Prochaska, "are chronic pre-contemplators and contemplators. They never get to the 'action' stage". And even if they do get to the point of actually wanting to change, the question remains, "How do they initiate change, and once done, how is it maintained?"

How to change

Regardless of how much we may want something, the reason we often cannot get started is that we have developed mental attitudes that control our actions. We may consciously desire to study better, stop smoking, lose weight, get more exercise, or whatever, but we just cannot seem to get started, and when we do, we often give up before reaching our goal. Why? Because we have developed habits that are so deeply ingrained that our conscious mind cannot easily overcome them. Our subconscious is controlling us. Keep in mind that the subconscious mind does not think. Thinking is left to the conscious mind. However, the conscious mind can influence the subconscious, if and only if, we take steps to alter or change the subconscious mind. Throughout history, great philosophers, wise men, and leaders have agreed that what we think about is what we become. Known as a major influence on American psychology, William James said, "The greatest discovery of my generation is that human beings can alter their lives by altering their attitude of mind." James also said, "If you wish to be learned, you will be learned, if you wish to be rich you will be rich, if you wish to be good, you will be good - only you must really wish them and wish them exclusively."

The Italian psychologist Roberto Assagioli wrote, "Fundamental among man's inner powers is the tremendous unrealized potency of man's own will." The dictionary defines willpower as "control of one's impulses and actions." The key word here is "control." But how do we gain "control" so that we can get what we want? Understanding why we think the way we do and taking steps to use the power of our minds will go a long way to getting to the "action" stage. That will help us take control of our lives, rather than being victim to past experiences and learned behaviors that keep us from getting what we want.

The formula to get what you want is simple.

Decide what you want.
Set achievable goals.
Have a purpose.
Have a plan to achieve your goals and purpose.
Don't give up

Sounds simple enough. But if it is so easy, why do so many fail at achieving what they desire? There may be many reasons, but one of the main reasons is that they do not know how. The guidance provided in this book will provide insight and answers to how to "alter your attitude of mind" so that you can achieve whatever you choose in life, to include being an honor student, and so much more.

Chapter 3
How to Get What You Want?

Basic Principles for Success

Earl Nightingale, the well-known author motivational speaker on character development and success principles, said in his publication *Lead the Field*, "Our environment, the world in which we live and work, is a mirror of our attitudes and expectations." Nightingale also said that "success or failure is not a matter of luck, or the breaks, or whom you know—or many of the other tiresome myths and clichés by which the ignorant tend to excuse themselves. It is a matter of following a commonsense paradigm of rules—guidelines anyone can follow."

There are many accounts in history of people who overcame challenges to gain success. Consider these well-known people:

He failed every subject in 8th grade and was socially awkward—Charles Schultz, the creator of the famous comic strip Peanuts.

He suffered from depression, failed at business early in his career, grieved over the loss of his mother when he was 9, and the loss of a sister, and two sons ages 4 and 11. He became one of the most successful and beloved presidents of the United States—Abraham Lincoln.

Considered a failure by friends when he was 21, yet his persistence and belief in himself allowed him to invent devices that greatly influenced the world. Included among his inventions were the light bulb, the phonograph, and the motion picture camera—Thomas Edison.

As a young girl, she was described by her friends as shy and inadequate but became one of the most influential and admired First Ladies in American history—Eleanor Roosevelt.

His teachers called him a failure, yet Tony Blair became Prime Minister of the United Kingdom.

He struggled with a learning disability, yet Tom Cruise became a famous American actor.

Considered one of the brightest minds in history, he did not speak until he was 4, and teachers thought him lazy—Albert Einstein.

He suffers from dyslexia, struggled in school, and did poorly on standardized tests. Today he is one of the most successful business tycoons in the world—Richard Branson.

Twice rejected by the University of Southern California, he became the most successful filmmakers of all time—Steven Spielberg.

One of my favorite heroes who overcame extreme challenges is Sean Stephenson. He has a condition called osteogenesis, also known as brittle bone disease. Sean suffered over 200 bone fractures by the time he was 18 and grew to only three feet tall. Yet Sean became a psychotherapist, worked as presidential liaison for President Bill Clinton, lectures throughout the world, and has authored two books entitled: *How You Can Succeed: Transforming Dreams Into Reality* (2001), and *Get Off Your Buts: How to End Self-Sabotage & Stand Up For Yourself* (2009), coauthored with well-known motivational psychologist Anthony Robbins. "It isn't our problems that hold us back," says Stephenson. "It's how we handle those problems."

In his worldwide best-seller *Think and Grow Rich*, Napoleon Hill revealed the secret of successful people. Hill made his conclusion after 29 years of research and interviews with hundreds of people. More recently, in the number one New York Times best-seller, *The Purpose Driven Life*, Rick Warren made many of the same conclusions, only from a more spiritual perspective. My purpose in this book is to present basic success principles as espoused by those who have achieved success and happiness in life, with students specifically in mind.

"Soft skills" distinguish successful people from unsuccessful people, regardless of their physical, mental or environmental challenges. According to the National Association of Colleges and Employers often what is missing is having strong "soft skills." What are "soft skills?" They are the skills that define how you relate to others, school, work and life. Sometimes they are called "social skills" or "people skills." Communication, character traits, and attitudes are examples. What is important about people who have mastered "soft skills" is they learned to control their lives rather than allow circumstances to control them. Persons with well-grounded "soft skills" attributes accept themselves, regardless of their strengths and weaknesses, and are committed to high values. They seek self-improvement by continual learning and apply self-management skills and success strategies. They do not allow their pride to interfere with learning and personal growth. SECTIONS B and C list and describe the attributes necessary for success in school and beyond and with less stress.

In contrast, "hard skills" is having knowledge of a subject. It is the "hard skills" that are primarily (but not exclusively) taught in school. Certainly, they are essential to success. However, the most likely to succeed are those who have mastered and use "soft skills" in conjunction with the knowledge learned to master "hard skills."

TIPS
To Apply "The Secrets Revealed," To Daily Life

Believe. You can achieve your dreams and goals, but just don't just believe; believe with passion! Think you can't and you won't. Believe you can, and you probably will. Louise L. Hay, well-known lecturer and author, explains that we all have the inner power to reach our full potential. Hay has written many books on the subject, but for starters you may wish to check out *The Power Is Within You*. The title says it all. Many of us have desires. But we rarely realize our desires because we miss a few critical components.

Assess. Honestly assess your strengths and weaknesses. Give focus on your strengths and try to shore up your weaknesses.

Learn. The more you know, the fuller your life will be. Practice the principles provided in this book. Seek educational opportunities. Learn from others. Read! Watch educational programs. The more you know, the more value you will be to yourself and to others. Do what you love, and success will follow.

Develop a strong character: Character traits count. Do this by always being honest and doing what you know is right. Tap into your spirituality. Appreciate life's blessings. Show charity and kindness to others. Find the surrounding good. Do your part without being asked. Listen more and talk less. Take responsibility for what you do and what you do not do. No excuses. No blaming. Get rid of thoughts and words such as "can't" and "won't," and replace them with "can" and "will." Don't let others steal your dream. Develop the skills and traits for success and happiness, which is explained in Chapter 9.

Plan & Prioritize. Set goals for yourself. To achieve your goals, you must have a plan. In other words, your goals tell you what you want; your plan shows you "how" and "when." Do the most important things first. Prioritize your daily tasks and just do them. Goals without a plan are but dreams, and dreams are unrealized goals.

Persistence. Don't give up on yourself. Give credit for progress yet allowance for failures. Strive for progress, not perfection.

Ask for help and guidance. Find a mentor or coach. The most powerful letter in the English language has only three letters: A-S-K. You might be surprised at how many are willing to help. But when turned down, don't be discouraged, just ask again. One thing is for sure: If you don't ask, the answer is a guaranteed "no.

Be involved. You have heard the term, "Practice makes perfect." So, to be the "best you can be" (to quote the U.S. Army slogan), it is not only essential to be aware of the success principles presented in this book, it is necessary to use them. One of the most effective ways is to be involved. If not already, seriously think about joining a youth group that promotes the traits and skills presented in the book. Scouting, 4-H, Future Farmers of America, church youth groups, school clubs, and athletic teams are valuable resources that can help teach you essential life skills and can reinforce the success principles contained herein.

Have fun on the journey: There is a saying there is as much fun on the journey as there is in reaching the end of the trip. There is satisfaction in knowing you are headed toward achieving your desired goals. The steps taken towards achieving your goals takes up most of your time, so you might as well enjoy the ride.

I am not going to wish you "luck" because "luck," as Nightingale stated, has nothing to do with achieving. "Choice," on the other hand, has everything to do with it. Choose it, and it will be yours for the taking. What does all this have to do with getting better grades? Regarding schoolwork, the first step is to acknowledge that you want to make good grades. Visualize getting exam papers back with an "A" written at the top of the page. Sense the good feeling you would have about receiving that grade. Start your journey to academic success with a positive mental attitude. Many confuse willpower with self-denial. For example, how do most people make New Year's resolutions? By stating: "I will make better grades," "I will lose weight," "I will stop procrastinating," etc. These are okay, but these resolutions state what we desire, but do not state how they are to be achieved. If combined with positive action, resolutions would be more powerful. For example, "I will lose weight by taking a daily walk with my dog." This combines the resolution of what we want with an action. The best resolutions also intertwine the action with an incentive that is pleasurable. In other words, the walk can be enjoyable and help one to lose weight. In contrast, if the resolution states, "I will lose weight by dieting," and if you don't like to diet, the odds of giving up before the goal is achieved is much greater.

Avoid focusing on the negative, such as how difficult or boring something is. Rather, focus on the positive. There is always something positive one can focus on, regardless of how challenging the task may be. For example, thinking about the rewards that will be gained upon completion of the task, or of the things that can be learned during the process, can help make the process much more palatable. When we focus on the positive, the incentive becomes more powerful with chances of success much greater. Focus on the positive results rather than the challenges of the process. Saying to oneself, "I will read this chapter, but I don't want to do it. I would rather watch TV," provides less of an incentive than, "I am reviewing this chapter instead of watching the TV program because it will help me get a better grade, and I can see myself getting an 'A' on this test." Note that the first example includes the negative words, "but I don't want…," nor does it state a reward for the effort. The second example affirms the reward…" because it will help me get a better grade." The fact that it states, "I can see myself getting an 'A' on this test" helps to reinforce the affirmation.

In the following chapters, I will provide more actions you can take to help get what you want. A good strategy is to write your desire on a 3-by-5 card or something similar and post it in your room where you can plainly see it. This little trick will help remind you of your goal and embed it in your subconscious mind. You will be surprised how you act to achieve what you want.

SECTION B
Steps to Overcome Any Challenge

Change your thoughts and you change your world.
Norman Vincent Peale

Chapter 4
The Miracle of Goal Setting or Keeping Your Eye on the Road

Let's go on a road trip. Where do you want to go? How are we going to get there? When do you want to go? I find it interesting that we humans will ask and answer these questions when we wish to go someplace, but we will not do so when planning our lives. To plan a trip, we decide where we want to go. This is the same as having a goal. A goal is the desired result that a person sets for him or herself. In other words, goals tell us "what" we want. They point us in the direction we want to go. With goals, we create our future

Unfortunately, many confuse "goals" with "tasks." Just as we prepare our car for our road trip, it has nothing to do with what direction we will be heading. The car doesn't care; it just needs to be taken care of. Shopping, mowing the lawn, picking up a messy room are "tasks," not "goals." What's the difference? "Tasks" are things that need to be completed and are usually assigned and routine. They have little to do with contributing to our dreams and visions for the future. It has been repeatedly demonstrated that people who have goals are more successful than those without them. Could it be that those without goals do not know where they are going?

TIPS
To Reach Your Goals

Follow these steps to increase your odds of reaching any goal you set for yourself.

Goals must be realistic and achievable. This is the key to effective goal making. To set a goal of graduating from high school at age 13 may be a bit of a stretch, and for most, unrealistic. On the other hand, to set a goal to be invited to take a few AP courses while a sophomore or junior is realistic, and for some achievable.

Goals must be specific and written. People who have set goals that are specific and written are generally more successful than those who have goals but did not make them explicit nor have them in writing. In 1950, the famous success guru, Earl Nightingale, stated in a presentation *The Strangest Secret,* "Of 100 people who at the age of 25 had a desire to be a success in life, by the age of 65 only one would be rich, four would be financially independent, five would still be working, and 64 would be broke." How could this happen? In answering this question, Nightingale reveals part of the secret, which is no real secret at all. The people who failed to achieve the success they wanted in life had developed no real purpose for their lives. They also had no or weakly developed goals.

To go on a road trip, you should first know where you want to go. Next, you figure out "how" you are going to get there. You think about and decide on the mode of transportation, route, time, expenses, etc. Imagine what would happen if you began your trip without knowing where you were going, or not knowing how to get there? Interestingly, this is precisely what many of us do with our lives. We will plan a trip, but we fail to plan our lives. Having a goal is not enough. To make the power of goal setting work, you must be clear about what you want. Be as specific as possible.

A student who resolves to always start studying at 7 p.m. is more likely to meet that goal than the student whose goal is to just "study harder."

Once you decide what you want, write your goals down. Look at them daily. Another powerful tool in achieving goals is to strongly believe rather than merely hoping or wishing. The stronger you imprint on your mind that which you want to achieve, the greater chance you have of getting what you want.

Purpose. Although some use the word "purpose" synonymously with the word "goals", others, to include myself, define "purpose" on a broader scale. A life purpose helps to define long-, intermediate-, and short-range goals. For example, your "purpose" may be to serve others. How you do this will be incorporated into your goals. (See Chapter 8 for a more in-depth description of "purpose.")

What is the difference between long-, intermediate-, and short-term goals?

A long-term goal is something you desire to acquire or achieve in the distant future. For example, it may be a desired degree or profession, or a desired income, a social cause, a political endeavor, or possibly an athletic milestone. Long-term goals help point you in a direction. If you have direction, you will make progress. You can always change course, but if you have no goals, you will meander around aimlessly wasting time and energy with little to show for it. Let's assume you want to become a registered nurse. You just don't automatically become a nurse because you want to. Steps must be taken to achieve this long-term goal. An intermediate goal helps you achieve your long-term goal. If becoming a registered nurse is your long-term goal, then graduating from high school, followed by getting your bachelor's degree in nursing, would be intermediate goals. Other intermediate goals may include completing required courses or achieving a specific grade point average.

Short-term goals would be anything needed to meet the established intermediate goals. An example of a short-term goal would be to get an "A" on an exam. To this you might add, "I will study tonight and tomorrow from 6:30 to 8 p.m., then review the night before the test."

Short-term goals should always point towards helping to achieve the intermediate goals, and the intermediate goals towards achieving long-range goals. Whatever your goals are, to make the goals more effective, establish a specific timeline. For example, setting a deadline to have a report outline completed tomorrow, a rough draft done before the upcoming weekend, and the final paper completed by next Thursday is more effective than planning to have the report done next week. Why might this be? Well, mainly because it is easy to procrastinate, avoid or even forget things when we have not set clear benchmarks for ourselves.

Bumps in the road. Sometimes you will not reach your goals when or how you may have expected. When this happens, ask yourself what happened. Learn from mistakes, because they are opportunities to learn. Disappointments, frustrations and challenges are inevitable. These are just mere "bumps in the road" on your journey. Accept them. They are only temporary. If you find your road blocked, take a different route. If you are spinning wheels (feeling stuck), take a break and come back later or ask for help. There is more than one road to the destination. Just make sure you keep your eye on your purpose and goals. Be patient! You will get where you are headed. It may not be in the time or on the route you initially anticipated, but if you keep your eye on the road and are persistent, you will arrive.

Chapter 5
The Cornerstone of Success,
"Be Prepared"

WHY IS IT ESSENTIAL?

Before we pack our car and head out, we need to plan what to take with us and get the proper maintenance on the car. How many travelers have driven many miles from home only to get a flat tire and then discover that the spare tire is flat as well? Or opened their suitcase to find they forgot to pack their bathing suit, or accidentally locked their car keys in the trunk and had no spare key in their possession? The World Association of Girl Guides and Girl Scouts (WAGGGS) share the same motto as the Boy Scouts: "Be prepared." In the third part of *Scouting for Boys,* the founder of the Boy Scouts, Robert Baden-Powell, explains the meaning of the phrase, "You are always in a state of readiness in mind and body to do your duty." Baden-Powell explains that to be "Prepared in Mind" is having disciplined yourself to be obedient to every requirement, and also by having thought out beforehand any issue or situation that might occur, so that you know the right thing to do at the right moment, and are willing to do it." Being "Prepared in Body is making yourself healthy and active and able to do the right thing at the right moment."

Being organized is one of the key elements to making your life easier and more successful. I am often amused when people attribute good fortunes and success to "luck." Oh, I am not suggesting that there is not an element of luck that may help contribute to a positive outcome. But often "luck" occurs because the situation has been made conducive to the opportunity. A football thrown to a wide receiver bounces off his hands into the arms of an opponent's outstretched arms who has a clear path to the goal line. Many may have considered the player who intercepted the deflected pass to be lucky because he was at the right place at the right time. Maybe so, but he was able to capitalize on the opportunity only because he was prepared, and that has nothing to do with luck. Being "organized" is being "prepared." More about "being prepared" in Chapter 5. Regardless of whether you are naturally organized or not, here are some TIPS that can help students

As the Scouting programs teach youth to "Be Prepared," so must we learn to be prepared in school and in our daily lives. Once your car is prepped and you are packed and satisfied that you have everything you need for your journey, you can get on the road. Just as there are potential obstacles on your road trip, there are many forces that come into play that will divert your attention from achieving the goals and dreams you have set for yourself. Proper planning, focus, determination, and formation of positive habits will help you to be prepared for whatever might come along that could deter or divert you from achieving your goal. The driver of an automobile makes sure his car is prepped by checking gauges, sets his destination on a map or GPS, and when driving is constantly aware of driving conditions, hazards, other drivers, and traffic laws. Similarly, in life we must keep focus on preparation, where we are going, and monitoring surroundings and progress. Doing so in a routine and conscientious manner will help ensure that we arrive at our destination. Interestingly, as simple as this seems, many do not follow this simple yet highly effective strategy, and that is why, as **Earl Nightingale stated, "Few in life end up achieving the success in life that they dream about." Don't be one of them. Have written goals, be prepared, plan, and you will be one of the few who do achieve their goals.**

Chapter 6
Murphy's Law: If Something Can Go Wrong, It Will, (And what to do about it)

Now that you have an idea of where you want to go, we must acknowledge that everything might not always go as we had hoped or planned. "Murphy" is hanging around! Who, you might ask, is "Murphy?" The adage has been around for centuries. One theory can be traced to the English County of Yorkshire when farmers used the term "sod's law" to describe how things could go wrong if proper precautions were not taken. In 1949 the term grew in popularity when an engineer named Edward Murphy was working on a project to see how much sudden deceleration a person could withstand in a crash. In one failed test, Murphy blamed a technician. Mocking Murphy for failing to take responsibility for not checking the technicians work, team members adopted the phrase "if it can happen, it will happen" and called it, "Murphy's Law." The project leader, Dr. John Sapp, at a press conference, was asked why no one had been injured during the rocket sled tests. Stapp replied that it was because "Murphy's Law" was always considered, meaning it was essential to consider all possibilities that could go wrong before performing a test. In other words, to ensure success, don't accept mediocrity. How is this done? By committing to doing your best. By practicing principles of self-discipline. By being willing to change. By not accepting excuses or allowing others to pull you down.

Early 20th century writer and poet Rudyard Kipling provided some valued guidance through his poem "If." Persistence, Determination, Willpower are the words that come to mind when I recall his poem. Here is an excerpt of the poem.

If you can keep your head when all about you
Are losing theirs and blaming it on you,

If you can trust yourself when all men doubt you,
    But make allowance for their doubting too;
If you can wait and not be tired of waiting,
    Or being lied about, don't deal in lies,
Or being hated don't give way to hating,
    and yet look too good, nor talk too wise.
If you can dream - and not make dreams your master,
    If you can think - and not make thoughts your aim;

If you can meet with Triumph and Disaster
    And treat those two imposters just the same;
If you can bear to hear the truth you've spoken
    Twisted by knaves to make a trap for fools,
Or watch the things you gave your life to, broken,
    And stoop and build 'em up with worn-out tools;
If you can make one heap of all your winnings
    And risk it on one turn of pitch-and-toss,

And lose, start again at your beginnings
    And never breathe a word about your loss;
If you can force your heart and nerve and sinew,
    To serve your turn long after they are gone,
And hold on when there is nothing in you
    Except the will which says to them, "Hold on!"

Here is an example of how my son used "Persistence," "Determination," and "Willpower" to help overcome a traumatic event in his life. Riding his bicycle on a gravel road, going downhill at a rapid clip, the front wheel of my son's bicycle came off. He took a nose-dive, head-first into the gravel road. He sustained serious multiple injuries to his forehead, nose, mouth, tongue, wrists and teeth, and his jaw was broken. Bleeding profusely and feeling disoriented, he somehow managed to find his way home, which was fortunately only about 1/3 of a mile away. Only our exchange student was home when he stumbled through the door. My wife and I were out to dinner when I received the frantic call from the 16-year-old student. "Can you put him on the phone?" I asked. "I am not sure," she replied. "He seems pretty confused, but I will try." She was able to get him on the phone. "My face, my face," I heard him wail. I called 911. I then called neighbors who might be able to help. No one was home. After about 15 minutes the rescue squad had arrived. He was transported to the local shock-trauma hospital where he underwent five hours of surgery.

Our son also has been challenged because of drug addiction. His physical trauma, and his roller-coaster ride with his recovery process, could have caused him to react with blame, anger or withdrawal. Yet, he chose to accept the circumstances encountered. He looked upon the issues as obstacles that had been placed before him to help him grow. He told me he was inspired by the words in Kipling's poem ... *meet with triumph and disaster and treat those two imposters just the same.* He also recalled the first two lines of the poem, *If you can keep your head when all about you are losing theirs and blaming it on you.* He recalled these words when others tried to tempt him to make choices that would result in relapse. I am proud to say he is "Holding On." He has recovered from his physical and mental trauma, established goals, found a purpose, and is thriving.

TIPS
To Help "Hold On"

Many people have achieved great success in life without a formal education, resources to get started, or even special abilities or capabilities. But none have succeeded without the will to do it. Another way of expressing a lack of will is a lack of "self-discipline." Improving self-discipline is creating new habits to help reach goals. We all have "Murphy's" to deal with. Barriers that Murphy likes include lack of confidence or knowledge, shyness, a disability, etc. Regardless of our obstacles, to beat anything that is getting in the way of reaching goals and dreams is to acknowledge them, then face up to them.

Like a car that is stuck in the snow, so too can we feel as if we are not moving forward, regardless of how hard we try. There can be several reasons for this, but often it is because of what psychologists call "defense mechanisms." Examples are avoidance, denial, repression and rationalization. Unfortunately, the defense mechanisms do little to help get rid of past experiences that are holding us back. The only way to get rid of the little devils is to face up to them, acknowledge their existence and our feelings about them, and the consequences they have on our lives. Do this, and they will begin to go away. Conversely, if we hold on to them, guess what? We get to keep them. In some cases, facing up to the garbage in our lives requires the assistance of a professional counselor and/or a support group.

As I stated earlier, the most powerful word in the English language has only three letters: A-S-K. The Bible says, *"Ask, and you shall receive."* In fact, most of the religions of the world teach this. Yet, many of us will not ask for help when we need it. Why? The answer is fear. What are we afraid of? It can be any number of things. Examples are rejection, shame, showing vulnerability, being hurt, fear of failure, etc. According to psychologist William DeFoore (*Anger: Deal with It, Heal with It, Stop It from Killing You*) and other anger management therapists, few of us recognize that the emotion of "anger" is fueled by the fear of something. When we feel anger at someone or something, we are projecting our own anger. So, if you note yourself harboring feelings of anger, look hard at what may be fearful for you. If you are unwilling to face up to anything that is getting in the way of your goals and dreams, you will not be able to move forward. Keep doing what you have been doing, and you will keep getting what you have been getting. Be willing to change. Choose to change. Once you do this, you will begin to take the steps necessary to move forward, and miracles will happen.

We have already addressed the importance of having goals. Without goals, you have no direction. Unfortunately, many do not establish goals because they do not have the knowledge or willpower to do so. Or if they do have goals, they lack the desire to follow through on them. And "willpower," according to the Merriam-Webster Dictionary is "the ability to control yourself: a strong determination that allows you to do something difficult." What is behind the challenge of accomplishing what you want? I have addressed how "fear" may block us from achieving what we want. Another is **"habit"**. Once a habit is formed, it is difficult to change. The Oxford Dictionary defines a habit as "a settled or regular tendency or practice, especially one that is hard to give up." It can be an automatic reaction to a situation, or an addictive practice (psychological and physiological dependence).

Addictions. Unlike a habit, an addiction is a compulsive form of a habit. A person who has an addiction has little or no control of their actions. According to the *Free Dictionary* by Farlex, "Addiction is a persistent, compulsive dependence on a behavior or substance. The term has been partially replaced by the word *dependence* for substance abuse. Addiction has been extended to include mood-altering behaviors or activities. Some researchers speak of two types of addictions, substance addictions (alcoholism, drug abuse, and smoking); and process addictions (gambling, spending, shopping, eating, and sexual activity). There is a growing recognition that many addicts, such as polydrug abusers, are addicted to more than one substance or process."

According to the National Institute on Drug Abuse (NIDA), "Addiction is defined as a chronic, relapsing brain disease that is characterized by compulsive drug seeking and use, despite harmful consequences. It is considered a brain disease because drugs change the brain; they change its structure and how it works. These brain changes can be long-lasting and can lead to many harmful, often self-destructive behavior."

If you want to fail, to be unhappy, to make those who love and care for you unhappy, to sabotage your chances for success, then experiment with drugs. Everyone who has become addicted started out by just trying. Once addicted, it is extremely hard to recover. So, the best course is to just say "no" when some fool tempts you to try. If you already on the path of self-destruction, you probably will not even be reading this book. But if, per chance, are one of the very few who are, then seek professional help immediately. The longer you wait, the harder it is to break the cycle of addiction. More about addictions in Chapter 24, "Obstacles to Achievement."

TIPS
To Change Unwanted Habits

Self-discipline is training one's self to create new and desired habits from unwanted habits, thus improving the opportunity to reach one's goals.

Identify which habit (s) you would like to change. Then choose to change. Be totally committed to it. Rather than saying to yourself, "I would like to stop losing my cell phone," say, "I am tired of losing my cell phone, it causes frustration, it is a waste of time looking for it, and I am determined to fix the problem right now."

Write down your goals (the habits you would like to replace).

Visualize. Relax, close your eyes, and then visualize what it would be like when you have replaced the harmful habit with a new positive one. Use affirmations as described in Chapter 20 and Appendix C.

Take action. Start small. Don't attempt to suddenly become an organized person. If your habit is to drop clothes on the floor, or lay your cell phone, backpack, books, and wallet or purse in the first convenient place encountered, then don't try to address all such issues at once. Instead, choose one or two to start, and then work on these, and only these. For example, you may select your cell phone and backpack. Decide on a specific place to put your cell phone EVERY TIME you enter your bedroom. You may choose your desk, for example. Then when you go to bed, transfer it to your bedroom nightstand. Commit to yourself that these will be the only two places you will ever place your cell phone when not actually using it while in your bedroom. Avoid the temptation to set it any other place, i.e., your bed, dresser, floor, etc. Make a similar commitment for your backpack. When you arrive home from school, for example, rather than merely dropping it at the front door, place it at your preferred study area, 100 percent of the time. The following week choose one or two more tasks, such as picking up clothes and where you place your wallet or purse. Decide on a specific place for your wallet or purse, then always, always put it in the exact same spot. Rather than unconsciously dropping clothes on the floor, conscientiously try to place clothes in your laundry hamper, drawers or closet. Keep in mind that to change old habits it takes a concerted effort over several days, or in some cases, weeks. When you find yourself lapsing, force yourself to return to performing the desired new habit. With a determined and conscientious effort, you will soon replace old inefficient habits with new efficient ones.

Manage your time. One of the most essential components of self-discipline is the ability to manage time efficiently. And the ability to manage time is critical to success. See Chapter 7 for great TIPS to help manage time.

Be vigilant. Studies have shown that it takes a few weeks to several months to change a habit. Thus, it is imperative to pay close attention to temptations to not to revert to unwanted habits. It requires self-discipline, and self-discipline is a matter of choice, a sincere will to achieve, and a commitment to stay focused on reaching your goals. Hold on!

Reward yourself. When you have successfully done what you have wanted to do for a few days, reward yourself with short-term incentives. For example, if you picked your clothes off the floor and properly placed them in designated places, Monday through Friday, you could reward yourself with a trip to the mall. Also, stay focused on the long-term rewards. You will be delighted that you will no longer have to look for your belongings. You will also be able to walk around your room without having to maneuver an obstacle course of stuff, not to mention getting your parents off your back about your messy room. These are rewards realized for your efforts. More importantly, you will have started a process that will contribute to the value of efficiency throughout your life.

Chapter 7
Organizing Space and Managing Time Effectiveness vs. Efficiency

So we now know where we are headed and are prepared to deal with obstacles and detours along the road. Great! But wait! Just because you have determined when you are going, how you are going and prepare the car and your personal effects, does not necessarily mean you are going to be effective and efficient on your trip. What do I mean? Well, if your goal is to drive from Pittsburgh to Philadelphia across Pennsylvania, you can take one of several routes. Assuming your goal is to get from Pittsburgh to Philadelphia in the fastest and most economical way, you would take the Pennsylvania Turnpike. Approximate driving time is five hours. But let's say you drive the more northern route through Altoona in the middle of the state. You have added two or more hours to your trip and $2 to $4 to your gas bill. What does this analogy have to do with school and life? The answer lies in knowing the difference between "effectiveness" and "efficiency." Both routes were effective, that is they got you to your destination. However, one way was slower and costlier, thus not very efficient. Many use these two words synonymously, but they are entirely different. Here is another analogy that helps explain the difference.

I knew a gentleman who held an M.D. and a Ph.D., yet he was one of the most disorganized persons I have ever known. Let me qualify. Although his office was a disaster, he compensated by applying many other success principles, such as having well-defined goals and being persistent. He admitted to me, however, that although he was successful, he often did not make it easy on himself. In other words, he accomplished his goals (effective), but not necessarily doing so with the least use of time and resources (efficient). My friend knew that he could have done things smarter rather than harder throughout his many years of formal education and professional career if he could have been more organized. "Why," I asked him, "could being organized have made a difference since you achieved professional success anyway?" He told me that although he had gained success, he could have done so with much less effort had he been more organized. He expressed frustration with himself because he lost a lot of time looking for things that had been misplaced, sometimes missing or being tardy for meetings, or having to re-do work because he "lost" the original copy. I asked him why he thought he had such difficulty with organization. He replied that some people have an inclination for organization, and others do not. "But," the doctor added, "he was convinced that people who are not naturally organized could learn to be so." He went on to add, "Habits, regardless if they are inborn or conditioned, are hard to break, but the process can be made much easier if parents teach organization skills while children are young. Although my parents supported and encouraged me," he said, "they did not teach me good organizations skills. Since being organized did not come naturally to me, I never acquired the self-disciple to change my habits."

TIPS
To Improve Organization

Organize your study area. Have a place to study that is clear of distractions, uncluttered, and well lit. Make sure you have all the necessary materials, such as paper, pencils and pens, books, erasers, etc. Remove anything that could cause a distraction, such as cell phones, or books and magazines that are not relevant to what is being studied.

Organize study materials. Make sure all necessary textbooks, notes, and class instructions are on hand before sitting down to study. Organize notes by subject in separate binders or notebooks. Create a system for filing loose papers and handouts. Make sure these papers are secured so they will not get lost. Absolutely avoid placing such documents in textbooks—you know, folding the paper and stuffing it between the pages! Although we all may have different preferences regarding how we like to organize our study materials, I personally think a 3-ring binder divided by subject is better than spiral binders. Why? Because there is no place to insert class handouts in a spiral binder. Pockets are OK, but only for the temporary holding of papers until they can be placed in your three-ring binder. A spiral notebook can be embedded in the three-ring binder instead of loose-leaf paper but should not be used instead of the three-ring binder. Try to arrange handouts in chronological order, most recent on top. Any instructions provided by the teacher that explains the course purpose, grading methodology, class guidelines (often called a prospectus) should be placed in the front of the binder so that it can be referred to frequently. Knowing and following the teacher's guidance is not an option. It is imperative! Before you can improve your "organization" skills, you may have to change habits. Go back to Chapter 6 and review the TIPS on how to change unwanted habits.

Time management. To increase efficiency, students must be a capable manager of "time." If you study the secrets of productive people, you will realize that a common trait they have is their ability to make maximum use of their time. Those who use time wisely will be most productive. Those who do not will struggle. In Appendix III of this book, I provide a few life lessons from Benjamin Franklin. Regarding time management, he says, "Your time is your life. If you waste your time, you are wasting your life. I've never met a successful person who didn't value their time, and I've never met an unsuccessful person who did." Let's look at a few ways you use time wisely to create your success.

TIPS
To Manage Time

Make an honest assessment. To improve the management of your time, you must be aware of how you currently spend your time.

To do this, take a piece of paper and list the hours of the day from awakening to bedtime. Make a sheet for each day of the week. Now keep track of what you do for every hour for the entire week. This exercise will help you get a clear picture of how you spend your hours and how much time you devote to various activities throughout the day. Once completed, compare your timesheet to the areas you consider most important in your life. Now ask yourself the question, is the time you devote commensurate with the things that are most important to your success?

Prioritize. Now write down everything you wish to accomplish. Prioritize your "to-do" list by marking the most important as "Need to do today" (priority one); "Important to do within the next few days" (priority two); "Would like to do soon" (priority three); "Not important" (priority four). Absolutely do not let the day go by without working on your priority one tasks. When completed, begin working on priority two tasks. Every two days or so, re-categorize your list. Some priority twos may move to ones, and threes or fours may move to a higher priority on your list. Of course, new tasks will be introduced—probably daily. Prioritize these as well. You will, no doubt, notice by using this system, you will gain a good idea of what needs to be accomplished and in what order. You will also be more inclined to achieve the tasks in a timely and more efficient manner. This will also help increase your self-confidence that, in turn, further incentivizes you. If you regress, do not be discouraged. Just get back on track. When you manage your time, you will accomplish more and do so faster.

Evaluate how much time is needed to study for each class. Be realistic about this! Some teachers and some classes will require more study time than others. So, don't be tempted to allocate equal amounts of time to every class. Just because you say you are going to study 20 hours a week when you know you would never adhere to that is only setting you up to break the schedule you set for yourself. So, if you can just spend 10 hours per week, then allocate those 10 hours to your plan. Consider that every week will be a little different depending on workload, assignments, test scheduling, and extracurricular activities.

If you are sincerely honest, you know that you will be tempted to do other things that you prefer to do than study. It is only natural to be seduced by things that are pleasurable and avoid that which is less so. How does one "discipline" themselves to do what is most important rather than most pleasurable? A challenge, indeed! Here are a few tools to help keep focused.

Make a list. Having a "to-do" list with suspense dates and times is a powerful tool that helps to remind you of what needs to be done and when it needs to be done. The adage "out of sight out of mind" suggests that if we don't keep it in our face, we will tend not to think about it and; consequently, forget about it. We have all done this from time to time. Besides serving as a reminder, there is another benefit to having a "to-do list." That is, when we complete a task and cross it off, we get a sense of gratification. We are rewarding ourselves by the simple act of marking off a completed job. This simple act when repeated often will contribute more to our self-discipline than practically anything else we can do to help maximize efficiency and productivity.

Have a schedule. Our bodies and minds work better when they are provided with routine schedules. This is not to suggest that occasional spontaneity should be avoided. Instead, most of our daily lives should adhere to a regular schedule. Planning appropriate study time, with a commitment to sticking to it, will result in many positive results to include accomplishing more, meeting deadlines, better outcomes, and better self-esteem, just to name a few of the benefits. Also, forming the habit of making and adhering to a schedule will have a profound positive impact on other areas of your home, extracurricular, and work-life. My suggestion is to start your week by making a weekly schedule on Sunday evening. Review what needs to be accomplished for the week. Check your goal list to make sure your weekly planning is on track with your established goals. Coordinate with family and friends to make sure your plans consider others' activities and commitments. Study periods must be strictly adhered to. Otherwise, the routine and psychological factor will be compromised. Try not to tie yourself into a rigid schedule that will be difficult, if not impossible, to stick to. Instead, create weekly schedules that are realistic for your situation and that you can keep without frustrating yourself.

Energize yourself with energy-boosting activities such as a few moments of relaxation, power nap, exercise, a walk, or jog. How can such activities help efficiency? Because they boost mental sharpness and increase energy level. Be reasonable in allocating your time. If you are a runner, unless you are training for a marathon, run a mile or two, not ten. If you are a walker, walk for 30 minutes. Take a 30-minute nap, not an hour.

Eliminate time wasters. We are continually bombarded with internet ads, apps, announcements, and media hits. We are tempted to check many of them out, if for no other reason than curiosity. So if you find yourself checking Facebook, Twitter, podcasts, ads, etc. to the detriment of accomplishment of more important tasks, then STOP checking such things throughout the day. A good time-saving strategy is to set a reasonable time for spending on activities and stick to the schedule. Cut out games entirely if you can! Why do I say this? Because for many students' video games become addictive, resulting in prioritizing this to all else. If you absolutely must spend time playing, limit it to weekends, or as a minimum only after you have devoted productive time to what is most important to your success. Apply these time-saving activities, and you will find that your productivity will increase dramatically. In fact, if you "save" just one hour a day, that amounts to 28 to 31 hours a month. two hours a day amounts to 56 to 62 hours a month. Wow! New "found" time. Imagine what you can do with so many hours that otherwise would be "wasted" on insignificant activities that contribute "0" to what you set as most important to you.

Multi-task. There are tasks we must do every day, brush teeth, shower, study, chores, etc. These click away the minutes on the clock. To save time, try combining activities. If you need to speak with someone on the phone, use a headset or your cell phone speaker while you are doing your house chores, but not while driving or doing another task that requires focus. Record lessons that require review or memorization and review them while riding to school or working around the house. Listen to audiobooks unless your teacher wants you to read the text version. I am sure you can think of other ways to capitalize on your time by doing more than one thing at a time. But be careful! Too much multitasking can increase stress levels, and we certainly do not want this. So it is OK to try and combine a few tasks if they are reasonable and productive, but avoid multi-tasking when concentration on a single task is essential or if it causes you a bit of stress.

In this chapter, I have defined the difference between effectiveness and efficiency. We can see how being efficient can be invaluable to one's effectiveness in life—not only in school but in your daily routines, today and for years to come.

SECTION C
Building Blocks for Success and Happiness - In and Out of School

Remember, happiness doesn't depend upon who you are or what you have; it depends solely upon what you think.

Dale Carnegie

Chapter 8
Building a Solid Structure

The most powerful investment we can make in life is ourselves.

Franklin Covey

How do you define "success"? There are many theories about what it takes to be a success. Some specifically apply to success in school, some with relationships, business, financial success, and more. In fact, what constitutes "success" differs from one person to another, from one organization to another, from one culture to another. Generally, "success" describes the attainment of a goal, aim, or undertaking. Some define "success" not just as the "attainment" of a goal, but also the initiatives taken to achieve that goal. Influencing factors on goal achievement include, "morals," "ethics," "skills," "values," "traits," What are the differences between these terms? Let's look at each.

Morals. The word "morals" comes from the Greek root word "mos," which means "custom." Thus, "morals" is defined as the social and cultural beliefs that are considered generally right or wrong principles of a group or society. Many moral philosophies differ from one society to another. The individual can either accept or reject the morals of the group. Since morals are framed and designed by the group, there is no option for the individual to think and choose. Although the individual can either accept or reject the moral principles of the community, he/she cannot change them. According to Jon Haidt, an expert on moral foundation theory "moral systems are interlocking sets of values, virtues, norms, practices, identities, institutions, technologies, and evolved psychological mechanisms that work together to suppress or regulate selfishness and make social life possible." The moral foundation's theory measures five foundations that have been identified as universally accepted. Included are caring, fairness, loyalty, respectful to authority and traditions, and spiritually pure. Because society expects us to comply with these principles does not necessarily mean we will do so.

Ethics. The word "ethics" comes from the ancient Greek root word "Ethikos," which means character. Ethics is the guiding principle of an individual or group that defines how we should respond in a situation. For example, our "ethics" will determine the degree to which we will be loyal, generous, and honest. Whereas morality describes what is "right or wrong," as defined by the community; ethics deals with what is "good or evil." This helps to explain why one's ethics stay with them regardless of the society in which they live. One's ethics will define how a person conducts themselves in a specific situation. An ethical person will be loyal, for example, not because society expects it, but because he expects it of himself. Another example is a person who stands up for what he/she knows is right even though others try to influence him/her to think or do differently. Often when we do something we feel is unethical, we feel guilt.

Skills. A skill defines the ability to perform a task competently. Being a good athlete or dancer are acquired "skills" developed through hard work. When asked what we do well, we will most often describe a skill rather than a value, trait, or ethic. Our values, traits, and ethics have a significant influence on our success at becoming proficient at a skill.

Core values are the fundamental principles or beliefs a person has that help to guide how they behave, relate to others and the world around them. Values help define how a person should live their life. We have different values, some more important than others. For example, one person may place a higher value on the environment than another, or on independence rather than conformity. For the less important ones, we might choose to change based on new perceptions and life experiences. Values that are more important can become essential; therefore, we are not willing to compromise. Many beliefs can be categorized as a "value." Included are security, self-direction, tradition, conformity, caring for others and self, and spirituality.

Character traits are the aspects of a person's behavior and attitudes that help to contribute to a person's personality. Character traits come from the core values as defined by the community and culture in which we live. A person's values influence their personal traits and help to define who they are, and how a person interacts with and responds to others, their community, and the world.

Character traits can sometimes be distinguished from values by watching how a person acts. There are many traits that people can have. Examples include openness, conscientiousness, extraversion, and agreeableness. Negative character traits include neuroticism and dishonesty.

A bit confusing, isn't it? Let's just simplify things. In this Chapter, I have chosen five core values, and in Chapter 9, 10 traits that, when conscientiously followed, will significantly increase the odds for success and happiness.

Let's compare values and traits to building a structure. Two essential components of a building are the sub-structure and the super-structure. The super-structure is the portion of the building above the ground. The super-structure includes the slab, floor, frame, the walls, and the roof. We can see these. So, just as we can see the super-structure, we focus on how much we accomplish and on material things as measures our self-worth, success, and happiness.

The sub-structure lies below the ground. It is the foundation that transfers the load of the building to the earth. It bears the weight. If not built on solid ground, the building will fall. The sub-structure can be compared "spirituality." As humans, we have difficulty identifying with what we cannot see or touch even though is essential to our values. In addition to spirituality, we can identify four other values important to success. Let's label them as Purpose, Emotional/Social, Mental Health, and Physical Health. Let's symbolize them as columns that provide support to the structure.

It is important to know that one or two columns cannot stand alone. It takes all four to provide stable support for your structure. What happened to the Philistine temple when Samson pulled the columns down? The temple came crashing down. Likewise, our personal temple will fall if we do not have strong columns.

Are not good grades, diplomas, degrees, jobs, money, and the things we can buy with that money important? Won't these things bring happiness and peace? Indeed, they can make life easier and more fun. But do they bring true continual peace and joy to your life? Do you remember the pleasure you had the last time you got a new "toy" such as an electronic device, clothes, accomplished something, received an award or trophy? How long did that joy last? Once the pleasure wore off, you were seeking something else to give you pleasure. I am not saying this is wrong. We all do it. But when we make such aspirations our primary goal we are, in effect, robbing ourselves of internal and ongoing peace. There are many financially successful people (and have a lot of material possessions) who are unhappy in life.

On the other hand, I have known people of limited financial means who are very content. I am not suggesting that being financially secure is not important. Being so helps to make life easier which, in turn, relieves stress—sometimes. But wealth does not create contentment. If it did, why do so many wealthy people lead lives in which adverse outcomes are common, such as unstable relationships, divorce, drug and alcohol abuse, depression, and even suicide? Look at the lives of many of the rich and famous. Although they may lead glamorous lives that does not mean they are content or even happy. Watch the news and read the tabloids! Daily, the news tells us of another "fallen star." So how can this be? It is because they have established as the foundation of their life something other than one of the five values. Or, they have compromised their morals, ethics, or values.

It is good to have a passion, such as music, theater, art, career, etc. How well we perform at these is determined by how solid our structure is. The substructure is your spirituality. It holds up the other five core values. Let's look at the essential core values needed to construct a solid structure.

Spiritual: Belief in a higher power.

Purpose: Establishing a life purpose and direction.

Emotional/Social: Constant daily deposits into self, family, and personal relationships.

Mental Health: Learning about and caring for psychological, emotional and social well-being.

Physical Health: Dedication to physical well-being for self and others.

Spiritual

One definition of "spirituality" is your way of loving, accepting, and relating to the world around us. Some call it "faith" or "spirituality." Often people say "spirituality" and "religion" are the same. Not for everyone. "Religion" is organized and openly displayed by rituals and various church doctrines. For some, "spirituality" is more personal and private. This is not to suggest that religious people are not spiritual. It is just that one's spirituality is practiced and expressed in different ways. Regardless of one's personal philosophies on spirituality, for most, it is an integral part of having a balanced, happy, and successful life. Some believe in a higher being; some are certain there is no supreme being (atheists). Some are not sure (agnostics). Carl Sagan, the astrophysicist, defined an agnostic as "somebody who doesn't believe in something until there is evidence for it." Some have belief in a supreme being but are just not engaged in exploring what that might mean.

Over the millennium and across the world, the concept of a supreme being (God, Yahweh, Elohim, Allah, Jehovah, Shangdi, Waheguru) has incorporated many beliefs. Yet all religions have accepted as fact that a supreme being created the Earth and everything that is in it. He is the provider and savior. Those who believe in a supreme being accept that God, as I will refer to Him, will provide contentment in this life and eternally. The challenge to human beings is that God has given us free will. That is, we can make our own choices, good or bad. Humans make many poor choices, often driven by such negative feelings as greed, selfishness, prejudice, jealousy, stubbornness, vanity, antagonism, lack of caring or love, or some other dysfunction. So, if Scripture tells us how to live, and that by living according to God's word, we can attain peace and happiness (with less stress) why do many ignore it? Arrogance, laziness, ignorance, skepticism? The Bible is the best-selling book of all time. The wisdom of Scripture has helped millions to attain direction and contentment.

Many academics argue against the existence of a higher being, citing scientific evidence to support their positions. They are inclined to do this because they are trained to believe according to rational thinking. That is, if it cannot be proven according to the scientific method, or if there is no physical evidence, then it must not be so. Put another way, they have difficulty with that which is too difficult to explain (infinity, the creation, God as omnipresent). So, they justify their atheism by arguing against the existence of a supreme being.

On the other hand, those who believe, regardless of their specific religious persuasion, have accepted the belief that the universe is so highly exacting and intricately interdependent that our world could not have been created by cosmic happenstance. Interestingly, the more many scientists learn about our universe, world, and ancient history, the more they are convinced that it was created with a purpose. Dr. R. David Marshall in his book, *The Truth Behind the New Atheism*, states, "Scientists who become theologians know how dynamic and intellectually challenging God-study can be. For a Christian, every breakthrough in science, every new reading in history, every discovery of a new culture, every philosophical insight cast new light on the nature of God, and how He interacts with the world He made." Dr. Michael Guillen in his book *Amazing Truths, How Science and the Bible Agree* said, "After decades as a scientist, after reading and analyzing scores of creation theories, I'm struck by the similarity of the narratives offered by science and the Bible."

There are many things that science can explain, and countless others that it cannot. Man can understand why there is a balance of nature yet cannot explain how the highly exacting and phenomenal that power came to be. Nevertheless, we accept it knowing that if it were not so, we would cease to exist. Carl Sagan wrote in his book, *The Demon-Haunted World: Science as a Candle in the Dark*, "Science is not only compatible with spirituality; it is a profound source of spirituality. When we recognize our place in an immensity of light-years and in the passage of ages, when we grasp the intricacy, beauty, and subtlety of life, then that soaring feeling, that sense of elation and humility combined, is surely spiritual. So are our emotions in the presence of great art or music or literature, or acts of exemplary selfless courage such as those of Mohandas Gandhi or Martin Luther King, Jr. The notion that science and spirituality are somehow mutually exclusive does a disservice to both."

In January 2019 Time/Life published a special edition entitled *Miracles of Faith*. The publication is filled with examples of acts that cannot be explained by man. Some call these "miracles." In the Introduction the authors state, "A miracle is commonly defined as a divine action that extends beyond natural law which cannot be explained within the natural powers of man-and therefore, must be the result of supernatural intercession." Nearly all religions cite miraculous happenings. Both the Hebrew and Christian Bible describe over 100 prophesies that have come true. For Christians, the revelation of Christ's birth, death, and purpose long before He was born is central to their faith. The Old Testament prophesied the coming of a Messiah and His birthplace (Micah 5:20). The New Testament cites 40 miracles performed by Christ. Some like to debate that such a phenomenon cannot be by divine intervention, yet they cannot provide a plausible explanation. Those who believe state that there are so many prophesies and miracles in history that there can be no explanation other than they must be the result of the power and grace of God.

There are countless stories of persons challenged with misfortune, sadness, anxiety, loss, mistreatment, discrimination, hatred, etc. yet were able to deal with such challenges when they were willing to believe in a greater power. In the book *Alcoholics Anonymous*, in Chapter 4, "We Agnostics," it explains how thousands of men and women, "in the face of collapse and despair, in the face of the total failure of their human resources, they found that a new power, peace, happiness, and sense of direction flowed into them." Those who give testimony as to how this change occurred in their lives state that it was the "consciousness of the presence of God." It never ceases to thrill me when I witness and hear the testimony of persons whose lives have been turned for the better when they admit that the presence of God was the most powerful reason for the change.

Faith gives our existence meaning, provides hope, and helps give mankind a foundation on which to build his/her life. It helps give purpose to our lives, without which we would have little direction. There are many ways that humans express their spirituality through organized religion, of which there are hundreds. Sadly, many have allowed their spirituality to be influenced by how others practice their religion. Please do not let your opportunity to receive the benefits of a sound spirituality to be negatively influenced by how others may or may not choose to worship or not.

Since this book is about helping to reduce stress levels for students, and this section is about spirituality, then it is reasonable to ask, "can spirituality help reduce stress levels"? Research tells us the answer is "yes." According to an April 23, 2016, Mayo Clinic newsletter, "Stress relief tools are very tangible: exercising more, eating healthy foods and talking with friends. A less tangible — but no less useful—way to find stress relief is through spirituality." In an article by Dew, et. al. *Religion/Spirituality and Adolescent Psychiatric Symptoms* in the publication of Child Psychiatry, Human Development, (Volume 9, December 2008), 115 articles were reviewed that examined relationships between religion/spirituality and adolescent substance use, delinquency, depression, suicide, and anxiety. "Ninety-two percent of the articles reviewed found at least one significant relationship between religiousness and better mental health. Evidence for relationships between greater religiousness and less psychopathology was strongest in the area of teenage substance use."

I have observed in my lifetime, most who had a strong faith were generally optimistic, had strong relationships, and a positive quality of life. Scripture helps us to live happier lives and gives hope for the future. I am amused by academicians who teach theories that explain ways people can achieve happiness and contentment in life, often as if they are new revelations. Yet, they are all in the Bible and have been for thousands of years. In fact, nearly every principle addressed in this book can be found in the Bible. Many just have not bothered to read or study Scripture. Don't believe me? Study the Bible, Koran, Torah, or Vedas, according to your religious preferences and draw your own conclusions. Be cautious, however, as many misinterpret passages of Scripture. To truly understand Scripture, it needs to be studied. Although loaded with wisdom, Scriptures are thousands of years old and often written in a manner that is not always easy to understand. I urge you to seek out a priest, pastor, rabbi, academic expert, or minister who knows Scripture well and can deliver the messages in an understandable manner. Bible study groups are also very beneficial.

Struggling with addiction, my son achieved success with the spiritual-based Alcoholics Anonymous (AA) and Narcotics Anonymous 12-step programs. He and most of those dealing with addiction agree that spirituality was the key to a successful recovery. He has had a few "miracles" in his life. I call them "divine intervention." even though others may call them coincidences. Here is one. When in a recovery program, Teen Challenge, instead of being asleep in the dorm, he went to the Chapel and prayed for courage to accept the trials that had been placed before him and asked how he could help encourage others to deal with their challenges. Suddenly inspired, he started to draw a picture of the face of Jesus just after His crucifixion. With a fine tipped ink pen, he began to create the image of Jesus, using a technique called pointillism, which entails making thousands of tiny dots like the pixels in a photograph. He had only been drawing for seven months at the time. He had never had an art lesson. The image has inspired many and is displayed in homes, recovery centers, and in the offices of several pastors. He recognized his gift and is now using his talent professionally.

The First Amendment to the United States Constitution prohibits the government from making laws that prevent people from worshiping as they so choose, or from interfering with citizens to worship as they so choose. The writers of the Constitution did this to prevent the government from doing what governments in Europe, the Middle East, and even in some parts of Colonial America had been doing for centuries, often resulting in conflict. Many interpret this "separation of church and state" as meaning that religion must be excluded from public life. Some also believe that those who wrote the First Amendment were not spiritual. Nothing could be further from the truth. In fact, 24 of the 56 signers of the Declaration of Independence held seminary or Bible school degrees. The following quotes from some of the founding fathers attest to their spiritual convictions and undoubtedly influenced the principles on which our country was founded.

"Whereas it is the duty of all nations to acknowledge the

providence of Almighty God to obey His will, to be grateful for His makings, to humbly employ His protection of faith." George Washington

"He who should introduce into public affairs the principles of Christianity will change the face of the World." Benjamin Franklin.

"The Bible is a book worth more than all the other books that were ever printed." Patrick Henry.

"The perfect morality of the gospel rests upon the doctrine which, though often controverted has never been refuted: I mean the vicarious life and death of the Son of God." Benjamin Rush

Although not signers of the Declaration of Independence, many other influential Americans testify to the importance of spirituality.

Abraham Lincoln said, "It is the duty of nations, as well as of men to own their dependence on the overruling power of God, to recognize the sublime truth announced in the Holy Scriptures and proven by all history that those nations only are blessed whose God is Lord."

"The religion which has introduced civil liberties is the religion of Christ and His apostles. For this, we owe our free constitutions of government." Noah Webster.

"My religion consists of a humble admiration of the illimitable superior spirit who reveals himself in the slight details we are able to perceive with our frail and feeble mind." Albert Einstein.

TIPS
TO FIND YOUR SPIRITUALITY

Study. If you are currently comfortable with your spirituality, as you define it. Good! If on the other hand, you are not sure of your spirituality or questioning your life's aim, your reason for being, or what you want out of life, I would implore you to spend some time with more study on the subject. Read, ask, discuss. If you currently do not have a spiritual center, visit different centers until you find one in which you are comfortable. For many, spirituality, regardless of how you define and practice it, helps to determine direction. One of the most important things to keep in mind is that spirituality brings you an inner wealth, not the monetary kind—that is external. External things can be transitory and even lost. So, if you want peace in your life, invest in spiritual wealth.

To be curious and have doubt is normal. The Apostle Thomas was both. In John 14, Jesus told his apostles that he was going away to prepare a heavenly home for his followers and that one day they would join Him there. Thomas reacted by saying, "Lord, we don't know where you are going, so how can we know the way?" (John 14-5). John 20:24-29 tells how Thomas, often called "doubting Thomas," had heard that Jesus had appeared to the other apostles after His crucifixion. Thomas was skeptical. He said, "Unless I see the nail marks in His hands and put my finger where the nails were, and put my hand into His side, I will not believe." (John 20:25). It was not until Jesus appeared to Thomas and invited him to touch his wounds did Thomas believe. Because he was able to seek out the answers to his questions, Thomas gained a deep faith. He went on to share the Gospel in Syria, ancient Persia, and India. Thomas acknowledged his doubts but was not content to accept them as valid until he explored the facts. Should we do no less? "Ask, and it shall be given you; seek, and you shall find; knock, and it shall be opened unto you." (Mathew 7:7). (Scripture quoted by permission. MacArthur Study Bible. New King James Version. Nashville, TN, Thomas Nelson. 1997). Put another way; one must take the initiative. Many will take the initiative to learn a trade or gain an education but will not take the initiative to enhance their spirituality.

Keep an open mind! Be your own person, and do not allow the skepticism, doubts, and negativity of others to influence you. Some religions attempt to dictate rules on church members that are not based on Scripture. Strategies that elicit fear and intimidation are sometimes used. Your church should make you feel good, not bad, provide peace, not anxiety. If you find your self-worth is being challenged, inner conflict increasing, or doubt about who you are as a person, look elsewhere! Also, I would implore you to not make up your mind about spirituality and how you may choose to live it before you have done some research on the subject. You cannot properly debate the subject if you have little or no knowledge. Do some study. You may be pleasantly surprised.

Purpose

An essential element to your life's direction is a "purpose." So just what is a "purpose"? According to Richard J. Leider, author of *The Power of Purpose*, it is "the conscious choice of what, where, and how to make a positive contribution to our world." Your purpose significantly helps to answer the questions of who you are (values and traits) and contributes to providing your meaning in life. Will your life help make a mark in the world, or will your life be a gift wasted? A life-purpose helps provide direction to your life.

Rick Warren, one of Americas most influential spiritual leaders published in his best-selling book *The Purpose Driven Life*, "Knowing your purpose gives meaning to your life." Warren further explains that "When life has meaning you can bear almost anything; without it, nothing is bearable." A by-product of having a purpose is that it helps relieve negative stress.

When a person has discovered and is practicing their life's purpose, they will find that they are more goal-oriented, balanced, happier, and successful. In Chapter 4, I defined "goals" and provided TIPS on how to achieve your goals. I provided an analogy for planning a road trip. Before you begin your trip, you must first determine why you want to go on the trip. This constitutes your "purpose." After that, you must decide how you are going to implement your purpose — this is your "plan." Incorporated in your plan may be long-, intermediate- or short-range "goals." This will include answers to questions such as: What transportation means you are going to use? What direction are you going to go? When are you going? How long will it take? When will you take rest stops? Even though we incorporate such plans and goals when planning a trip, we will often leave out one or more of these essential steps in preparing our life's direction. If you do not know where you are going, it is hard to get there.

TIPS
To Help Identify Your Purpose

To help identify your "Purpose" ask yourself, "what are you passionate about?" Music, art, computers, animals, helping others, sports, etc.? If you are not sure, do not worry. It will be revealed to you in time. You can determine what might become your purpose by considering what strengths you have. Consider your talents, and "yes," you do have talents; everyone does. For many, a powerful life purpose is when it is devoted to the service of others. Leader suggests a way to help discover your purpose is to write on a piece of paper the words; "My purpose in life is..." Then in a sentence or two try to write down what you feel your purpose presently might be. Don't worry, if you struggle with this. Discovering your life purpose is a process and may take time, even years. But it is essential to start thinking about it. It will be revealed to you sooner or later. Ask the question, "Why do I want to do this?" If you have difficulty answering the "why," then revisit what you are considering as a "purpose." By the way, discovering your life purpose must come from inside you. If you look for it outside of yourself, realizing your purpose, your goals, and your dreams will be a far more significant challenge.

DREAM! Another thing that can help you determine your purpose is to dream. Daydreams and night dreams can be valuable in helping you develop your life purpose. Dreams help inspire, clarify, and give direction. Dreams are a way that your subconscious speaks to you. Listen to it!

Emotional/Social

Emotional/social skills are the ability to understand the feelings of others and manage his or her own feelings and behaviors. It is necessary to develop the skills for successful and effective personal and social interaction.

Did you know that we lie to ourselves? Thoughts (which can be manifested as "habits") are automatic but may not necessarily be correct. Through lifelong experiences, our brains are "programmed" to think specific thoughts. These thoughts may be valid or invalid. Often, we will act on those thoughts. If the views are negative, we will get negative in return. If the thoughts are positive, we will get positive in return. We may not know when or how we will receive the negative or positive, but it will happen. Don't take my word for this. It is a universal truth espoused by nearly every religion and philosophy in the world.

When we recognize a thought or habit as being a roadblock to achieving our desires and goals, then we must change those thoughts. We can train our thoughts to be positive and hopeful. Once you are aware of what you can do with your thoughts, you can choose to think positively. One way to learn how to change your thoughts is to notice them when they are negative and talk back to them. If you think a negative thought and do not challenge it, your mind believes it, and your body reacts to it. This results in psychological changes such as fear, depression, and (yep) stress and anxiety, and/ or physiological changes such as high blood pressure, irregular sleep patterns, aches, pains, etc. Indeed, such manifestations can sabotage any efforts for adequate study, not to mention our overall mental health. **Since it is our beliefs about a situation or event that triggers our feelings, if we alter those beliefs, we can influence our emotions.** At first, implementing these strategies may seem a bit daunting, but be persistent! Make sure you practice them daily! Do not skip! Experts say it takes about 28 days to change a habit and longer for more deep-seated psychological issues.

TIPS
To Create Positive Results for
Emotional and Social Life

Here are a few TIPS that you can use to help create positive results in your life. It will take a bit of effort, but the results will be well worth it.

Organize your life and world. Establish a clear set of rules to follow. Set timelines for completion of tasks. Give yourself rewards and consequences. Prioritize daily tasks.

Recognize that the past is the past, and you cannot change it. Try not to dwell on that which you have no control. Acknowledge your feelings (fears, guilt, and anger). Take measures to address them. Seek professional and/or spiritual help if need be.

Be open and honest with others, but more critical of yourself. Honestly and objectively assess your own philosophies, biases, and feelings. A realistic assessment of your strengths and weaknesses will have a direct bearing on your feelings of self-worth and self-respect. This, in turn, is essential to making wise choices to help improve and avoid making poor decisions. The better you know yourself, the better you will be able to manage yourself.

Communicate effectively. The ability to effectively communicate is essential to success academically, socially, and professionally. Most misunderstandings are the result of ineffective communication. Communication involves listening, speaking, writing, body language, and facial expressions. Effective communication is not as easy as you might think. In fact, poor communication is cited as one of the most significant reasons for school, relationship, family, and business problems. The good news is effective communication techniques can be learned. For a few strategies see Chapter 11 on good communication strategies.

Listen to music, read books, watch television, and movies that lift your spirits. Minimize those that are negative and can pull you down emotionally. If after viewing a show that leaves you tense or anxious, it would be wise to change to programs that are more calming to your nerves.

Have a hobby. If you don't have a hobby or activity, find one! Have fun with it! Activities and hobbies are a great diversion from the normal routine and help to provide balance in your life. Note I said "balance." Too much of any one thing will throw you off balance, and that is not healthy.

Cultivate relationships. Constant daily deposits into the self, family, and personal relationships are vital to one's life balance and success. Develop healthy support systems and support others. Give more than you expect to receive. Social media can be an excellent thing in helping to stay connected with others. Unfortunately, there appears to be a trend away from frequent face-to-face relationships by Millennials and Generations Y and Z. This is impacting on such things as community service. For example, volunteer social organizations that do so much good for communities are having difficulty recruiting people in their twenties to mid-fifties. Many members of such organizations (seniors) feel that a reason for this is the trend towards self-entertainment (primarily focused on technology) and distracts from personal face-to-face contact and fewer volunteer initiatives. One of the fundamental principles to success in life is a focus on others rather than self. Technology can help to inform and connect, but when used in excess it interferes rather than helps to cultivate meaningful relationships and community service. Earl Nightingale said, "Our attitude towards others determines their attitude towards us." And the best way to help develop relationships and service is in person.

Forgive. Life is not fair. Bad things happen. When an injustice occurs to us or someone we care about, we feel hurt. A natural reaction is to retaliate and inflict pain on the person or persons who caused our hurt. In a Ken Burns special on "The West," in Season I, Episode 9, a Lakota Native American named Albert White Hat describes his struggle with forgiveness. He spoke of two massacres of Native Americans by U.S. soldiers. One occurred on November 29, 1864, on a Cheyenne and Arapaho reservation at Sand Creek in southeast Colorado. Six hundred seventy-five soldiers killed and wounded from 70 to 163 Native Americans, including many women and children. The second massacre occurred on December 29, 1890, at Wounded Knee in South Dakota. It is estimated that 150 to 300 Native American men, women, and children were killed. Congress later admitted the wrongdoing, but that did little for the grief and anger that descendants felt about the atrocities. After years of harboring such feelings, White Hat realized that his anger was steadily growing inside of him, and that if he did not address it, he was susceptible to doing something he would regret. He observed others who had hung on to their anger, eventually attempting to relieve their inner turmoil with displaced anger and blame, drugs and alcohol, or some other negative response. After days of prayer and meditation White Hat realized that the only way he could rid himself of the anger gnawing away at him was to forgive. "Besides," he said, "this is history, and there is nothing anyone else can do about it anyway." The persons who committed these massacres are long dead, so carrying around negative feelings about incidents that occurred 122 to 154 years ago was only pulling him down. Realizing this, White Hat chose to commit himself to remember his ancestors with memorials. But he would no longer allow unresolved anger to control his happiness, and the only way to do that is to forgive.

In her book, *The Power is Within You,* Louis Hay said, "When you are unwilling to forgive, you limit your growth. Forgiveness allows you to right a wrong, to have understanding instead of resentment, to have compassion instead of hatred." Fourteen passages in the Bible address the importance of forgiveness. Do you think that the willingness to forgive just might be a great value to help ensure a stress-free and happy life?

Be humble! Boasting, self-focus, placing oneself before the needs of others will do little to impress others. Ironic, isn't it? The braggart is trying to impress when they are doing the opposite. So avoid the temptation! Since one of the success principles is focus on others, one cannot do so when they focus on themselves. What do you think when others always consistently talk about themselves and their accomplishments?

Conversely, what is your impression of those who speak little of themselves, instead take more interest in others? This is not to say that a person should ever consider their own needs and wants. It is just that they should always be sensitive to the needs and desires others as well.

Mental Health

Success in school and in life is more mental than physical. Before we can act on our goals, we must first have the right mental attitude. Earl Nightingale said in his best-seller *Acres of Diamonds,* "We must believe, and not wish, but firmly **believe.**" Nightingale also said—

- *That success is based on effort, not luck.*
- *There is power in perseverance and determination.*
- *Have confidence in your parents, caregivers, teachers, mentors, coaches. If you lose confidence in others to help guide you, find others who you have faith in you. Then listen to them and respond!*
- *That you can achieve whatever you set your mind to.*

Nightingale uses the words "effort," "perseverance," "confidence" to achieve whatever you set your mind to. Critical to these is sound mental health. We live in a world that inundates us with constant stimulation. Our brains need rest, just as does the rest of our body. Consistent doses of over-stimulation can lead to adverse outcomes to include depression, loneliness, anxiety, etc. We can relax by watching television, surfing the net, communicating on social media, or listening to music. There is nothing wrong with such activities, but these activities provide our minds with external stimuli that block true effective mental relaxation. Chapter 20 will provide simple meditation strategies that will help relax the mind which, in turn, will help minimize mental stress and enhance learning. More advanced forms of relaxation (some term it "enlivening" the mind) can be achieved through practices such as Zen, Chopra, Tai Chi, Yoga, and breathing exercises. **If you experience ongoing anxiety, sadness, or depression despite any individual efforts you have tried, seek professional help!**

TIPS
To Increase Mental Health

Franklin Covey, a well-known leader and consultant on individual and organizational efficiency advises that mental self-fulfillment requires steady doses of learning through group interaction, reading, and study. Here are a few of his guidelines.

- Organize and prioritize, as explained in Chapter 7.
- Take a few moments every day to relax. Try meditation exercises.
- Watch television shows and movies and listen to music that are emotionally uplifting.
- Exercise regularly, eat healthily, and get proper rest, as described in the next section.
- To Covey's advice, I add — read, understand, and follow the advice presented in Chapter 24, "Obstacles to Achievement."

Physical Health: Nutrition, Sleep, and Exercise Nutrition

Nutritionists and scientists have proven over and over that healthy eating sharpens minds and improves health. A study from the University of Essex, United Kingdom, showed that children who consumed healthy foods scored higher in English, science, and math. Children eating healthy food also were calmer in the classroom. Regrettably, our food industry is not always our best advocate, although their marketers would have you believe differently. However, you can take charge of our dietary habits by taking a few crucial steps. The sooner healthy eating habits are introduced, the easier it will be to create lifelong practices that will contribute to health and positively affect outcomes in and out of school. I will offer general suggestions in this chapter, but I encourage you to consult authoritative sources, such as your pediatrician, primary care physician, or a nutritionist if you have any specific concerns.

According to the Dietary Guidelines for Americans, U.S. Department of Agriculture, Department of Health and Human Services. Alexandria, VA, healthy eating promotes optimal growth and development in children and prevents disease, such as diabetes, cardiovascular problems, and cancer. A healthy diet also prevents obesity, iron deficiency, and dental cavities. The *Dietary Guidelines for Americans* recommends that youth eat food rich in fruits and vegetables, whole grains, protein, and fat-free or low-fat dairy products. The guidelines also recommend that children, adolescents, and adults limit intake of solid fats (saturated and trans-fatty acids), sodium, sugars, and refined grains. Unfortunately, most young people are not following the recommendations outlined in the *Guidelines*. Eating a healthy breakfast is associated with an improved cognitive function (especially memory), reduced absenteeism, and improved mood.

TIPS
To Help Ensure Proper Nutritional Health

Limit eating out and fast food meals. Besides being expensive, eating at restaurants, and buying prepared meals are not always the healthiest choices. This is not to suggest that you should never enjoy a night out, just don't rely on restaurants as a means for avoiding the effort to cook at home. Fast food meals or quick-fix meals may be OK as an exception. They should not become the routine.

Do not overeat. Grandma may have insisted that you eat all the food on your plate, but current thinking is that it is not a good idea as it encourages over-eating. So, to resolve this issue, limit portion size.

Healthy snacks. Instead of unhealthy snacks, try fruits, whole grains, veggies, and nuts. Drink lots of water.

The American Heart Association recommends that sugar intake for children be limited to 12 grams (3 teaspoons) a day. Keep in mind that sugar is included in bread, canned goods, frozen dinners, ketchup, and fast foods. When these are combined with cookies and sweets, the amount of sugar intake will far exceed the daily recommended amount.

Avoid soda. One 12-oz soda has about 10 teaspoons of sugar. That is more than three times the daily recommended limit for children.

Sweets. Cut down on sugar in recipes. Candy, cookies, and ice cream should be a special treat, not a routine. Make your own snacks.

Limit processed foods. White bread, cakes, and pies are full of sugar.

Limit salt intake. One teaspoon of salt contains about 2,300 mg of sodium. Some guidelines for the maximum salt consumption suggest about 1,900 milligrams per day for children between the ages of 4 to 8, 2,200 milligrams for children 9 to 13, and 2,300 milligrams for teens 14 to 18. If only one teaspoon contains the maximum recommended amount, given the amount of salt included in processed food, it is simple to see how easy it is to exceed the daily recommended amount. Limit or try to avoid, packaged, restaurant, fast food, and salty snacks. Choose low-salt or reduced-sodium products.

Vitamins and minerals. Children require more vitamins and minerals to support growing bodies than do adults. Essential vitamins and minerals can be adequately obtained from fruits, vegetables, milk, yogurt, fish, eggs, poultry, lean meat, and unsalted nuts, and whole-grain foods such as whole-wheat bread, wheat, oats, barley, and brown rice.

Fats. Fats are essential for daily nutrition. Know the difference between the kinds of fats.

Trans fats must be limited. These are found in processed foods made with partially hydrogenated vegetable oils, vegetable shortenings, and most snack and baked foods. Healthy fats include monounsaturated fats that are found in canola oil, peanut oil, and olive oil — also, avocados, almonds, hazelnuts, pecans, pumpkin seeds, and sesame seeds.

Polyunsaturated fats. (Omega-3 and Omega-6 fatty acids) are found in fish such as salmon, herring, mackerel, and sardines. Polyunsaturated fats are also in unheated sunflower seeds, corn, soybean, flaxseed oils, and walnuts.

Natural remedies for stress and anxiety. Because prescription medication for stress, anxiety, and depression have side effects, many are turning to natural and herbal supplements. This does not mean that there are side effects with non-prescription supplements. It is important to understand that emotional issues cannot always be "cured," rather symptoms can be reduced temporarily. When emotional issues are experienced, it is essential to discover the cause, and this can best be done with the help of medical professionals. As more research and experience is known, certain supplements have been shown to be effective. A supplement that works for one person may not work for another. Supplements can also interact with other supplements or prescription medications. It is strongly advised to check with your primary care provider before starting any supplement. Here are a five of the more popular supplements that have shown to be effective for stress and anxiety.

Vitamin B Complex. Low levels of vitamin B have been linked to stress, irritability, and restlessness. Vitamin B is essential to maintain proper brain function.

Gama Aminobutyric (GABA). Deficiencies of this amino acid have caused anxiety, stress, and depression. GABA helps the body make endomorphins, a naturally produced chemical in the pituitary gland of the brain. The morphine-like chemicals help produce positive feelings and reduce stress.

Magnesium. Low magnesium levels can cause nervousness.

L-Theanine. An amino acid found in green tea that produces feelings of relaxation and reduces anxiety.

Niacin. A type of B3 vitamin that is necessary to create Serotonin. Deficiencies of B3 can cause anxiety, poor concentration, irritability, and apathy.

Iron. Numerous medical journals report that low iron levels resulted in higher behavioral problems in study groups. A study published in the *Archives of Pediatrics and Adolescent Medicine,* states that "the majority of children with ADHD have significantly lower levels of iron than children without ADHD." Although too little iron can cause problems, too much iron can cause grave illness, and even death. So, the best advice is to get iron from iron-rich foods such as beef, poultry, salmon, tuna, whole grains, eggs, dark leafy vegetables, shellfish, lamb and pork and shellfish. Iron supplements are OK but check with your primary care physician.

Sleep

According to WebMD, children ages 7 to 12 require from 10 to 11 hours of sleep every night. Adolescents from 12 to 18 need 8 to 9 hours of sleep. Other sources, such as Nationwide Children's Hospital, suggest at least 9. Mindell JA and Owens JA authors of *A Clinical Guide to Pediatric Sleep: Diagnosis and Management of Sleep* state that teens typically do not get enough sleep for a variety of reasons. Included is the fact that many school districts require students to be at school as early as 7 a.m. Thus, some students must get up as early as 5:00 to 6:00 a.m. Homework, after-school activities, and socializing can often lead teens to get to bed later than they should. When adolescents don't get enough sleep, it can lead to moodiness, irritability, and frustration. The JAs also report that sleep-deprived teens are more likely to engage in risky behavior, to include drowsy driving. Attention, memory, and decision making can be affected which, of course, will adversely affect schoolwork.

TIPS
TO HELP ENSURE ADEQUATE SLEEP

* Maintain a regular sleep schedule.
* Take short afternoon naps if needed.
* Turn off televisions, cell phones, computers, tablets, and non-soothing music.

- Avoid stimulants containing caffeine and sugar.
- Avoid oversleeping on weekends. Doing so will throw week-day sleep patterns out of balance.

Exercise

The U.S. Department of Health and Human Services recommends one hour of physical activity for youth every day. Included is moderate or vigorous aerobic activity daily or at least vigorous intensity at least three days a week. Muscle training and bone training should be included in the daily activity, or as a minimum three days per week. But even low-intensity exercise, such as walking can have beneficial results. A combination of low-intensity workouts and mind/body exercises can have dramatic effects on both physical and mental health.

TIPS
For Proper Physical and Mental Exercise

Moderate aerobic exercise includes walking/comfortable strolls, moderate-intensity hiking, skateboarding, bicycle riding, brisk walking, and dancing.

Vigorous aerobic workouts include sports such as soccer, swimming, tennis, and track.

Muscle strengthening includes push-ups, sit-ups, and resistance exercises.

Bone-strengthening includes skipping, jumping, basketball, volleyball, and baseball.

Mind-body exercise includes Yoga, Tai Chi, and Qi Gong.

Check out Yoga breathing strategies. Deep breathing strategies can re-balance the autonomic nervous system, thus help to relieve stress.

A combination of low-intensity workouts and meditation can have dramatic effects on both physical and mental health.

Chapter 9
Ten Essential Traits

One's character is set at an early age.
The choices you make now will affect
you for the rest of your life.
I hate to see you swim out so far you can't swim back.
"Flipped" by Wendelin Van Draanen

The "Foundation" (Spiritual) and "Columns" (Purpose, Emotional/ Social, Mental Health, and Physical Health) presented in Chapter 8 answer "what" we should incorporate into our daily lives. They answer the question of who we want to be as a person, or how we want to live our lives. The essential traits listed in this Chapter define how we relate to the world. Although we can list many, I have selected ten that are essential for success in life.

Character traits can be both good and bad. Readers may wish to add or substitute other traits they think apply to most you. For the ten I listed, I challenge you to review them, then honestly quiz yourself how you think you have incorporated or intend to incorporate these traits into your life.

Character traits are essential for success in higher education and in careers. As stated in the Preface, families and the community play a significant role in the successful education of children. To compliment what is taught in the home, youth programs such as Scouting, 4-H and Future Farmers of America teach skills that that help prepare youth for college, choose a career path and be successful.

Some people think only intellect counts:
knowing how to solve problems, knowing
how to get by, knowing how to identify an

advantage and seize it. But the functions of
intellect are insufficient without courage,
love, friendship, compassion, and empathy.
Dean Koontz

Caring. I care about others and try to understand their viewpoints.

Several words help to define the spirit of "caring." Kindness, concern, compassion, support, empathy. It is essential to listen to the viewpoints of others and try hard to see things from their point of view. You do not need to agree, only to understand. We can care for others but not experience the feelings of another. Although having empathy is difficult to achieve, it is an emotion well worth striving for. By so doing, it enhances the ability to care. Because we have our feelings and opinions, it is often difficult to set these aside, even momentarily, to objectively and without prejudice "hear" what others are trying to tell us. If we do not hear, we cannot understand. If we do not understand, it makes the ability to care more complicated, and if we cannot care, we cannot achieve empathy. Get it? Daniel Goleman in *Social Intelligence: The New Science of Human Relationships*, said, "Self-absorption in all its forms kills empathy, let alone compassion. When we focus on ourselves, our world contracts as our problems and preoccupations loom large. But when we focus on others, our world expands. Our problems drift to the periphery of the mind and so seem smaller, and we increase our capacity for connection or compassionate action."

Integrity is telling myself the truth.
Honesty is telling the truth to others.
Spencer Johnson

Integrity. I know being honest will cause favorable outcomes.

According to Wikipedia, "Integrity is the practice of being honest and showing a consistent and uncompromising adherence to strong moral and ethical principles and values." Honesty reflects who you are as a person. Being honest means others can count on you to do the right thing and doing what you committed doing. Thus, it affects your reputation and ultimately, your success and happiness. The tabloids and newspapers continually report on successful people who have fallen from grace because of a single act of dishonesty. There is a saying, "One aw crap wipes out a dozen attaboys." This can apply to many things, and assuredly when one is dishonest. Living a life of complete honesty is difficult. We are human and susceptible to influence and temptation.

I indeed have been guilty. If I told you I had done nothing I have been ashamed of, I would not be honest. To this day I carry shame for not being truthful to my mother when I was a teenager. I had scratched a favorite figurine of hers. She asked my brother, sister, and I who had done it. I never owned up to it. Although the infraction was relatively minor, the dishonesty for me has not been insignificant. My mother probably had long forgotten the incident when she was living, yet I still carry the guilt. Had I owned up to it, it would have been done and over with many years ago. The point is that the effort to cover up a dishonest act will have long-lasting adverse effects than the temporary consequences resulting from being truthful.

Dishonesty has a direct bearing on one's reputation. Poor reputations cause loss of friends, jobs, and opportunities. Your reputation is one of your most valued assets. When you have a good reputation, you feel good about yourself, and others feel good about you. Do all you can do to preserve your reputation. Keep asking yourself, "Is what I'm doing contributing to or taking away from my reputation?" Agree with yourself to make decisions that will only reflect well on you, your family, your organization, and your country. Do not allow the poor choice of others to sway or deter you from doing what you know is right. If you do, the price you pay could cost you dearly.

Besides being honest with others, it is also essential to be honest with yourself. If you lie to yourself, you will be unable to be honest with others. It also means being frank with others. It does not mean being insensitive or rude. A person can be honest with another while expressing thoughts and feelings tactfully and gently. It also means not compromising your convictions even when others are pressuring you to do otherwise. I think this following quote by Barbara DeAngelis, the well-known relationship consultant, and TV personality says it well. She says that living with integrity means "not settling for less than what you know you deserve in your relationships. Asking for what you want and need from others—speaking your truth, even though it might create conflict or tension. Behaving in ways that are in harmony with your values. Making choices based on what you believe and not what others believe." To DeAngelis' remark I add, follow her advice and do so with gentleness, sensitivity, and tact.

One more quote (sorry about that). I think Denis Waitley, a favorite motivational speaker, author, and consultant on how to be a winner, well defines the significant consequence of when integrity is compromised. He said, "If there are no moral absolutes, if morality depends on the situation and circumstance, if people do what 'feels good,' ultimately they will lose their integrity and self-respect." To that, I remind readers that "self-respect" is your most valued possession. Guard it as if your happiness depends on it! It does.

All our dreams can come true if
we dare to pursue them.
Walt Disney

Confidence. I can do this.

Confidence is a belief in oneself and your abilities. Having self-confidence is the key to success. Lack of confidence is one of the most significant roadblocks to achieving success. To accomplish, one must take chances (reasonable ones) and seize opportunities when presented. Over-confidence can cause one to take risky chances or to come across as self-centered or cocky. So, a healthy balance is essential. You can gain confidence by following the guidance provided in SECTIONS A and B. Also, seek out support groups and friends who help build your self-esteem. If others (to include family) do not help you feel good about yourself, learn to ignore those who would put you down, and turn to those who help build you up.

My attitude, not my aptitude, will determine my altitude.
Zig Ziglar

Attitude. I know my attitude will determine my destiny.

An "attitude" is one's feeling or position about something or someone. Attitude has a considerable influence on how we perceive our world. I sincerely believe that how we look at our world makes the difference between happiness and sadness, success, and failure. Put another way, one's mental attitude often is the determining factor in success in life. How you think about things is the foundation of everything in your life. Earl Nightingale, who through his publications and presentations motivated hundreds and thousands of people to achieve top success in life, wrote, "Our environment, the world in which we live and work, is a mirror of our attitudes and expectations." Negative thoughts and emotions such as anger, resentment, jealousy, shame, and bitterness leave us in a state of unhappiness and depression. Harmful actions such as dishonesty, lying, blame, deceit, gossip, complaining, and stealing also create a mental state that brings one down and severely interferes with happiness, the impression others have on us and, ultimately, success. Positive people look at what they have rather than what they don't. They view the wonder of the world about them. They create a mighty mental attitude that fosters positive outcomes in their lives.

When I was doing behavior counseling, I provided this scenario. "If I have a magic wand and I wave it in front of you, then suddenly you have lost your life's partner, you are no longer employable, your health is failing, and you know that your days on Earth will soon end, would this depress you?" Everyone I asked replied, "yes." "Well," I continued, "this is what many of our seniors go through." Few with whom I asked realized the connection of the scenario with seniors. Then I continue with this story. My father was in this situation when he was 84. My sister would look in on him from time to time.

One day after a visit, as she was leaving, she turned to him and said, "Dad, your glass always seems to be half full." "No," he replied. "Uh-oh," Lida thought to herself, "maybe he is not as optimistic as I thought." My father then added, "My glass is overflowing." How is it that a man can view his glass as "overflowing" when he was facing the life challenges I described? If you knew my father, it would not be hard to understand. He looked at what he had, not at what he did not have. He was living in his home, had relatively good health, was financially comfortable. He had a loving family and many friends. He was not overly religious, but he was spiritual. He also accepted where he was at in life and did not try to control events. He enjoyed reflecting on the happy memories of his past yet lived in the moment. A wounded combat veteran of World War II and Korea, he did not dwell on the negative memories of his past. He also continued to serve his community with his active involvement in The Military Orders of the World Wars, whose motto is, "It is nobler to serve than to be served." When we feel gratitude for what we have, rather than what we don't have, we will experience more joy in life. At this point, you may be saying, "This may seem easy in principle, but it is just not so easy just to say, I am now optimistic and grateful." True, it is not necessarily easy. But there are ways to help see the "glass as overflowing" or at least "half full."

My father-in-law, a man of limited means and fragile health, also had the right attitude. One of his philosophies was to live life simply. "Don't want things too nice," he advised. In a society in which we place so much value on materialistic "things," it is indeed sound advice. Pap, as we called him, also had his priorities right—faith, family, and all else in that order.

Here are a few truisms that can help.

- How you think about things will determine your attitude, and your attitude determines your life.

- No one controls your attitudes other than you.
- When you control your thinking, you control your life.
- You have the power to change the way you think.

Focus on what is going right. When one or two things go wrong, we are tempted to think everything is going wrong. When we are in this state of mind, it is easy to forget what is going right. When you change your negative thoughts to positive ones, your attitude changes, and that your experiences change for the better. So how do we turn a negative situation and negative thinking around? When you are experiencing negative emotions such as stress, anxiety, worry, sadness, loneliness, envy, and insecurity, to name a few—try to recognize the underlying feeling behind the thought. Often it is **"fear."** The Matrix websites provides good advice on dealing with stress, anxiety, and depression for high school students. (https://www.matrix.edu.au/coping-with-stress-how-maintain-your-mental-health-during-hsc/)

It may be hard but try to uncover what it is you are fearful. If you cannot readily identify your fears, you may need professional help. Don't be timid about getting help. You are not unique. Everyone has something they are afraid of. The benefits of getting a good handle on our emotions far outweigh the negatives of holding on to old beliefs.

Recognize that outer circumstances can determine your feelings, but they need not control your attitude. Tell yourself that you will not allow external events to affect your attitude. Easier said than done, I know, but tell yourself this anyway and keep telling yourself! By so doing, you will gradually shift your thinking from reacting negatively to responding positively.

A key component of one's attitude is their perspective, or to quote from one of the best children's books ever published, "it all depends on how you look at things… it all depends on how you look at things." The quote comes from the book *The Churkendoose*, by Ben Ross Berenberg. I think the story so well describes the value of "attitude" that I feel compelled to share a portion of it with you. The book is the story of an odd little bird hatched from an oversized egg in the barnyard. He was born with the head of a chicken, the body of a turkey, the legs of a duck, and a mouth like a goose. He had one ear that stuck out from the back of his head.

Being different, he was not accepted by the other barnyard animals and was ignored. Regardless, he allowed his differences, as was exemplified by his words, "Well, I'm not a chicken, and I'm not a duck. I have more brains than I have luck, I'm not a turkey, and I'm not a goose. Can't you see? I'm a Churkendoose." He goes on to ask the other animals, "Must I be a chicken or a goose? Can't I be a Churkendoose?"

Nevertheless, he was thrown out of the henhouse because he was just too ugly. He wonders why others do not like him. "Can it be that I am such a sight? That when others see me, they take fright?" One day he hears a commotion in the barnyard. He quickly returns to see a fox in the henhouse. When the fox sees the strange bird, he is frightened away. Of course, the Churkendoose is welcomed back as a hero. Confused by his sudden notoriety he states, "No, no wait. Before you caused me tears, now you're giving me three cheers. 'Cause I chased the fox and set you free. Well, I don't want the tears, and I don't want the cheers. Can't you like me just because I'm me?" The hens see their hypocrisy and begin to like him, not for what he did, instead because of who he was. The Churkendoose then states, "What fun we have. Now we help each other and learn from each other. Making friends can be a pleasure cause a good friend is a treasure." The book concludes with my favorite line when the Churkendoose exclaims, "It all depends on how you look at things—it all depends on how you look at things." When we strive to see things from other's point of view, we gain understanding.

When we increase understanding, our attitudes and relationships change for the better. The Churkendoose did not allow the prejudice of the others to affect the views of himself. He accepted himself as he was. Just as significant was the attitude change of the chickens. Their attitudes towards the Churkendoose changed when they looked beyond his outer appearance to see his inner spirit.

Learn to accept criticism as an opportunity to learn, even if the person making the criticism does not come across with tact and sensitivity. Grow from your experiences. If you keep making the same mistakes, you will continue to get the same results. Be open to learning from others but stay in control of your feelings about yourself. You are the master of your life, not others.

Happiness will come to you when it comes from you.
Success will be yours when you choose to
take responsibility for making it so.
Author unknown

Responsibility. I take responsibility for what I do or fail to do.

Responsibility means being accountable. When you make excuses or blame others, you are relinquishing your power to grow emotionally.

Taking responsibility also means doing what is necessary to make sure a task is completed. A project or idea will never come to fruition if the desire to follow it through to completion does not exist. The key is planning. Planning entails, setting goals, then devising a strategy to meet those goals. The approach requires the use of tools to facilitate the process. The "tools" help to organize, prioritize, check, and correct. What are the tools? Planners, calendars, file folders, organization boxes, labels, award stickers, bookcases, etc.

If you are challenged with taking responsibility, review the suggestions provided in SECTION B.

Children must be taught how to
think, not what to think.
Margaret Mead

Judgment. I will make good choices.

Although I have labeled this skill as "judgment," in effect, it is based on the power of making choices. The most significant strength we have over our destiny is the ability to make choices. Let me rephrase this. *We create who we are through the choices we make.* The choice you make every minute of every day determines your life. Every word, every action (or inaction), every decision, determines your destiny. Sadly, jails and graveyards are full of good people who made bad decisions. The way we view our world and how we respond is the result of the choices we make.

A student may have little choice whether to go to school or not or what core courses to take. The student must decide if they want to study or not, to do an assignment promptly, or even do it at all, to participate in extracurricular activities, play hooky, go on to higher education and, if so, where to go. What to major in what career course to pursue? Making choices can often be a daunting task, especially if you do not know where you are headed. The challenge is the fact that many college students in their first or second years do not have a clear vision of what they want to major in or what career path they would like to follow. According to a study conducted by the National Association of Colleges and Employers (NACE), as many as 80 percent of college students change their major at least once. Some change their majors two or three times. Reasons that influence why a student may choose a major include inspiration of a teacher or professor, earning potential, family desires, friends, or just "drifted" into a new major. Only about 66 percent choose majors based on career interests, reports NACE. Many do not choose their majors based on their heart or talents. Of course, switching majors usually results in an increase in cost and added coursework.

Making choices can often be made easier by discovering what your calling may be. The earlier in life this can be ascertained, the easier decisions will be later. To help, ask these questions: What are your strengths and weaknesses, likes and dislikes, your passions, preferences, tastes? Do you have a purpose? Once you get a handle on such questions, the choices become easier. My father said that the sign of a rich man is not how much money he makes; instead, could he look forward to going to work every day. The same applies to school. If you are not afraid to follow your passions, your dreams, and to use your talents, you will have done yourself a great favor in creating for yourself a content and happy future.

If nothing is ventured, nothing is gained.
Sir John Heywood

Initiative. I will take the necessary action to resolve issues or find solutions.

Taking the initiative means doing something because you choose to do it, not because someone told you to do it. All around us, all day long, we are the beneficiaries of the initiatives of others. Electronics, transportation, education opportunities, defense, health and medicine, social advances. The list is endless. Such gifts did not grow out of the ground, instead were created by the initiatives of people. For many, it is their potential that drives them to take the initiative to create, to invent, to improve. Indeed, many will take action to help to make the world better, even if only in a small way. Some will choose to take no or little initiative. Some people are "reactive" to life events. In other words, they will do what others direct them to do. Others are "proactive." That is, they take the initiative to accomplish things on their own without waiting to be told. If you want to be appreciated by others, to get ahead in school and the workplace—take the initiative!

Nothing great was ever achieved without enthusiasm.
R.W. Emerson

Motivation. When I want to do something badly enough it, I will do it.

When someone wants to do something, they become motivated. Although this book describes study strategies (SECTION D), and classrooms strategies (SECTION E), to help ensure academic success, if a student is not motivated to learn how to study smarter, no approach will help. Humans naturally seek out which is most enjoyable. If an activity is perceived as dull or uninteresting, it is difficult to want to do that which is of little or no interest. So, the challenge is to inspire. Many of the TIPS contained in this book address ways to motivate. The key is to get started. The best way to do that is to actively visualize rewards, then set goals (Chapter 4) and timelines. Once that done, take small steps to achieve those goals. Apply incentives for yourself. Doing these little things helps to boost confidence and improves attitude, which enhances motivation.

> ## *Talent wins games, but teamwork and intelligence win championships.*
> ### Michael Jordan

Teamwork. I recognize that I must be a team player and that there is power in numbers.

Although personal skills are necessary for success, achievements are often dependent on cooperative efforts with others. In sports, a single outstanding player cannot win by him or herself. To win, a collective effort by all team members is necessary. This is true with team sports such as soccer, baseball, volleyball, as well as individual sports, such as golf, swimming, track, skating, etc. All athletes benefit from the teaching and guidance of coaches, from the encouragement of fans and family, and the support of fellow team members. Collaboration is, of course, not limited to athletics, but is essential in practically all endeavors in life, be it with family, social or work. We have developed in our society a high emphasis on competition. This is not a bad thing and will help to establish essential success skills. However, an over-emphasis on a "win-lose" philosophy that promotes "getting over on" an opponent can encourage confrontation, poor sportsmanship, and lack of integrity. Thus, it becomes a detriment to fostering a cooperative spirit. The "win-win" philosophy strives to win, but encourages competition that is respectful to opponents, adheres to fair play, and promotes the enjoyment of the activity for all regardless of who wins or loses. The "win-win" philosophy applies not just to athletics but to any group endeavor to include family, school, clubs, and business. Persons who do not embrace and consistently practice proper teamwork skills will, at some point, find themselves off the team. They have forgotten to apply the essential success principle of working honestly and cooperatively with others.

Whatever your goals, don't give up!
Amy Grant

Perseverance. I will not give up.

The ability to remain constant to a purpose, goal, or task. Many talented people have not achieved their dreams or not amounted to much in their lives. There are countless stories of persons who are physically or psychologically challenged yet have realized extraordinary accomplishments. Why? The answer is simple. Perseverance! Put another way; it is the personal quality that one will follow jobs through to completion. The difference between persons who try and fail and those who try and succeed can often be traced to the level of their perseverance. You can help motivate yourself to persevere by having a Purpose and by following the guidance provided in SECTION B.

When things are not going right.

When contemplating the ten essential traits, assess your strengths and weaknesses, and set goals to make yourself the best you can be. Everyone will fall short from time to time. Do not fret; we are human. When you find yourself faltering, or when things are not going your way, remember that you have the power to change the way you look at things.

Chapter 10
How to Be a Great Leader

If you inspire others to dream more, learn more, do more, and become more, you are a leader.
President John Q. Adams

Many young people would like to perform in a leadership role in some capacity. It may be captain of a sports team, leader in a junior or senior reserve officer training program, an officer for a youth club or organization, or a peer leader in a non-organized activity. If a young person does not aspire to a leadership role, that is perfectly fine. Not everyone wants to be a leader. For those who would like to assume a leadership role, read on!

What exactly does "leadership" mean? Although many differ on precisely what makes up a "leader," as a retired U.S. Army officer, former manager and leader in public, private and volunteer organizations, and a student of leadership theory, I feel confident that I can adequately identify and describe the attributes that effective leaders have in common. Before I do, however, I would like to distinguish between the term's "leadership" and "managership." Although the two terms are often used synonymously, there is a difference. Managers focus on details. So too should leaders, but they must go a step further. Before a person can lead, they first manage themselves. The best distinction I have ever seen that defines the difference between a "manager" and a "leader" was published in the Wall Street Journal in 1986 by the United Technologies Corporation.

People don't want to be managed,
They want to be led.
Whoever heard of a world manager?

World leader, yes!
Educational leader. Political leader. Religious leader. Scout leader.
Business leader.
They lead! They don't manage.
The carrot always wins over the stick.
Ask your horse. You can lead your horse to water, but you can't
manage him to drink.
If you want to manage somebody, manage yourself.
Do that well, and you'll be ready to stop managing...
And start leading.

I think this passage well distinguishes the difference between a "manager" and a "leader." Few employees have been spared the agony of having to work for a "micro-manager," or a manager who focused so much on details yet failed to inspire subordinates to do their best. Sadly, some of these managers can climb the ladder to a position of leadership. Often such people turn out to be ineffective in the leadership role. The result for their organization is a struggle and even failure. Why? Because the skills necessary for managing are not the same as the skills required to lead. For example, a manager's priority is to focus on procedural details, whereas a leader will focus on inspiring others to carry out duties to accomplish specified goals. I am not suggesting that leaders do not manage, and managers do not lead. Good managers and leaders do both effectively. Another reason why some managers fall short of being effective leaders is that they did not adequately learn enough self-management skills. So, if one cannot correctly manage themselves, how can they accurately manage others, much less lead others? The best leaders in history were also good followers. So, if you are not willing to follow, how can you learn to lead? Would others be more willing to support you if they knew that you had the experience and knowledge of being a follower?

Self-management is only part of the equation. Poor leaders also lack or are weak in one or more of the "10 Essential Traits" described in Chapter 9. Indeed, personal characteristics can contribute to a person's ability to be a leader, but studies have shown that leadership traits can be learned. Specific attributes have been identified as typical of good leaders. Note, I said, "good leaders." Adolf Hitler, Atilla the Hun, Genghis Kahn, and Ivan the Terrible were leaders who killed millions of people. They may have been effective in getting others to fight and die, but they were not good leaders. In fact, they are among the most hated leaders in world history. By studying and practicing the characteristics described below, you too can be a leader and be a good one!

The U.S. Army has identified the primary attributes common to good leaders. There are three categories: BE, KNOW, and DO with specific attributes assigned to each group. All the Ten Essential Traits (attributes) described in Chapter 9 can be attached to each of the three categories. I have slightly modified the Army's description, but the basics are the same. I have also added two not included in the Ten Essential Traits: "Knowledge" and "Communication." The reason for this is that the "Ten Essential Traits" deal with personal characteristics, whereas the traits described in this Chapter (Knowledge and Communication added) deal with traits necessary for interacting with others. Essential Traits are essential to be a leader. That is why I say "manage yourself first" before striving to "lead" others.

BE

"BE" describes your character. Traits that apply to you as an individual

Care. Caring for yourself, others, your country, your team, and your organization are essential to be a good leader. If you don't care, then get off the team!

Integrity. Team members want their leaders to be honest, fair, and forthright. Treat others the way you want to be treated. To be honest with others, first, be honest with yourself. Doing so will result in respect, and without respect, there is no pride, and without pride, the game is lost.

Confidence. Belief in yourself! When you are confident in yourself, your team members will be as well. Don't let the doubts of others deter you! Develop competence in your team. Instill in them the attitude they can accomplish whatever they set out to do.

Attitude. Be positive! Do not allow negative attitudes to pull you or your team down. Pay no heed to those who say, "can't," "won't," "too hard," or verbalize other such negativisms. Promote positive thinking and optimism. Be excited! Have fun!

Responsibility. Take responsibility for your own actions or inactions, and those of your team. Doing so fosters respect. Admitting mistakes may be painful in the short run, but in the long term, forgiveness is probable and ultimately promotes more goodwill than to deny, blame, or cover-up. When you must decide, once you have enough information to make that decision, make it, even if it may be unpopular. Although it is nice to be liked and respected, it is more important to be respected. People will follow leaders whom they respect, not necessarily those they merely "like."

KNOW

"KNOW" describes the knowledge you have about the subject and group you are striving to lead.

Knowledge. The more involved you are, the better leader you will be. How can you guide and lead others if you do not know what you are leading for? Study, practice, review, teach!

Judgment. In Chapter 9, "Ten Essential Traits," I addressed "judgment" as it relates to making good choices for oneself. Leaders have the additional challenge of making sound judgment calls for the highest good of the group. There are countless examples in history in which persons in leadership positions have faltered and even failed because they made poor judgment decisions. According to Merriam-Webster, "judgment" is "the act or process of forming an opinion or making a decision after careful thought; the act of judging something or someone; the ability to make good decisions about what should be done." Even after striving to look at all variables before deciding, sometimes things do not go as planned. This is life. Move on. Subordinates rely on their leaders to try to make the best decisions for the group, given the information available.

DO

"DO" describes how you go about applying the traits described under "BE" and "KNOW."

Initiative. Being proactive and not waiting for others to tell you what or when to do things. On your own, make assessments, plan, and act based on the task at hand. This does not suggest that you do not seek or seriously consider the advice of others before making decisions.

Motivate. Have a vision of what you want your team to achieve, then motivate others to embrace that vision. Inspire them to do what it takes to succeed. Promote creativity, encourage initiative.

Teamwork. Strength comes from people working together in a cohesive, synergistic manner. Effective leaders get people to work in harmony. Leaders support team members. For people to do their very best work, they need an organizational environment that encourages them by making it safe to take reasonable risks, to tell the truth, and to speak up—without being punished for doing so. Support your team by creating this kind of environment.

Persevere. Highly effective leaders aren't afraid to be decisive and to make tough calls quickly when circumstances require it. Once they have all the information needed to make an informed decision, they make the decision then stick with it, unless there is a particularly compelling reason to change it.

Communicate. In any organization, knowledge is power. Great leaders ensure that they provide every team member of the organization with complete and up-to-date information about the organization's goals, performance, successes, and failures. To achieve this level of connection, leaders also provide ample channels for two-way communication between team members and the leadership team. Acknowledge ideas offered, whether adopted or not. Great care must be taken to ensure that information which flows up the chain is not distorted. Help ensure that communication from subordinates is accurate and timely. Do this by maintaining an open line of communication with team members at all levels of the organization. Good leaders will have an "open door" policy that allows subordinates to speak with top leadership without interference from middle managers.

One of the most effective leaders I know is retired U.S. Navy Command Master Chief Charles "Chuck" Baldwin. His last military assignment was the chief enlisted leader of the 5,500- sailor, nuclear-powered aircraft carrier USS Dwight D. Eisenhower, and a finalist for the top non-commissioned officer of the U.S. Navy. Baldwin later used his leadership skills to co-found one of the finest high school military academies in the country, the Delaware Military Academy. He also served as a Junior ROTC instructor, middle school principal, president of the Charter School of Wilmington (DE), and consultant in the creation of the First State Military Academy. He has received many awards and recognition for his accomplishments and serves on several boards and commissions. Baldwin embraces and espouses 10 leadership principles for anyone who aspires to be a leader, both youth and adult. The model is "Deckplate Leadership" that he lists in his book *From Carrier to Classroom*. These principles are:

1. Always accept challenging assignments and situations. Be known as the one who gets it done.
2. It is okay to question an order and display apprehension. Remember though, that proper procedure is to use the chain of command before you act.
3. Learn all the skills of an assigned position to gain the respect of subordinates.

4. Use respectful language when dealing with people; never be demeaning or hurtful. If you slip, apologize sincerely.
5. Praise in public, reprimand in private.
6. All students are great kids.
7. MAP—daily performance is composed of Moral, Academic, and Physical activities.
8. Know your people.
9. Be known by your people.
10. Be enthusiastic.

Final Thoughts on SECTIONS A, B, and C

Make a point of practicing the "BE, KNOW, DO" leadership attributes, and Chief Baldwin's "Deckplate Leadership" principles, and you will be destined to be an effective and even great leader, regardless of the type organization you are affiliated.

In SECTIONS A, B, and C of *Student Success with Less Stress*, I have provided the essential actions, values, traits, and attributes a person needs to be a success. Challenge yourself to apply the principles to your lives. Know them, practice them, be them! This is not to suggest that you will have a few bumps in your road, you will. But the more you use and apply the skills and traits, the better you will be able to deal with challenges, and your "bumps" in the road will stay as bumps and not turn in to obstacles to success.

SECTION D
Clever Study Strategies

Let us train our minds to desire
what the situation demands.
Seneca

Chapter 11
Communication Strategies to Get Ahead

One of the most famous lines often quoted is from the 1967 movie, "Cool Hand Luke," starring Paul Newman, *"What we've got here is a failure to communicate."* Why is the line so often quoted? Because it reflects the fact that the failure to properly communicate results in misunderstanding, confusion, failures, discord, and stress. For complete communication to occur, three critical elements are involved:

1. The message must be sent.
2. The message must be received.
3. The message must be understood.

Although the three critical elements are true for all types of communication, in this section, I am only addressing face-to-face communication, not written as in letters, notes, email, or texting. Since we cannot usually control how messages are sent (especially in a classroom), I will also not address this; however, we can control how we receive messages. This is done visually and auditorily. The art of communication is the most under-schooled and improperly used communication tools utilized in our society today. Think about it. How many times have you missed valuable information because you did not "hear" or possibly "understand" what others were trying to communicate to you?

If the message is not received, it cannot very well be understood, can it? There are many reasons that a message sent by another may not be "received." Maybe we did not understand the other due to language barriers, external interference, or perception. More often, however, we "block" our ability to listen effectively. When we "block" the messages of others, we are "passive listeners." Passive listeners often lose what is being said by others, thus suffer the consequences of missed messages and necessary information.

Barriers to communication

- **Information Overload.** We are surrounded with a pool of information. It is essential to control this information flow or else the information is likely to be misinterpreted or forgotten or overlooked. As a result, communication is less effective.
- **Inattention.** Not paying attention.
- **Time Pressures.** Often in school and in daily life, we are required to perform within a specified time period, the failure of which has adverse consequences. In a haste to meet deadlines, the formal channels of communication are shortened, or messages are partially given, i.e., not completely transferred. Thus, enough time should be given for effective communication.
- **Distraction/Noise.** Communication is also affected by noise and other distractions. Physical distractions include poor lightning; uncomfortable sitting, or ineffective room arrangement.
- **Emotions.** Emotions effect communication. If the receiver feels that the communicator is angry, he interprets that the information being sent is bad. If the communicator is happy and jovial the message can be interpreted to be good and interesting.
- **Poor retention.** Human memory cannot function beyond a limit. One can't always retain what is being told, especially if he is not interested or inattentive.

Non-verbal communication

Effective non-verbal communication is essential not only for academic success but for positive human relationships and career success. Based on his research, Dr. Albert Mehrabian, author of

Silent Messages, said less communication is conveyed through words than through nonverbal features such as facial expression and body language. Other researchers agree that the most communication is nonverbal. What is included in "nonverbal" communication?

- Body language and body movements and posture.
- Eye contact.
- Physical closeness.
- Voice tone, pitch, speed.
- Facial expressions.

According to the research of R. Adler, L. Rosenfeld, and R. Proctor, *Interplay: The Process of Interpersonal Communicating,* adults spend an average of 100 percent of their time engaged in some sort of communication. Of this, an average of 45 percent is spent listening, 30 percent speaking, 16 percent reading, and 9 percent writing. Research suggests that we remember only about 25 percent to 50 percent of what we hear. That is not very good. Even if "heard," how much have they "understood" the intent of the speaker? Studies have shown that effective listeners, also termed "active listeners," have more friends, have greater self-confidence and make higher grades at school. What does it take to be an "active listener"? First, let's look at some of the things that interfere with being an "active listener."

When we should be listening attentively, we may tend to do one or more of the following activities that block our listening ability, rather than focusing on what the other person is saying. When we do not focus on what is being said, we often miss important points the other is trying to convey.

Here is a list of some of the things we do that interfere with effective listening.

Mind read. Trying to figure out what the other person is really trying to say or feel.

Rehearse. Thinking about what you are going to say.

Judge. Placing labels on other's opinions before you know the facts, such as "they are unqualified, prejudiced, hypocritical, etc."

Dream. Thinking about other things.

Advise. Providing opinions before you have heard all the facts or understood their position.

Debate. Taking a strong position on an issue before considering the other's viewpoint.

Strive to be right. Unwillingness to admit that you may be wrong or made a mistake.

Tuning off. Changing the subject because you have lost interest.

Lose focus. Not intently paying attention. For students, this is often caused by excessive note-taking. If you try to write down everything the speaker is saying word-for-word, you will miss much of what the speaker is saying.

Multi-task. Inattentive listening because you're doing something else while the message is being delivered.

The first step in improving non-verbal communication skills is to assess which blocks most apply to you. Be honest with yourself about this. We all use them from time to time. If we are unwilling to recognize in ourselves the block we use, it will be impossible to grow into an active listener.

What are some strategies that can help to overcome "blocks" to be an effective listener? Active listeners can better identify main points, filter out extraneous information, and integrate new information with prior knowledge. Active listening helps with concentration, thus facilitates the ability to recall information. Active listeners do not have to spend time seeking to find the answers to questions missed the first time around and fixing mistakes. Passive listeners, on the other hand, often lose what is being said by others, thus suffer the consequences of missed messages and necessary information. Let's examine the art of listening and how you can improve your listening skills. Listening is a process that has three essential steps.

1. **Hearing.** "Hearing" means listening enough to catch what the speaker is saying. For example, you can "hear" another

speak a foreign language, but you may not understand the message the sender is trying to convey. We hear sounds, but that does not mean we understand those sounds.

2. **Understanding.** For effective communication to occur, one must know what the sender is trying to tell us. When you have heard the message, and understand it, then effective communication has taken place.

3. **Judging.** Since we all have different perceptions, values, and points of view, we often interpret what we hear and understand in different ways. Does what the speaker say make sense to you? Can you set aside your views and prejudices to try and objectively understand what the speaker is saying? This does not mean you necessarily have to agree, just "understand."

TIPS
FOR BETTER COMMUNICATION SKILLS

When you are communicating with another

Realize that much communication is, in fact, non-verbal. So, to foster your non-verbal communication skills:

- **Sit or stand close enough to the speaker**, so you can clearly hear what the other is saying. If sitting, lean slightly forward in the direction of the speaker.
- **Maintain eye contact.**
- **Indicate to the other person that you are listening** by an occasional nod or verbal acknowledgment such as "yes," "I understand," "right," "uh-huh," etc. Of course, this is not appropriate in the classroom.
- **Be aware of body language** and facial expressions that can convey interest, disinterest, agreement, or disagreement.
- **Remove or get away from distractions.**
- **Be committed to understanding the other.**

- **Stay focused!** Give your full attention to the person who is speaking. If you are unable to focus, maybe it is because your mind is on something else or you may be not emotionally open at the time, ask to postpone the conversation to a more opportune time. Of course, this strategy will not work in a classroom.

Don't interrupt! Let the speaker finish before you begin to talk. Speakers must be allowed to complete their thoughts without interruption or others changing the subject.

When you are the speaker

- **Make your point as briefly** as possible to lessen the listener's temptation to tune out.
- **Express yourself so others will listen.** Clearly state what you have observed, think, feel and want. Be sincere. Avoid gossip, blame, or accusing others. Show interest in others.
- **Clarify.**
- **Ask questions.** "Can you give me an example" or "Have you ever felt that way before"?
- **Paraphrase.** In other words, state in your own words what you think the other is saying. Example: "So, in other words, you are saying…" or "My understanding is…."
- **Feedback.** This means talking about your reactions or perceptions of what the other is saying. Feedback provides the other person the chance to see if you understood what he/she was trying to say. When providing feedback, it is appropriate to tactfully and respectfully give your thoughts and opinions. It is not OK to be critical, condescending, rude, or argumentative. Doing so will quickly result in a breakdown of effective conversation.

When you are the listener

- **Listen with empathy.** Try to be aware of how the other person feels about the subject. Give allowance for their thoughts and beliefs. It is OK that you may feel or think differently.
- **Listen with openness.** It is difficult to efficiently listen when you are trying to judge, find fault, or blame the other. Also, when you have strong feelings or opinions on a subject, it is not easy to set those aside, even momentarily, to objectively listen to the other's viewpoint. "Agree to disagree." In other words, you don't always have to agree, but you should at least hear the other persons views and story. Before drawing your own conclusion, get as much information from the other person as possible. You just might be surprised at how much you do agree on some things. If nothing else you will at least have grown to appreciate the other's opinions and views, even if you may not entirely agree.
- **Listen with awareness.** Try to relate what the other is saying to your own experiences of life and your knowledge. In other words, try to determine the facts of what is being said by what you know to be true. Also, watch the other person's facial expressions, voice, and body language. Do these fit with what is being said? Sometimes a good listener needs to be as a "detective" in attempting to determine the whole and truthful message.
- **Listen for main ideas.** The main ideas are the most critical points the speaker wants to get across. They may be mentioned at the start or end of a talk and often repeated. Pay particular attention to statements that begin with phrases such as "my point is...," or "remember..."
- **Identify key points.** Ask yourself what the speaker is trying to convey. Then listen for evidence that supports the ends.

Listen for the "who, what, why, when, and where" of the conversation.

- **Summarize.** Mentally summarize what you have heard. When you can, write down the key points and answer the "who, what, why, when, and where" questions, if applicable. Listening is such an important element of communication that I have dedicated an entire section to it. I must confess that, as a verbal person, I have had to practice hard to program myself to be a better "active listener," and still must continuously work on it. My wife would agree that I am not a candidate for a gold award when it comes to hearing what she is trying to tell me. So, I would be advised to "practice what I preach." Practice the non-verbal communication strategies, and active listening TIPS provided, and you (we) will reap the benefits.

Chapter 12
Sensible Notes

How important are notes to making excellent grades? Essential!
Most studying is done from notes. Think about it! Teachers and
professors spend a great deal of time preparing lesson plans for their
classes. Most of the lessons include lecture. Often the lectures are
supplemented with readings, written assignments, and projects. To
take good notes, the student must be able to listen effectively. If you
have not already done so, I encourage you to go back to Chapter 11
and review the part on "listening."

TIPS
TO TAKE GREAT NOTES

Look at the speaker. Don't daydream, look out the window,
or allow others to distract you. When you look at the person who
is speaking, you will hear more of what they say. Looking helps
to maintain focus. Remember, much of communication is done
with body language and facial expression. If you only hear what
the speaker is saying, you will miss the "unspoken" part of the
communication process.

Focus. The mind works faster than the spoken word. Thus, it is
easy for your mind to wander. When you catch your mind wandering,
re-focus! Sit up straight, lean forward, and fix your eyesight on the
speaker. Concentrate on the speaker's words. Mentally ask questions,
and then listen for answers.

Listen for main ideas. Main ideas are the most critical points
the speaker wants to convey. How do you know when the central idea
is being spoken? Usually, it is at the start of a lecture, then repeated
at the end of the talk. Often, they are repeated several times. Look
for clues! Listen for the lecturer to give a "hint" such as" my point

is..." or "remember this..." "as I mentioned previously....". Also, watch body language, such as when a lecturer shakes a fist or finger, underlines a word or phrase on the board, or raises his/her voice. Such gestures are a strong clue of essential points that you may well see again on an exam.

Ask questions. Often students will not ask a question for fear of sounding stupid or thinking they should have understood the points. Don't fall into this mental trap! The truth is there are probably other students who are also unclear and will be happy (and relieved) that someone else had the guts to raise their hand and ask. Also, keep in mind that teachers want you to understand what they are striving to teach, so when a student asks a question, the teacher is not offended, instead are happy that the question is being asked.

Summarize your notes in your own words. Don't try to write down everything that the instructor is saying, instead focus on understanding. Highlight, underline or mark sentences in your notes that the lecturer emphasizes.

Make your notes your notes. Take advantage of how you learn and write your notes according to that style. Some students prefer to use an outline; others would prefer to write in narrative form. Draw pictures if it helps. There is no one right or wrong way. Do what suits you most. Just make sure your notes are legible. If you have trouble reading your notes, they will be of little use.

Get it all but use shortcuts. Copy key points written on the whiteboard, slides, PowerPoint, or projector, especially the outline. Skip words like "the" and "a." Make use of abbreviations.

Consider splitting your notes into two columns. Keep lecture notes on one side. On the other side write questions on points you are unsure of. Doing so will help clarify points or questions from the lecture and enable you to associate the answer with the relevant material.

Review. Many honor students will review notes taken in class as soon as possible after class. The reason for this is to make corrections or modifications while the class lecture is still fresh in mind. Is key information missing? Check with classmates or the teacher to fill in what you missed. After class review also helps to reinforce the key points made in the lecture. An excellent strategy is to type your handwritten notes, or if the teacher permits, type directly on the iPad or notebook. Typed notes will also make it easier to review before quizzes and exams. Review your notes (all of them) periodically throughout the marking period. DO NOT make the mistake of looking at notes for the first time the night before an exam. Doing so will result in a cram study session, and unless you have an outstanding ability to memorize, this is an ineffective study technique. If you are a good memorizer, review anyway. Why? Because many who can memorize well are good at recalling facts short term but are challenged when it comes to recalling the same facts long term. By "long term," I mean the time between an exam or quiz taken early in the semester or grading period to mid-terms and finals. So, don't take a chance on good memory—review.

Chapter 13
Dynamic Reading

Reading can be simplified if done correctly. In this chapter, you will learn strategies to help read faster while remembering more of what you read. Let's call it "Dynamic Reading." In school, we are required to read, read, read. Middle school students may have to read several books a year, high school students a dozen or so, and by college over 20 per academic year, or more if you are an English or history major. In Western culture, we are taught to read every word in a sentence. Unless one has taken a reading dynamics course (speed reading) and learned to take in multiple words at a time, our eyes will laboriously move across a line 15 to 20 times (or however many words there are on a line of print). The result is the ability to absorb, comprehend, and memorize is challenged, and our eyes (and minds) quickly become tired. Given all the material we are (and will be) required to read in and out of school is indeed a daunting task. Wouldn't it be wonderful if you could learn to read faster and more efficiently? In the early 20th century William James, known as the father of American psychology, wrote, "men habitually use only a small part of their powers which they possess and which they might use under appropriate conditions." James studied the research of Bulgarian psychiatrist Georgi Lozanov, who developed a remarkable approach to accelerated learning by using the whole brain rather than just part of it, as we do in traditional reading. There are several steps to be a super reader. Let's check them out.

TIPS
READING STRATEGIES OF HONOR STUDENTS

Read with a purpose. Before you even start to read, ask yourself these questions: "Why am I reading this?" "What can I learn from this, and how can it apply to my learning of the subject?" Also, "given my purpose in reading the material, how much time do I need to spend on the reading it, given the complexity and length?

Get "In the Zone" as described in Chapter 20.

Study to understand, not memorize! A mistake that many students make is that they jump right into starting an assignment before they have a clear understanding of the "big picture." In other words, in their haste, they think to themselves, "I must read the chapter, why should I take the time to skim the entire chapter?" Because "previewing" helps with understanding the material which, in turn, helps one to recall crucial facts. Having a good idea of the general idea of the subject makes it much easier to understand and remember the details.

Find answers to key questions as you skim through the text. Look for the main topic and the author's primary purpose. Note how the is the book organized. Start with the Table of Contents, then look at the chapter and section titles. Don't forget pictures, charts, diagrams, and illustrations. The author will include such visuals that he/she wants to emphasize. If the text has a section or chapter summary, read them! They include what the author feels is most important. How long does it take to do this? A few minutes. By doing this it will give you a pretty good understanding of the material, and you have not even started to read the main content. Skimming also helps to set the stage for a compelling memorization strategy called "mind mapping" that I will explain in Chapter 16.

Increase reading speed. A concern that students have is that if they read through assigned material quickly, they will miss important details. It is true that if the reading material is skimmed over too quickly, relevant information and facts can be overlooked. However, the mind has an extraordinary capacity to take in large amounts of data very quickly if trained to do so. In western culture, we have been taught to read word by word. This is a slow process. Our mind works at a much faster pace than the rate we read. So, our mind begins to wander. Have you read something and then realized you had no clue as to what you just "read"? That is because your incredible, fast-paced mind became bored and it began to think about other things than what your eyes were looking at on a page. That brings us to the question, "If you could take in more written words faster, would your mind be better able to stay focused?" The answer is, "Yes."

How to read faster? Like anything, if you want to improve it takes practice if you want to improve. You can take a speed-reading dynamics course. However, if you do not have the time or resources to do so, you might try these strategies.

- At your regular reading speed, move your fingers cross the line in a steady, rhythmic pace as your eyes take in the written words. Try not to "lip read." That is, read to yourself by whispering the words you are reading. At this point, it is not necessary to focus on understanding all that you are reading. Just make sure your fingers and eyes move across the lines at a steady pace. Do this for about a minute. Remember, at this point, you are not reading for comprehension. You are training your eyes and mind to take in more of the written word faster.

- Now repeat the process but read two lines at a time. Do this for a minute, then do three lines at a time. Work your way through the whole paragraph. Repeat the exercise several times a day. Push yourself! It will be uncomfortable at first, but as you practice, you will find the discomfort begin to subside. You will also soon realize that you can read, understand, and retain the groups of words you have looked at without having to focus on each word.

Break it down. Read as if you are a detective. Find the main topic, then identify the supporting information provided to help clarify or explain the topic. Always strive to answer the questions: Who, When, Where, Why, and How. Jot down notes to answer the main idea of each paragraph or section. Write down words, phrases, or points you do not understand. Later try to find the answers through further reading, research, or asking others. If you still do not understand, then move on and come back later.

Review. Now go back to your notes. Are you clear on the main points? What conclusions are made? How did the author come to these conclusions? What are your thoughts and opinions on the subject? Can you relate the text to class notes or handouts? If your notes are unclear, re-write them. Study from notes, not the text... it is easier. Try to explain the main points in your own words. Remember, tests are written to test your ability to recall the material and to see if you understand the concepts.

TIPS
WHEN IN A TIME CRUNCH

When you are pressed for time, try these strategies.

Read book summaries. Read the book summaries to identify the plot, theme, and motif. Check out Cliff Notes, Sparknotes, or Wiki Books. If you know the main issues ahead of time, you can start highlighting any reference in the book that is related.

Search out abstracts and journal articles. These will help to discover what others think of the book and can give you ideas. I am suggesting this only to help you gain different perspectives. Do not forget to cite the source, otherwise, you may be guilty of plagiarism.

Take notes. Once you have identified the plot and major themes, write them down! Note the book pages and write a brief comment as to why you think the section supports the plot and theme. These notes will be beneficial if you have an essay assignment on the subject.

TIPS
WHEN READING TECHNICAL TEXTS

Technical texts. What about technical texts, such as science and math? Such documents require an organized, step-by-step approach. Technical books have lots of terms, formulas, concepts, and theories.

Thus, the reading strategy is different than it is for reading non-technical texts. It is essential to identify the progression of thought to understand and retain the information. Scientific and mathematical concepts are laid out in a logical sequence of facts and theories. Each prepares the student for the next idea. Knowing and understanding details does not have to be a complicated process if specific rules are followed.

Make sure you understand definitions and terms. Write them down. Use index cards. Write the word or phrase on one side of the card and the meaning on the other side. Carry the cards with you and look at them throughout the day as opportunity permits, such as riding in a car or bus. Using this strategy uses downtime and helps with memorization.

Pay close attention to examples, cause-and-effect relationships, comparisons and contrast, description, problem/solution. These suggestions also apply to non-technical texts.

Look for signal words to indicate what is being asked. For examples, cause-and-effect questions ask for certain events, concepts, or facts that effect other events, concepts or facts. Words often used are: because, as a result, in order to, also, accordingly, due to, since. Comparison and contrast ask how two or more persons, places or things are alike or different. Signal words include: similar to, compared to, different from, on the other hand, although. Descriptive questions describe an event, person, place or thing. Look for words such as to illustrate, for instance, for example. Problem/solution questions present a problem and ask for possible solutions. Words to look for may be: "the question is...", "an answer is..." or "a solution is...".

Pay close attention to provided examples, graphs, diagrams, and definitions. They help to visually see what sometimes is challenging to picture in your mind or described in the text.

Explain in your own words the concepts—first to yourself, then to another.

When the other person understands, you will have ensured

that you also are clear in your understanding. This is an especially effective technique for those who are verbal learners.

Connect new ideas with ideas and concepts you are already familiar. This strategy helps to link known facts with new, thus facilitates later recall of the new material.

Chapter 14
Improve Vocabulary and Spelling

Proper vocabulary is crucial for success. What you say and how you say it, whether verbally or in writing, determines your ability to get your message across in the most efficient way possible. A useful vocabulary does not just apply in English class, it is essential in all classes. The reason for this is simple. The better a student can express themselves, the better grades they will make, and ultimately, the more successful they will be. Often it is not how smart you are; it is if you can get your message across. A key component of strong social skills is the ability to connect with others through excellent communication. When it comes to success in the real world, employers value the employee who can verbalize and communicate and connect well with others. One's aptitude does not always result in better outcomes. Instead, it is how a person comes across, both verbally and in writing, that makes the most significant difference.

TIPS
FOR IMPROVED VOCAB AND SPELLING

Here are some TIPS on how you can improve your vocabulary and spelling skills.

Read!! In today's high-tech era, many students spend more time watching television and on social media than reading books. Because they do not read much, exposure to new written words is lacking. So try reading more. Pick up books that are of special interest and force yourself to start reading. You may find yourself beginning to enjoy it. Another way to help improve vocabulary is to make a habit of learning at least one new word every day. A good idea would be to use SAT or ACT word bank lists. An advantage of computers and smartphones is that the definitions of words, phrases, and other information can be easily looked up. Take advantage of the opportunity's technology affords.

Texting? Does texting adversely affect vocabulary and spelling? According to a Nielsen survey, teens text an average of between 3,000 to 4,000 texts per month. That's more than 130 texts per day. Many adults feel that young people's reliance on cell phones is contributing to a decline in the quality of vocabulary, communication, and writing abilities. Others point out that it is not worse, just different. There seems to be evidence that texting and computer use helps improve spelling. An article published in the February 2011 issue of the *Journal of Computer Assisted Learning* (Volume 27, Issue 1) cited a study that concluded texting was "actually driving the development of phonological awareness and reading skill in children." The *Scholastic Teacher* website reported similar findings. So did Dr. Michelle Drouin of Purdue University who published in the *Journal of Literacy Research,* (vol. 41, no.1) that text abbreviations, such as "msg" and "2nite" help students understand sounds, letters, and word relationships. Another advantage is that students sometimes use text abbreviations when taking notes, especially from a fast-talking teacher or college professor. My suggestion is to limit texting to specific times so that you do not form poor spelling and grammar habits.

Use "Spell Check" to learn. When you use Spell Check in Word, look at the correct spelling before you replace your misspelled word. That way, you are learning the correct spelling. Grammarly is a paid service that is more comprehensive than Microsoft Word's spelling and grammar checker. Grammarly also provides suggestions for punctuation, sentence structure, writing style, and plagiarism. Others spell and grammar checker programs are Grammarly Checker.net, and Reverso Speller, Paper Rater, to name a few.

Pay attention to roots, suffixes, and prefixes. These are the essential parts of words and understanding how they put together will help to understand the meaning of words as well as better know how to spell them. The central part of a word is called a "root." An example of a root would be "rad," which means "moving away from." Words with the root of "rad," include *rad*io, *rad*ius, *rad*iant. The root "auto" means "self." Words with the root "auto" include *auto*matic, *auto*nomy, and *auto*graph. A "suffix" is a letter or letters added to the end of a word that changes how the word is used or the meaning. Examples include peace*ful*, arrange*ment*, swimm*ing*, and popp*ed.* "Prefixes" are letters that are "pre," or go before the beginning of a word to change its meaning. Examples include *re*do, *under*fed, *in*active. When reading, try to identify the roots, suffixes, and prefixes. Look up a list of root, suffix, and prefix words on your favorite search engine (Google, Yahoo, AOL), or web browser (Explorer, Firefox, Chrome) and print them out. Memorize them. Don't fret! They are not difficult. You use them all the time during your everyday vocabulary. You have probably not thought to focus on the precise meaning. However, once done, you will find you will be able to quickly figure out what those long and often perplexing words in the English language mean.

Pay attention to new words. When we come across a word we do not recognize or one challenging to pronounce, most tend just to move on. That is a mistake! When we pay attention to new words, we are significantly increasing our vocabulary. First, pay attention to phonetic sounds. Phonetics is the study of the sounds of human speech. Phonics is a method for teaching reading and writing in the English language. When you see a new word, especially words with many syllables, sound it out. Listen to how the words are pronounced. Repeat the new word aloud. Use it in a sentence. Doing so will help you to memorize the word, how to spell it, and understand the words meaning.

Associate with others who have proper grammar. Listen to them and copy them. For goodness' sake, don't emulate the inappropriate language heard in movies, TV, and music. The actors, actresses, and musicians who speak this way may well not talk poorly in real life.

Chapter 15
Awesome Papers

The dreaded essay paper! For most students, having to tackle a composition can seem daunting. The process can be quite enjoyable if the following strategies are followed. Essentially, the ability to write an awesome paper is a step-by-step process. So, just like anything, when something substantial is broken down into smaller pieces, the "mountain" becomes a "molehill". Here goes...

TIPS
FOR WRITING PAPERS

Read your teacher's or professor's written assignment carefully. When I taught a college course, I had a promising student who completely misread the assignment and turned in a paper that missed the focus of what was asked. She also did not listen effectively when I verbally explained expectations. What made it worse is that she provided incorrect information to other students who also received poor marks. Lesson learned—pay attention to what is expected. Don't entirely rely on other students; they may not have correctly understood the assignment either.

Make a timeline for writing your report. If your paper is due in a month from the date assigned, DO NOT fall into the trap of thinking, "I have plenty of time, I will get started later." Here is a true story that happened with two exchange students that lived with my family. They came to me and asked for help with a written assignment for their theology class. The teacher had written specific instructions. I read the teacher's guidance, who clearly stated, "use at least three reference sources...not 'online' sources." OK, I thought, we will have to visit a library. Then I noted that the due date was the previous week. What? After my panic, the girls explained that the teacher had extended the deadline by a week due to snow days. "OK," somewhat relieved, "so when is it due now?" I asked. "Tomorrow," they replied. "What?" Panic again set in.

I pointed out the teacher's instructions stated that they were required to use a minimum of "three non-internet sources." What gave me even greater frustration is that I had provided the girls with a journal with guidance on how to study smarter rather than harder. One of the guidelines provided was to understand the teacher's instructions clearly. Then, establish a timeline for doing the project. The girls did neither, and now at 9 p.m., they were about to start on a project that had been given to them two weeks earlier. I could have said, "Too bad; lesson learned," but I tend to be soft, so together we started. In the next-to-last paragraph of this chapter entitled "Writing a paper in a time crunch," in the TIPS section of this chapter I will tell you how to we managed to complete the papers in six hours. Although the girls placed themselves in a precarious situation, we did manage to finish their essays. Indeed, it was not a preferred way to do it, and they did not get a full night's sleep. They will not make that mistake again. Hopefully, the lesson learned was more valuable than completing this one paper.

Determine your "topic." The topic provides a general subject of the paper. An example might be, "British and U.S. Relations During World War II." This sentence provides the reader with a clear yet brief understanding of what is to be discussed. Develop your paper using resources from experts in the field to elaborate on your topic.

Once you are confident, you know what is expected, you can take the next step. With the subject matter precisely in mind, gather your sources. Books, online resources, interviews, periodical, news sources are the primary resources used. Don't try to read everything, preview to ascertain if the resource contains the information you will need for your report. Bookmark the pages that pertain most to your subject. The length of the paper will depend on how many resources you will need. Be careful not to choose a topic that is too broad, assuming the teacher did not provide it for you. On the other hand, try not to pick a subject that is too limiting, as you might have difficulty writing even one page. Once you have gathered your resources, browse through them, and choose those that are the most relevant. Then divide them into groups that best support your topic. Number each of your resources as this will be helpful when putting together your notes.

Be passionate and excited about your topic. The more interest you have in your subject, the more enjoyable it will be to research and write. Since you will have to defend your position, it is far easier to do so if you have a strong opinion on the subject.

Develop a robust "theses statement." A theses statement is one or two sentences that tells your reader what they can expect from your paper. It is an interpretation of a question on the topic and often presents an argument, point, or counterpoint. Your thesis is the foundation of your paper. A strong thesis can facilitate the development of content and a better essay. A weak thesis will probably result in a weak paper. Here are some ideas that can help develop an excellent thesis.

- **Focus:** Make sure your thesis remains focused on one primary theme of the topic. If you don't, your paper could get confusing for the reader.
- **Be specific.** Be clear about what you are going to write. By so doing, you will better prepare your reader as to what to expect.
- **Empower your argument.** Do this by using adjectives that show the reader you genuinely believe in the points you are making. "I felt that the race to space was cool" Is not as strong as "The race to space was one of the fascinating events in the 20th century."

Here are examples of weak and strong thesis statements:

Weak Thesis: "The United States provided Great Britain with military aid during World War II with the passage of the Lend-Lease Act."

Strong Thesis: "After France's surrender to Germany, the British approached bankruptcy. Thus, America passed the Lend-Lease Act, which authorized military aid so long as Britain promised to pay the loan back after the war.

Categorize your notes into five sections: Introduction, Background, Facts, Arguments, Conclusion. Depending on the assignment, you may have to add pages and sub-categories under each section. Remember, in almost any planning activity you will be answering several questions: **Who, When, Where, What, and Why (or How).** For example, if you are to write a paper on philosophy, you may choose to compare and contrast Karl Marx and the *Communist Manifesto*, with Ayn Rand and *Atlas Shrugged*. **Who** were they? **When** did they live? **Where** did they live? How were their philosophies different (**What**), and (**Why**) did they have a different view?

Now go back to your references and read in detail. Be a detective and answer the questions of Who, When, Where, What, and Why. As you read, look for facts that support your theses.

Your "Introduction" is a statement of your thesis and definition of your topic. In the example provided, you might state why you chose the subject, such as to compare the two philosophies and how they have impacted the relations of Communist countries with free enterprise countries. The "Background" provides historical facts that may have influenced the theories of Marx and Rand. In other words, did when they live, where they live, and their life experiences influence their philosophies? In the "Facts" and "Arguments" section using details, facts, data, and information, extrapolate on how these might have influenced their philosophies. If required, build your point of view on the subject. Provide any opposing or different perspectives. In the **"Conclusion"** section re-state your thesis, then summarizes the key points presented. Review the best arguments and submit your final thoughts on the subject in support of your theses.

Some extra TIPS:

- In your introduction, to capture your reader's attention, provide an exciting piece of information that encourages the reader to want to read on. It can be in the form of a question or statement.
- In your conclusion, provide a synopsis that is brief and dramatic.
- Proofread the draft several times. Have someone else read it. Edit and check for spelling, grammatical mistakes, sentence structure, or phrases that may need clarification.
- If you have appropriately worked your timeline, you will have time to put it aside for a day or two, and then go back to it for a final review before submitting your final copy. By distancing yourself from the paper for a day or two, you allow yourself to return to it with a fresh mind. Often this helps see things you didn't previously see. You may catch some errors that you did not when you were immersed in the project.

How to ensure a failing grade — plagiarize — and how to avoid it. According to the Merriam-Webster Dictionary, plagiarism is "the act of using another person's words or ideas without giving credit to that person." Wikipedia takes the definition a step further by stating that: "Plagiarism is the 'wrongful appropriation,' and 'stealing and publication' of another author's 'language, thoughts, ideas, or expressions,' and the representation of them as one's owns original work." If you copy or quote another person's work without giving proper credit, you are guilty of plagiarism. If you present as your own another person's writing, regardless of how you got it, you are guilty of plagiarism. Even if you change words around if they are not your own, give credit to the person whom you got the information. If a teacher discovers that you have plagiarized, they will provide you with a failing grade. Don't assume that your teacher is not smart enough to identify papers or portions of documents that have been copied. You can try it if you want to take the chance, but why take the risk when plagiarism can be easily avoided. Here is how — by correctly citing the source! Put another way, give credit to the source you are using in your paper. The citation (called bibliography, notes, or works cited) should tell if the source is a book, journal, website, or personal contact. If a fact, data or thought is considered "common knowledge" it may not need a citation. The Purdue University Online Writing Lab published a paper entitled, *Is It Plagiarism Yet?* (February 2008), "that there is no clear boundary on what is considered common knowledge. Even experts on plagiarism disagree on what counts as common knowledge. For instance, many sources only consider facts—current and historical events, famous people, geographic areas, etc.— to be potentially common knowledge. Others also include nonfactual material such as folklore and common sayings. Some sources limit common knowledge to only information known by others in your class; other sources look at what is common knowledge for the broader subject area. The two criteria that are most commonly used in deciding whether something is common knowledge is quantity (is it found in numerous places), and ubiquity (it is likely to be known by a lot of people). Ideally, both conditions are true. A third criterion that is sometimes used is whether the information can be easily found in a general reference source."

Good news and bad news. We live in an age with a plethora (how do you like that word) of potential resources that writers can use when researching a paper. Years ago, traditional sources were limited mostly to books, journals, and periodicals. Today we not only have these, but we can use internet web pages, multimedia, and e-books. Additionally, many traditional resources can be found "online." The bad news is that all these resources can make proper citations somewhat confusing. Do not fret, though. There are different styles used for citing references. Basically, the information is the same, only presented a bit differently. Included are the author's name, the title of the publication, the publisher, location of the publisher, and the date published. For example, "Russell, Christopher. *The Battle of Turkey Thicket: A True Story.* Baritone Books, Baltimore, Maryland, 2017." There are sources you can use that will clearly describe how to cite your sources. The most widely used formats are the Modern Language Association (MLA), American Psychological Association (APA), and Chicago Style formats. Your teacher will advise you as to what form he/she prefers. All three provide guidelines for placing references to sources in the text of the papers or list them alphabetically by the author's last name at the end of the paper in a bibliography called the "Works Cited" section (MLA), "Reference List" (APA), or Bibliography (Chicago Style). Citations can also be found within the text, called "in-text citations," or at the bottom of a page, called "endnotes" or "footnotes." There are too many ways to cite the many types of resources used to list them herein so procure an MLA, APA or Chicago Style reference manual to see the proper ways to cite both in text and end of paper resources used. You can get examples for all three "online" as well. An excellent guide is the Purdue OWL, *MLA Formatting and Style Guide.* Another excellent source is *The Essential Guide for Research Writing Across the Disciplines* by James D. Lester and James D. Lester Jr. that provides comprehensive guidance on finding topics, research strategies, organizing and prep suggestions, and writing the paper. The book also provides guidance on citing references.

When you are writing a paper in a time crunch. At the beginning of this chapter, I told the story of my two exchange students who procrastinated. Unfortunately, this is not uncommon for students. So, if you find yourself in the position of having to write a paper in a short time, here are a few hints that can help.

Most certainly the best way to write a paper is not to wait until the last moment. I suggest you not allow yourself to fall into this situation. Anyway, if you ever find yourself in this predicament, as my two students did, here are a few strategies that can be of help. First, we looked at the clock on the wall. It was 8:20 p.m. We listed the steps needed to complete the paper and assigned an approximate timeline. The purpose of this was to give us an idea of how much time was required for each step and to help keep the girls on track. It is not precisely what we used, as we had to gear their timeline to the requirements provided by their specific assignment, as you will need to do. The one that follows is generic but can give you an idea or how it works.

TIPS
TO WRITE A LAST-MINUTE PAPER

Take a deep breath, relax, and carefully review the requirements. (10 minutes/7:30 PM)

Research and gather resources. Under normal circumstances, this is a very time-consuming part of the process. But since this is crunch time, don't belabor this. Get a few good references, then move on to the next step (30 minutes/8:00 PM). Times are approximate.

Take notes answering the questions, Who, When, Where, What, Why (60 minutes/9:00 p.m.).

Develop the thesis statement (20 minutes/9:20 PM). Don't gloss over this too quickly because if you write down an inadequate theses statement, you will struggle when trying to write the main body of your paper.

Write your introduction (20 minutes/9:40 PM). Remember to stay focused on your topic. If challenged with coming up with a couple of good opening sentences, use your theses statement.

Notes. Defend Your Thesis. (30 minutes/10:10 PM). On a piece of paper list all the points that support your theses.

Write (2 hours/12:10 AM). Develop each of the points into supporting paragraphs. Make sure your thoughts are clear and easily understood. Think about what critics might say and respond to them.

Summarize your thesis in your concluding paragraph. (30 minutes/12:40 AM).

Review and edit. (30 minutes/1:05 AM) Check for spelling, grammar, syntax, flow.

Go to bed! Promise yourself not to do this to yourself again.

Chapter 16
Memorization Made Easy

Some can memorize with ease. For others, memorizing is a challenge. I was always envious of my classmates who spent minimal time studying, then waltzed into the classroom on exam day and aced the test. I, on the other hand, would spend hours striving to cram in names, dates, formulas, historical facts, places, and other trivial rubbish—well, at least I thought it was rubbish at the time. Frustrated with the extra effort and hours I had to put in, and often without the grade results of some of my classmates. I thought to myself, "There has to be a better way to input to my brain and recall all this required information." With a bit of research, I discovered that there are, indeed, many "tricks" to quickly and efficiently digest and regurgitate information (sorry for the crude analogy). When one or more of the techniques described below are combined with adequately applied study techniques, you will have the skills necessary to not only make high grades but have invaluable tools that will help in daily tasks and your career.

Have confidence. One of the first things I learned is that when students have difficulty memorizing, it is because they are not motivated to learn the material. If one does not want to do something, they will not do it. To help with self-motivation, set your goals (see Chapter 4), then believe you can memorize the material. Faith in yourself helps you to relax, which, in turn, helps facilitate the mental process for better memorization.

Understand the information. If one does not understand, it can be more of a challenge to retain the material you are trying to absorb. To better understand, first strive to look at the big picture. For example, before trying to memorize the names of the internal organs that make up the digestive system, it would help to understand how the digestive system works.

Focus on details. Here is a simple example. After being introduced to someone, a little while later, you are unable to recall the name of the person to whom you had just met. Has this happened to you? Why do we have difficulty recalling the name of a person whom we just met? Because you did not focus on the name. What would be the odds of you remembering the person's name had you looked at the person you just met, repeated his/her name, then visualized the person's name with some familiar object. See the TIPS section below for examples.

The more of your senses (sight, sound, smell) you use, the easier it will be to memorize. Scientists who study the brain and memorization state that information is recalled when previously stored in the memory banks of the brain. For more information, check out http://www.human-memory.net/processes/recall.html. Good memorizers have a bias towards visual and spatial learning. The more we see, the more we remember. Super memorizers convert things that we want to memorize into mental pictures. Several strategies for using visual memorization strategies are provided in "TIPS" below.

Repetition is the traditional method most useful to try to memorize facts. Although repetition is tedious, it helps remember facts you want to recall days, months, or years down the road. For example, if a friend tells you their telephone number or e-mail address, you will memorize it only long enough to record it in your cell phone or address book. Then you promptly forget it. If on the other hand you want to be able to recall the phone number, later you would probably repeat the information over and over until you felt that you could remember it in the future. But there are more natural, and more fun ways to put data into your long-term memory. Let's take a trip down, "memory lane."

TIPS
FOR MEMORIZING

Mental pictures. Use your imagination to create images in your mind that will help you to associate or trigger the information that you want to recall. In school, we are often required to remember names. More frequently we meet new people. In fact, in your lifetime you will meet many thousands of people. Let's look at a few tricks for recalling names. Supposing you have just been introduced to a person named Tiffany Payne. You might picture a "Tiffany" ring on her finger, but it is too small and giving her a "pain" on her finger. Silly, I know, but the mental picture will help you later recall her name. But what if an association of the person name is not so simple, such as Mike McNally? Visualize a mental picture like the technique just described, but this time, you will have to take more liberties with your mental picture. The last name is a bit more challenging then Payne. You might picture him reading a book into a microphone (Mike) published by the well-known publisher Rand McNally. If unable to think a word that can easily be associated, consider something like this. Since you know that a name beginning with "Mc" or "Mac" is Irish or Scottish, you might visualize him in a Scottish kilt. Then associate the name with something or someone you are familiar, such as the American songwriter, rapper-singer, Nelly. Picture the person singing rap, like Nelly, into a microphone wearing a Scottish kilt.

Let's presume you are to remember the year the Stock Market crash marking the beginning of America's Great Depression. Also, you are to know who the president was at the time. The date was October 29, 1929. The president was Herbert Hoover. Do you know of anyone whose birthday is in October? Think of them. Now picture them at age 29. Now you have the month, day, and year. Picture the Hoover dam leaking with water pouring out of holes. Visualize President Hoover trying to plug up the holes. What if you must recall the 24th President of the United States, Grover Cleveland. You might think of the Sesame Street character, Grover hanging out on 34th Street in Cleveland, Ohio. Silly, I know. Believe it or not, often the sillier the association, the easier it is to recall. By linking as many common factors as possible, you increase your chances of recalling the information later.

Here is another trick to increase your ability to recognize a person you just met. Rather than focusing on the person's eyes, as we tend to do, focus on the nose or to the right or left of the nose. The idea behind this is by focusing on the nose area you can visually take in the whole face, thus helping to recall the person better when you meet them later. If you combine this strategy with the mental pictures and visualization strategies described below, you will be able to recall their name better. Remembering names will impress the other person (even if they may not recall yours). A good strategy to help others recall your name is to say your name in the conversation. For example, you might say something like, "My mother told me, 'Carl' don't forget…" Another strategy might be to repeat your name when first greeting the other person. "Hi Dave, Carl, here…how are you?" If appropriate to the conversation, you might ask, "How do you spell your last name?" Hopefully, it will not be "Brown," this may make you seem a bit ignorant. So, you could respond with something like, "I just wanted to check because I once knew a fella who spelled it "Broun."

Mentally prepare. First, it is essential to "set the stage." By that, I mean recognize that a vital step for the process of memorizing is to prepare yourself mentally. Just as one needs to warm up before performing strenuous physical activity, so too is it important to prepare your mind for the exercise of memorization. To do this relax, close your eyes, take a few deep breaths then tell yourself that you can and will remember. By so doing, you are providing yourself with a positive affirmation that you can take in store and then later recall the desired information. It has been proven that your mind will often respond to what you tell it. When you say to yourself that you can do something, your mind will react accordingly. In other words, the mere intention to remember prepares the brain to better able to recall data. If you make use of this fact in studying, you will be able to recall more information. Of course, what you are asking of yourself must be reasonable and within your ability. Just because you tell yourself to fly does not mean that you will suddenly be able to fly. Had the Wright brothers not had the confidence that they could build a flying machine, they would never have accomplished their dream of doing so. But be careful, if you tell yourself that you cannot do something, the chances are that you won't. So be positive!

Use all your senses. When it comes to recalling information, we should recognize what works best for us. For example, some can be quite successful at reading silently to themselves, while others prefer to read out loud. Both are using their sight as the primary sense for taking in the written word. Others, however, can remember better by "hearing." By reading a lesson aloud, one would be using visual (the eye takes in the printed word), auditory (the ears hear the words) and transmits the information to the brain. This does not mean that one uses only hearing or only sight to learn. It is just a preference. So by using both auditory and visual, we can help maximize the learning process, as opposed to merely relying on one of our senses, alone. Later in this chapter, I address the use of visualizations, rhymes, songs, and mind mapping. These strategies utilize more senses than just visual.

Visualizations. Turn an abstract idea into an image of something as specific as possible. For example, visualize a scene or experience that you can associate. If you are studying events of World War II, you might recall a visit to a war memorial or museum that depicted an event or events that may help you picture in your mind facts that you are trying to remember. I recall seeing a diorama at the British War Museum in London of underground air-raid shelters that citizens had to live for protection from the Blitz bombings. When I think of this scene, it helps me recall that the most massive bombing took place in 1941 and 1942 and that around 40,000 civilians were killed—a figure that stood out in my mind as I read the description of the display. Of course, merely recalling the museum display will not, in and of itself, help me recall the dates of the bombings over Britain. I noted the three "4's"- "40,000 casualties during the years 1941 and 1942. I also noted that there were four mannequins in the diorama. So, in my mind, I connect the four mannequins to the number 4 in the casualties and two years of the attacks. I looked again at the diorama to see if I could make other connections. I noted four chairs around a table. I fix this in my mind as well. So, later I think about the four mannequins then "link" this to the dates and casualty number and that bombings took place in the 1940s. For "41" and "42" I simply think of the first two years of the 1940s.

Take breaks. When you find yourself getting tired, take a short break. It is often easier for us to remember the beginning and end of a study period than all the details in between. Claude Olney in his best-selling book *Where There's a Will There's An "A"* pointed out that students who studied using several short sessions were better able to memorize material than students who studied for one long session. In his audiobook by the same name, Mr. Olney cited a series of about 15 numbers to several students, then asked them to recall the numbers. None were able to recall the entire list. However, when he asked if they could remember the first and last number, nearly all the students were able to recall those two numbers. Olney explained that our concentration is at the peak during the beginning and end of study sessions. Olney stated that Tony Buzan (see Mind Mapping below) confirmed this fact in his book *Make the Most of Your Mind*. Experiment with what works best for you regarding break time. You might be surprised to learn that taking frequent yet shorter breaks, improves your ability to recall than when you study for long sessions with longer breaks. For example, if you have an examination on Friday in two weeks, study this week, then again on Monday of next week, then Wednesday, and review on Thursday. If you know you will have an exam in a couple of months, space your study sessions out over several weeks. Avoid cramming!! Doing so may help pass an exam the next day but will usually do little to help make a good grade on a mid-term or final exam.

Vary study places and strategies. Sitting at a desk studying for hours on end may work for some. But you might try to vary the mundane study at a desk silently reading to yourself by doing something active. For example, reading aloud, draw association pictures, or walking around while reciting. You might want to change your study location now and then. Quiet places in a park or near a gentle stream are excellent study places. In 1970 the University of Michigan conducted a study of two groups of students who split study sessions; one group in the same room, the other in multiple locations. The group that varied study locations were able to recall information 53 percent more than the group that studied in only one spot. This certainly challenged the theory that you must always study at the same place at the same time every day. Experiment and see what works best for you.

Study when you are most productive. Some are more productive in the morning, some at night. Everyone has their best study time. Find your best time to study and keep on that schedule. Doing so will make recall more effective.

Re-enforce. Once you have memorized your material, don't assume you will be able to recall it a day, week, or months later. To truly embed the stuff in your brain, periodically repeat the material. Experiments have proven that "over-study" resulted in much better retention. Often students make the mistake of not reviewing previously studied material. Does this sound familiar? "I am glad that test is over, now I do not have to worry about those chapters anymore." But wait! What about the mid-term and final exams? Chances are you WILL see that material again. And since you don't want to study for mid-term and final exams to be a re-learning task, instead it is far better to be merely a review of material already learned. In other words, it is wiser to reinforce recently learned material soon after as it is introduced to the brain, rather than attempting to re-learn weeks or months after first being introduced to the subject matter.

Repetition. One way to remember is to repeat. Although this method works, it is boring, and for many, it takes a long time. Although the brain responds well to the information that is repeated, a more straightforward and more efficient way is to combine repetition with an **association or linking** for memorizing, as explained in more detail, below. For example, when memorizing a poem or stanza, remember the first few lines then proceed to memorize the next few lines. Then go back and start at the beginning repeating the lines you have already learned, then add the following few lines. Proceed until you can recall the entire passage. By so doing, you are "linking" the lines. Put another way, when one line is embedded in your memory, the next line can be recalled easier because the mind will associate the previously learned line to the new line—more about linking later.

Acronyms. An acronym is an abbreviation for a phrase or a word made from the initial letters or parts of other words. Acronyms are pronounced as if it is a single word. Examples are: We refer to the National Aeronautics and Space Administration as NASA or North Atlantic Treaty Organization as NATO. Acronyms also use just initials, such as NIH for National Institutes of Health, U.S.A. for United States of America, or U.K. for United Kingdom. The acronym Benelux refers to the three neighboring countries in Midwestern Europe: Belgium, the Netherlands, and Luxembourg. Use of acronyms helps to remember words or phrases that otherwise may be difficult to recall. For example, to remember the Great Lakes, associate the first letter of each of the five lakes with the word "HOMES." Huron, Ontario, Michigan, Erie, Superior. To remember the Essential Minerals: Zinc, Calcium, Chromium, Iron, Potassium, Phosphorus, Iodine, and Magnesium you can think of the sentence Zebras Can Cluster In Pleasant Packs in Mass. You might want to even picture in your mind zebras grazing on a pile of minerals to help recall the acronym.

Write it down. Studies show that the process of writing down what you are striving to remember helps to speed up the memorization process. Again, you are using more than one of your senses.

Read out loud and recite back: The more active your study, the better the chance of recall. Thus, to help new ideas fix in your mind, read aloud, then try to recite back to yourself. Passive reading will result in less recall than when more of your senses are utilized. Active reading and describing key concepts back to yourself will help connect ideas to your core memory.

Recording. Recording and playing back information will combine, verbal, and auditory senses combined with repetition to help facilitate memorization. This can be especially helpful when learning vocabulary and for foreign language study. Recordings are also useful when played back at bedtime when the brain is relaxed and, in the zone, to remember.

Associating or linking by associating new ideas with facts already lodged in the brain we can better recall the new ones. Do you remember a time when you saw or heard something that reminded you of experience? A song, for example, that reminds you of an event or person in your past? How about a smell that "triggered" a memory, such as the smell of a freshly baked apple pie suddenly conjuring up an image of your grandmother's kitchen? When we associate or link information that has been previously anchored in our brain with a new event, it can help recall new information. This is done by "associating" familiar information with the new information. The sense of smell can be a powerful trigger. How can you use it to help study? One way would be to use incense or an aromatic candle when studying. When you begin a study session, use the aroma to help send a message to your brain. "OK brain, it is study time, so relax and get in the learning mode."

When attempting to learn the Spanish phrase for "What is your name." which is "Que se llama?" you might picture in your mind a cue (queue) stick with a big eye (se-e) by a llama (the animal). Silly, I know, but studies have shown that often the more outrageous a picture association is, the better it will be remembered. Don't ask me why it works, it just does. Want to remember the word "wanton" which means "irresponsible or lacking restraint"? Think. A *one-ton truck* is driving too fast for safety. To compare two unrelated objects. For example, she has a "bubbly personality", one's personality has nothing to do with bubbles, but so what? If it helps, you recall the meaning of the word, that is what counts. A simile (sounds like "similar"), on the other hand, shows the similarity between two different things. For example, "her smile was as radiant as a quarter moon." In this case, one can visualize a smiling face, much like the radiance of a quarter moon that looks like a smile. For more TIPS on using linking to recall facts, see "Mind Mapping," below.

Mental pictures. The mind stores pictures and images easier than the written word. For example, when you think of a pie, do you picture in your mind the letters "p-i-e," or a mental picture of a round object with a brown crust, maybe even sensing the aroma? So, to better recall, change words into pictures, then study the images. Use images that are familiar to you.

The Peg System. The pegging system associates a familiar "peg" word with new information that you want to remember. Often peg words are associated with a number then link or peg it to information that is already in your memory. With this system, you combine numbers with images. It is excellent for remembering PINs, phone numbers, locker combinations, and passwords. For example, 0 is hero; 1 is run; 2 is a shoe; 3 is a tree; 4 is a door; 5 is a hive; 6 is a chick; 7 is heaven; 8 is a gate; 9 is wine, and 10 is a hen. Note that the numbers rhyme with the letters. Of course, you can make up your own associations if you like. Here's how peg words work with the atomic numbers in the Periodic Table of Elements. Hydrogen is number 1. So, picture in your mind water (hydro means "water") running out of a faucet; Helium is number 2. Picture a heel of a shoe; Number 3 is Lithium so you might picture light in a tree; Beryllium is 4, so think a door made of berries; Boron is number 5, so visualize bees coming out of a hive to chase a wild boar, and the list can go on.

Another example is to make up a story using the numbers and images. Let's say your password for a web application is 017892. Choose words that rhyme with the corresponding number. Picture a hero (0), runs (1) to heaven's (7), gate (8), with wine (9) in his shoe (2).

To recall a password that combines numbers and letters, make up a story that can help you easily remember. So, you might picture your Mom in a tree, drinking wine on a farm with a hen and chicks. So, to remember M39@f10a6, mentally associate: M (<u>M</u>om), in a tree (3), drinking wine (9) at (@) a <u>f</u>arm (f), with hens (10) and (a) chick (6). If you want to memorize a series of numbers, such as a PIN, make up a sentence with each word having a predetermined number of letters. Then assign the number you want to recall to each word. So, assume your PIN is 1435. You may make up a sentence: "I (1-letter) like (4-letters), ice (3-letters) cream (5-letters)." Use your imagination to come up with your own peg words. Have fun!

Some good memorizers who use the numbers strategy will

associate numbers with objects that seem to resemble the number, then make-up lines or little stories that are associated with the numbers. For example, 1=stick, 2=swan, 3=breasts, 4=a boat sail, 5=a hook, 6=a unicorn, 7=a cliff, 8=a snowman, 9=a club, 0=ball. Let's say you want to remember Mexico's Independence Day. Contrary to popular opinion it is not Cinco de Mayo (May 5th), rather September 16th, 1810. So, using the numbers-object method, one might envision a Mexican warrior with a club (9 or the 9th month/September) with a stick (1), riding on a unicorn (6). So, September 16th. Now for the year 1810. Continue our mental picture by envisioning our Mexican warrior swinging his stick (1) at a Spaniard that looks like a snowman (8), also holding a stick (1) in one hand and a ball (0) in the other. 1810! The trick is the pairing of the words that help you memorize information quickly. Your mental images or stories can be as silly as you want. Sometimes the goofier they are, the easier it is to remember. By the way, you can combine the numbers-rhyming with numbers-objects strategies if you wish. The point is doing what works best for you. Experiment!

Rhymes and songs. It is easier to remember words when they rhyme or have rhythm. Make up a rhyme to help you memorize information. For example: "Brown vs. Board of Education ended school segregation." When possible link a tune to what you are trying to remember. I am impressed with how rappers can recall so many words and rattle them off at ward speed. The fact that the words rhyme dramatically facilitates their ability to memorize the lyrics.

Chunking. Break numbers down into no more than 2-4 digits long. So, 7378421975 becomes 737/842/1975. To further help, try to associate the numbers with something that will remind you of that number. For example, 7+3+7=17, your current age. 842 might be: "I ate (8) enough for (4) two (2)." 1975 might be the birthday of someone you know and can associate their birthday with.

Mind Mapping Mind. Mapping is a technique introduced by Tony Buzan, an English author and educational consultant who invented the thinking method of Mind Mapping. Mind Mapping is a strategy that uses words, images, color, rhythm, and logic, and spatial diagraming in pictures to facilitate recall. The unique way of organizing information helps to memorize information more smoothly and efficiently. The system also dramatically improves note-taking speed. I have included the seven steps to making a Mind Map, below. Note that Tony uses words such as: "image," "picture," "connection," and "association." The same words used in describing other memorization techniques are explained in this chapter. For further explanation and samples on mind maps go to your search engine and type in: "maximize the power of your brain." You can also search for Tony Buzan or Mind Mapping. Here is the general idea of how to Mind Map.

1. On a piece of paper, jot down the "who, what, why, when, and where"—and sometimes "how."

Start in the CENTER of a blank page. By starting in the center, it gives you room to spread out in all directions. Begin with an image relevant to the subject you are trying to remember. This image represents the central idea of your Mind Map. Images are easier to remember than written words.

2. You can write words, but pictures are better.

Use colors! Your brain likes colors. Plus, the use of colorful images makes your Mind Map more exciting and fun. Also, use curved lines instead of straight lines to help to make your Mind Map more interesting.

3. Connect your images to the central image. Develop your Mind Map further by connecting more levels. By linking your pictures, you are using the power of association to help you to remember.

4. Keep your Mind Map organized. Your mind gets confused with disorganization. Try to use a single word on each line.

As you gain experience, you may wish to vary from the rules provided. When developing your Mind Map, you are beginning the process of memorizing the subject matter.

Remember (no pun intended), as with anything you must practice the strategies provided in this chapter. By doing so, you are training your brain to memorize faster and more efficiently.

Chapter 17
Quizzes and Exams...No Problem!

Teachers use several tools to help determine a student's grade. Every teacher has their preferences, but generally, evaluations are by class participation, homework completion, quizzes, projects, papers, behavior, ability to follow instructions and examinations. Although teachers will give different weight to each of these areas, exams (tests) almost always are given the most weight.

TIPS
To Prepare for Quizzes and Exams

What Do You Want? In Chapter 4, I addressed "The Miracle of Goal Setting." So, when it comes to grades, to include examinations, ask, "What grade do I need to get on the next exam to maintain or increase my Grade Point Average?" By asking yourself this question, you are, in effect, setting a benchmark for yourself. An analogy would be like running a race and seeing the finish line in front of you. As you dash towards the line, you run a little faster. Would you do this if you did not know where the finish was? Unlikely.

To get started, do an honest assessment of where you might stand in preparation for examinations. Put the review in the form of questions an honor student might ask themselves. If you are not entirely confident of your answers, then turn back to the appropriate chapter in your text or your notes for help. When should you do this self-assessment? Not a day or two before the exam! Start early in the grading period, then update periodically throughout the grading period.

Planning. Ask yourself...

- What is my plan of study?
- What method (strategy) of study am I most comfortable for taking this exam?

- How much time do I need to study for the exam? How should I best allocate my time for preparation?
- Should I work with a partner or study group? Will reciting the material to another person help?
- Are my notes complete and precise? Am I missing any essential notes? (Chapter 12)
- Have I read and understood my textbooks and handouts? Have I answered questions and sought out assistance on anything I am uncertain? (Chapters 13)
- Am I using the strategies on memorization (Chapter 16) to help me better prepare for quizzes and examinations?
- Have I honestly identified anything that is interfering with my ability to meet my academic goals?
- Assess. How comfortable am I with the material that is to be tested? Do I have all the reference materials and handouts that I need to help me efficiently study? Am I missing anything and, if so, how can I get the information I need given the time I have before the exam? How much time do I need to devote to preparing for this exam?

Organization and preparation. In Chapter 7, I spoke about the importance of organization. Being organized can significantly help when it comes to exam preparation.

- **Schedule.** What are my requirements and priorities for other subjects, assignments, extra-curricular, family, and social commitments? How can I allocate my time so that I have enough time to devote for preparation for this exam?
- **How does your teacher format and administer tests?** How much weight does he/she place on quizzes and examinations? What kind of exams does he/she give, i.e., a multiple-choice, short answer, an essay, a combination?
- **Start preparing for quizzes and exams on the first day of class.** What? You may ask? "How can I do that, when I don't even know what is to be tested?" Here is how. Read

the class syllabus! Often, the teacher will tell you how he/ she determines grades. Recognize that everything you do for a class is helping to prepare for examinations-listening, note-taking, reading, and homework-starting on the first day of class.

Listen! In Chapter 11, I provided guidance on active "listening" strategies. Believe it or not, most teachers will give verbal clues as to what will be on an examination. How do they do that?

- Repeating essential points several times.
- Stating emphasis, such as "This is important," or "You must understand," etc.
- Pause during a lecture, to give students time to write down the information.
- Changing voice inflection for emphasis.
- Use specific words, such as: "to summarize," "most importantly," "as a result," "remember," "don't forget," etc.
- Watch for non-verbal signals such as dramatic hand gestures or tapping of a finger or pencil to emphasize a point.

Study your notes. If you have taken good notes (Chapter 12), you will be confident that essential points have not been missed. Review them carefully. Since you have reviewed them periodically throughout the marking period, by now the important information will be well ingrained in your mind. So this will be a review, not a first-time cram study session.

Review your textbook and any handouts. Just as with your notes, this too should only be a review, and not a last-minute effort to read material for the first time. Review the main points you have previously marked in your text. Look again at any charts, graphs, illustration, summaries, etc. the author (s) have inserted. If the text provides questions at the end of the chapters, are you comfortable that you know the answers? Re-review chapter headings, first and last paragraphs of all sections. Why? Because this is where the author provides essential points. If you are still unclear or wish to further review details, you can re-read for detail. If you have adequately reviewed throughout the grading period, you should not have to do re-read. If you feel you might have previously missed details or wish to re-review, then re-reading may be necessary.

Use the index. If the test is to cover specific chapters, see what pages are associated with those chapters, then turn to the index and review the terms associated with those pages. Make sure you are familiar with the terms used.

TIPS
FOR ESSAY QUESTIONS

I used to hate essay tests when I was in school. I am not sure why. I suppose it was because I was afraid that I would not be able to recall the facts needed for the test question. However, looking back, I performed better on essays than on objective tests. Why? First, because I knew more than I gave myself credit. After all, I had studied the material. Secondly, the teacher or professor would often give students a choice of answering 3 of 4 or 2 of 3 questions, or something similar. Thus, the students can pick the questions they are most comfortable. It also increases the odds of a better score as you can get partial credit on an essay question, whereas on objective tests, the answer is either right or wrong.

Read the question carefully. Make sure you understand what is asked. If you are asked to "define" something, don't "compare and contrast." If asked to "justify or support," don't "explain."

List. Before you begin to write, think about what you are going to say. If permitted to do so, on a separate piece of paper, jot down all the facts, and ideas you can think of that pertain to the question.

Organize your facts and ideas into some logical order. Try to answer questions using the "who, when what, why, where" responses to the question asked. Number your notes in the order you would like to write them on your exam paper to help with organization as you transfer the notes to your exam paper.

- **The first paragraph** should clearly state what you are about to say. Do this by introducing key points. Be concise!
- **Background.** Orient, the reader by providing historical knowledge, the philosophies, or theories that relate to the subject.
- **Arguments.** Elaborate on the key points mentioned in your first paragraph. What is the significance of the points you have made? Provide comparisons, arguments, cause and effects, conflicts, etc. that relate to the question.
- **End your essay** with a conclusion or answer as to why you made the points or arguments that you did. Avoid merely summarizing what you have already said.
- **Do not try to fill in space with unnecessary jargon.** Teachers are not fooled.
- **Clarity.** Use short, clear sentences. Write neatly! The teacher will appreciate it, and it could make a difference in your grade.

No clue? If you do not know the answer to the question, pass over it and focus on those you know something about. In other words, don't waste time.

Review. Look back over your essay. Check spelling, grammar, punctuation, and syntax. Unless your exam is written on-line or typed, if you find a mistake or want to change something, neatly draw one line through the incorrect word or words, and then write the replacement in the space above or below the marked-out word. Do not scribble out mistakes! It looks terrible. It is what children in kindergarten do.

Out of time? If you find yourself with only a few minutes left and a whole essay unanswered, then quickly list all critical points in an outline form. Even though you did not write your answer, most teachers will give at least partial credit if you listed some main points of the question.

Open book and take-home exams. Caution! You may think that an open book or take-home test is easy but, in fact, the take-home test can be the most difficult. Why? Because the teacher will expect more complete answers than closed-book tests. Often questions are more challenging than questions in a closed book exam. If faced with an in-class open-book test, prepare by using index cards and placing markers in your text so you can quickly find key points. Answer all the questions you can from memory, so if you must refer to your book, you will have enough time to do so. Another strategy is to summarize essential facts on a sheet of paper then cross-reference them to the text page in case you need to refer to them. An organized approach will help you find the information you are looking for quickly. For take-home tests, follow the same principles you would for an essay in terms of answering the "who, when what, why, where, and how."

TIPS
FOR OBJECTIVE QUESTIONS

Objective tests. Objective tests include true/false multiple choice, analogies, matching, sentence completion, or fill in the blank. Many students believe that because such tests only require fact recognition or memorization, it is easier. Not always true! Multiple-choice questions can be confusing because you are required to recall or recognize the correct answer from a list of incorrect answers. Short answer and fill in the blank questions require recall of specific information and facts. Because objective tests have more questions than do essay exams, more reading is needed, and cursory reading will result in incorrect responses.

Judgment. Because many short-answer questions ask students to choose between several possible answers, more than one of which may be correct, the students must eliminate incorrect answers or answers that may be less than correct than another.

Reasoning. Some objective questions ask students to figure out a pattern or relationship between numbers, words, or sentences.

Planning. How much time do you have to answer the number of questions? If questions are weighted, give allowance to those questions that count more towards your final grade on the test. Some students will divide the time allocated for the exam by the number of questions. Doing so gives them an idea of how much time to spend on each question. Although a good strategy, do it quickly. Do not spend too much time calculating and watching the clock.

Guess! Unless you know that you will be penalized for an incorrect answer, i.e., a deduction is made for every wrong answer (this is uncommon), you will increase your odds of a better grade by guessing if you do not know the correct answer. In other words, do not leave an answer blank on an objective test. Blank responses will be marked wrong, guessed answers might be right. When you use the process of elimination as described in the next tip, you also increase your odds of getting a correct answer.

The process of elimination. In multiple-choice questions, many times, there will be an option that is clearly incorrect. Here is an example of an actual government exam.

Why does the United States flag have 50 stars?

A. It looks good
B. For the number of states in the union
C. It was designed on the 50th anniversary of the Declaration of Independence
D. For the number of Founding Fathers at the Continental Congress

"It looks good" is an obviously incorrect answer. OK, you are now down to 3 out of 4. It could be the "designed on the 50th anniversary of the Declaration," but this is an unlikely response. Now we are down to 2 out of 4 and a 50/50 chance of getting the correct answer. Even if you do not know the actual number of Founding Fathers, it is improbable that it would have been precisely fifty. Besides, would that be a logical reason to place stars on a flag? That leaves only one likely answer—B. Of course, all incorrect answers will not be quite so obvious, but you get the idea.

Another example.

What are the two parts of the U.S. Congress?

A. House of Representatives and Senate
B. Senate and Parliament
C. Duma and House of Parliament
D. House of Lords and Parliament

Even if you were not sure of the names of the two parts of the U.S. Congress, but are more familiar with the British government, or even a little of U.S. history, then you could immediately eliminate B) and D). It could be C), but does "Duma" sound like an American term? That leaves only one probable answer—A).

After eliminating as many incorrect or improbable answers, you are still unsure of the remaining 2 or 3 responses, try one or more of these strategies to help increase your odds of choosing the correct answer.

Are the options provided reasonable given the context and content of the question? For example, in the same government exam, the question was asked:

The first three words in the U.S. Constitution are…

A. Life, Liberty and
B. We the People
C. In the beginning
D. Democracy for all

Think! Do the answers provided seem logical? Since the question asks for the "First three words in the U.S. Constitution," it would seem peculiar that the teacher would include a response that included the word "and" as one of the first three words. Let's eliminate A).

"In the beginning" sounds like something that might be used in a novel rather than a constitution. Cross that one-off. "Democracy for all" could be the answer, but an unusual way to begin a sentence. So, it just does not seem as if it belongs. Thus, the most reasonable "guesstimate" would be B) "We the People".

Although the above examples are simple, the strategies work for more complex questions as well.

Here are some more hints when taking objective exams.

Often correct answers are when the question has the words "some," probably" or "sometimes."

The answer is often incorrect when the sentence contains the words "always," "never," or "none."

Possible right answers often contain phrases as "all the above," "none of the above" and "one or more of the above."

Your first guess is often the correct answer.

When answering a question related to reading a paragraph, read the questions first. That way, when you read the section, you will be able to look for the facts asked for in the question.

When questions seem complicated, to help with your understanding of the question, re-read it and in your mind re-state it in your own words.

The elimination process also works well with matching type questions.

True/False Questions. The good thing about True/False questions is they give you a 50/50 chance of getting the answer correct. Read the question carefully. Broad or general statements are often incorrect. Since all portions of a correct answer must be valid, look for words that may show that any part of the statement may be wrong. If you are not sure of the right answer, often words such as: "no," "never," "always" are absolutes. Often absolute answers are incorrect. Conversely, words such as "usually," "rarely," "often," or "sometimes" will be contained in a "true" answer. Since T/F tests are a 50/50 proposition, unless you are being penalized for an incorrect response, guess!

Sentence completion or fill in the blank. Unless a word bank is provided, these types of questions require the student to know the correct answer. When unsure, and if you must guess make sure your response corresponds with any "hints" the teacher may have given. For example, if the word bank has two words, yet the blank space has only one space, the two-word option would be incorrect. So eliminate these. Sometimes you can find the answer buried in other questions on the exam.

Multiple choice math. Again, the process of elimination can help. Since often, one or more questions are clearly incorrect, the student can take an educated guess. For example:
900 divided by 71=

A. 1,000
B. 75.4
C. 2.67
D. 20

Immediately "A" can be eliminated as 1,000 is larger than the dividend of 900, thus not possible. It could be 75.4 but not likely as the divisor (71) would have to be much smaller than 75. "D" (20) could be correct, but multiplying 20 by 75 yields 1,500, a number much larger than the dividend of 900. So, the answer must be "C."

When possible, estimate the answer before calculating. This way, you will have an idea of the approximate solution and can eliminate apparent incorrect responses. Thus, when you do your calculation and are incorrect, you can still narrow the field and increase the odds of guessing the correct answer.

Look for answers that do not jive with the question. In other words, if the problem asks for weight, immediately eliminate any response that does not have a weight measurement, such as angle or exponent.

Simplifying math problems. After mastering the fundamental skills of addition, subtraction, multiplication, and division, mathematics becomes more challenging. Higher-level math problems involve multiple steps, thus require more in-depth reasoning and problem-solving skills. For many, this process can be quite intimidating, especially for those who are not naturally mathematically inclined. Math used to scare the heck out of me. But, like most things, when broken down into small, logical steps, the process becomes much less daunting.

In the following "TIPS" section, I provide more suggestions strategies to help make math simpler. Some techniques can be applied to higher-level math, but most apply to the elementary level. Although this is presented in PART I, which is primarily directed to students, there are several suggestions that parents can use to help young children with mathematics. Older siblings can help coach younger brothers or sisters as well.

TIPS
To Simplify Math

Use non-traditional math strategies. Several publications provide practical ways to do math in non-traditional yet effective ways. In the introduction to the book *"Short-Cut Math"* by Gerard W. Kelly asks: "Can you multiply 362 x .5 quickly in your head? Could you readily calculate the square of 41? How much is 635 divided by 2½? Can 727,648 be evenly divided by 8?" Kelly provides simple, short-cut tricks that provide faster, more natural ways to add, subtract, multiply, and divide. Kelly is not the only math wizard who can help simplify math concepts and calculations. Two other best sellers include *Verdi Mathematics* by Dhaval Bathia and *Secrets of Mental Math*, by Arthur Benjamin and Michael Sheoner. I will not provide their methodologies in this book, as it would add many more pages, and do not want to do that. I will let the experts describe their math strategies.

You may wish to read the online reviews and choose for yourself.

Use pictures and models. Since much of math is abstract, it is difficult for many students to visualize in their heads. Thus, pictures and models help students to understand the concept better. Fractions are difficult for young students to understand until depicted in the form of a circle or square. For example, if a word problem is given, it can often be simplified when illustrated in picture form. A useful resource is Cy Tymon's *Sneaky Math: A Graphics Primer with Projects.*

Break down problems into steps. All math problems are developed in stages. It is imperative that a student master a step before proceeding to the next. Failure to do so will make the understanding of all subsequent steps difficult, if not impossible. Because of this, missed lessons due to school absence can be critical. Make sure missed lectures and assignments in math are made up. Failure to do so will quickly result in the student falling behind.

Be neat! Numbers are easy to misread when not neatly written. Examples of numbers frequently misread when not written carefully include 1 and 7, 8 and 0, 6 and 0, 7 and 2, 4 and 9. Also, when numbers are not neatly written in columns, it will often result in mistakes. So make sure numbers are legible and written in straight columns. When copying a problem from one source to another, text to paper, for example, make sure it is copied exactly -double-check for errors. For TIPS on neat writing skills, see Chapter 19.

Practice! Basic math, such as the multiplication table and specific formulas, must be memorized. There is just no getting around this one. Use memory tricks described in Chapter 16. Parents can help young students by reviewing basic math skills while riding in the car while relaxing, or any moment that the child is not otherwise preoccupied. Older students can write the formulas, concepts, and rules on 3x5 cards and review on the school bus, in the cafeteria, library or whenever convenient.

Decimals and percentages. Decimals are easier to understand when converted to money. Lay coins out on a table and play money games. Percentages are simply a decimal with the dot in front, and when removed a percent symbol (%) is placed behind the number. When concepts are applied to money and stories, the decimals and percentages become easier to visualize. 10 cents=$.10=10% of 100. 100 cents =$1.00. And 10 cents is 1/10th of $1.00. Parents can show their child these concepts by playing a few games with the figures. Provide the child a dollar, then when shopping tells her she can buy some candy for 90 cents (or whatever amount). Can she tell you what percent it is of 100? You will be surprised how quickly they will pick up the concepts of decimals and percentages, especially when they get to buy that candy bar.

Algebra can be made easier when thought of as a game in which numbers are substituted by letters. When rearranged step by step, one can figure out the answer. Parents teach children to view it as a game. Find computer games that do this for you. Such games can help take the mystery out of algebra and contribute to alleviating any fear of problems that, at first, may seem intimidating.

Geometry is especially conducive to understanding abstract ideas with the use of models. A student can follow a geometric model in a few moments as compared to hours of study of abstract book examples.

Word problems can be scary. Why? Because they require reading, math, and reasoning skills. Word problems often contain a fact or facts that are not stated clearly. Also, math signs such as +, -, > or <, % are provided. So when all these elements are combined— yuck! However, just as with all challenges, when broken down into smaller pieces, the "problem" is simplified.

To summarize: The clue in doing a math problem is the procedure. Do each step in proper order. Read the question twice. How many steps are required? What math calculation is necessary, i.e., addition, subtraction, division? Check your answers by reversing.

Chapter 18
Extra Credit and Class
Attendance, Why Bother?

There is debate among teachers and college professors about the pros and cons of extra credit. If your teacher or professor does not offer additional credit, then there is not much you can do about it. You must accept what you earned with no opportunity to boost a grade or make up a missed class assignment or test. If a teacher or professor offers an opportunity for extra credit, it provides a chance to boost a grade view it as a gift and take advantage of it. When students take advantage of the offer, they send a message to the teacher that they care enough about the class to go above and beyond that which is required. Turn it down, and you may send a message that you don't care enough about the course or your grade to put in the effort.

Many high schools allow students to earn extra credits through online courses to supplement their school-based curriculum. Such an opportunity can lighten classroom instruction time or provide upper-level courses credit.

It is the rare graduate who did not skip class, or at least thought about it. But is it wise to do so? Let's look at the reasons why a student might consider skipping class vis-à-vis, not skipping class.

Why skip class?
- It is fun.
- It will not affect my grade.
- Everyone does it.
- It is a tradition.
- It's fun to get over on the "system."
- I am exercising my independence.
- I didn't finish an assignment.
- I need more sleep.
    I am sure there are more, but of those provided these

are often used "excuses." Of course, they are not legitimate reasons, such as being sick or having a doctor's appointment. Health or family commitments may be considerations. On occasion, a family outing can be an educational experience. The question must then be answered, "Does this outweigh the disadvantages of missing class?" As for the "excuses," I can think of no advantage, other than a temporary thrill. Honestly ask yourself, "do any of the reasons I may use outweigh the importance of attending class?" Here are the thought processes of honor students:

- If I miss class, work needs to be made up. Also, classroom instruction usually provides valuable information that helps me complete my homework. I will have to seek out classmates for the assignment, clarification, or notes. Going to class cuts out all the extra work.

- Instructor or class discussion may be missed that could be valuable when completing homework or helping in an exam. Relying on the notes or memory of another student is risky and may result in missed information.

- I know that my teachers note who puts in the most effort. If I receive an unexcused absence, it will send a message to the teacher that I am not serious about the class or grade. Since some portion of my final grade can be based on the teacher's impression, a missed class or classes may well tempt the teacher to grade down rather than up.

In high school, attendance is mandatory. Thus, excessive absences could result in the Attendance Office acting to notify parents. Unexcused absences also go on the student's record. Chronic unexcused absences must be reported to authorities and can result in fines against the student and the parent, believe it or not.

Colleges and universities often do not hold students to strict attendance mandates. Regardless, there are still negative consequences for missing classes. For example, many college professors take attendance and will factor in attendance records to final grades. Even if they don't that does not mean they might not notice those who seem to not take their class seriously. Remember, professors spend a lot of time preparing for the course they are teaching. If the student does not show they care enough to honor the professor's efforts, then why should the professor care about them?

- College students are paying megabucks for tuition. Skipped classes are a waste of money.
- Skipping classes can become a habit.
- Some college professors allow a specified number of days missed without consequences. Check your syllabus. If this is the case, be aware that this is offered in case the student encounters a legitimate reason for not attending class. If used for weak reasons, it could backfire if suddenly a legitimate one comes up, and you have already used up the quota on trivial purposes.

Often students skip class because they are pressured to do so by fellow students. If you allow others to influence you to make a poor decision, you are a sheep. Remember, it is your grade and future, not theirs. Besides, often the self-awarded time does not turn out to be as much fun as initially thought. Thus, the "reward" of a skipped class turns out not to be much of a reward at all.

Here are a few "Duhs." Skipping the first class of the marking period or semester, a review session, or a post-exam review. The information provided in such courses is, more often, not just "nice," but essential.

Look over the "Building Blocks for Success" presented in SECTION C. Personal traits and skills do not always come naturally, instead must be developed and reinforced. Then ask yourself, "By skipping class, how am I contributing to developing a work ethic that will serve me for the rest of my life?"

Ultimately, it is your choice to take advantage of extra credit when offered, or whether to skip classes. As in all decisions made in life, weigh the pros and cons before impulsively making a choice that you may later regret.

Chapter 19
How Handwriting Improves Grades

Do papers written or typed neatly make a difference, and if so, why? By "neatness," I mean papers, whether handwritten or typed, to be legible and pleasing to the reader. In this chapter, I will address handwriting as it applies to neat papers. Typewritten papers are pleasing to the eye because the letters are uniform, but errors in formatting, grammar, spelling, and syntax can make the document difficult to read. Sloppy handwriting, on the other hand, is not pleasing to the eye even if the content is letter-perfect. When you look at documents written by past generations, you will probably note that the handwriting is not only neat but attractive. Regrettably, many people have poor handwriting today. Often it is even difficult to read. What happened? In the late 19th century, the introduction of the typewriter started the trend. Word processing and computers, introduced in the 1970s, further transitioned longhand to typing. This trend made many believe that in our high-tech world, handwriting was less important.

Consequently, many schools started de-emphasizing the teaching of handwriting. Today, the Common Core standards, which have been adopted in most states, require teaching writing only in kindergarten and first grade. After first grade, the emphasis is on keyboarding. The result is that many students are unable to produce work that is neat and legible when written.

Another contributor to poor handwriting was the invention of the ballpoint pen. Before the ballpoint, people used fountain pens. Before the fountain pen, quill pens were used. To use these instruments effectively, the writer had to hold the pen lightly in the fingers, one of the essential techniques essential to good handwriting. Also, the writing tip of quill and fountain pens allowed for stylized writing. Ballpoint pens, especially cheap ones, tempt the writer to press harder which is not conducive to stylized writing. To prove my point, the next time you write with a ballpoint pen or even a pencil, look at the tip of your index finger. If you see a small indentation where you held the pen, you are holding it too tightly. Good hand writers do not hold the pen as if they are afraid it is going to jump out of their hand and run away. Instead, they hold it gently. Do this experiment. Try writing but hold the pen tightly, which for most of is our usual way of holding the pen or pencil. Now write again, but this time hold the pen or pencil lightly in your hand. Make sure you do not press your index finger into the pen or pencil. Notice that you write slower. Compare the two samples. Which one is neater?

Allow me to provide a few arguments that point to the fact that quality handwriting is still relevant, in spite of Common Core and others who feel script is unimportant. In his book and video series, *Where There's a Will, There's an A*, Claude W. Olney emphasized the importance of neat papers can have on grades. He described how an experiment in the university where he was a professor showed that documents sloppily written would frequently get lower grades than papers that were neatly written, even though the content was practically the same. In other words, although what was written was good work, the difference was in how the papers were presented. Studies by other scholars (Sheffield, 1996; Alston and Taylor, 1987) also pointed out that the quality of handwriting affected grading regardless of the content of the paper. Even though today most papers are typed, the point made by these scholars is as valid today as it was 20 to 40 year ago.

Some may ask, since I type my papers, why do I need to practice handwriting skills? Granted, these days most teachers and college professors require students to type their papers. Yet, typed documents can be challenging to read if not correctly formatted and contain spelling, grammatical, and syntax errors. When I was teaching college, even though students typed their papers, it was a chore trying to wade through a document that was poorly organized and had numerous grammatical, spelling, and syntax errors. In contrast, reading typed papers that had few errors was a pleasure to read. Even when the content may not have been as strong as it could have been, I would give points because the student took the time to make sure they handed in a paper that was edited correctly. A sloppily written paper signals to the teacher that the student doesn't care enough to do his/her best work. Consequently, the teacher will take that into account and grade accordingly. Handwritten papers do not have the benefit of the neatness of a typed document, thus making it more important to ensure that the script is legible and pleasing to the reader. Whether typewritten or handwritten, neatness counts!

Here are more reasons why good handwriting counts:

It reduces errors. A study in *American Demographics* as reported in the St Louis Post-Dispatch (MO) (Nov 20, 1994), estimated that U.S. businesses lost millions of dollars every year because of illegible writing and documents that were not clear. The article states, "The United States is experiencing a crisis in penmanship. The crisis takes the form of illegible memos, cryptic prescriptions, unenforceable parking tickets, and indecipherable mail addresses. It costs millions of dollars and even lives."

As a former health care administrator, I observed confusion and errors due to illegible physician notes and prescriptions.

Contrary to many of those writing school curricula, handwriting is not obsolete—taking notes, writing letters, filling out forms, and taking tests are often completed in handwriting instead of typed.

Ramon Abajo, author of *What Every Teacher Should Know About Handwriting,* stated, "Handwriting is the vehicle carrying information on its way to a destination. If it is illegible, the journey will not be completed. Despite the high quality of ideas and information, the writer will bear a lifelong burden. When handwriting flows, the writer has better access to his own thoughts and information."

Dr. Donald Graves, Professor of Education at the University of New Hampshire, a respected authority on the writing process, reports that young children want to write well but are often frustrated because they find handwriting difficult for little hands that are still learning coordination skills. Thus, when they perceive handwriting as challenging, when not adequately taught, they come to regard handwriting as unimportant. To become proficient at handwriting students must be shown, starting at an early age and continuing throughout their school years." With regular practice and encouragement, students will perceive handwriting as both stimulating and enjoyable. This will, in turn, help contribute to pride in their work and better grades. Besides, it will make the teacher's job easier.

Good handwriting has many other advantages. Here is what a few of the experts say:

Students who received instruction in handwriting showed improvement in composition fluency. Poor penmanship adversely affects spelling achievement. Berninger, V., and Graham, S. *Language by hand: A synthesis of a decade of research on handwriting. Handwriting Review, 12*, 11-25. 1998.

According to LD Online, a leading website on learning disabilities, research shows that handwriting instruction and handwriting skill impact student's overall literacy development and that early fine motor writing skills affect academic achievement.

Handwriting instruction taught at in preschool helps develop fine motor skills that facilitate better academic skills that are important for school readiness skill associated with later academic success, reported in the Mar 18, 2014, *Journal of Childhood Literacy* by Dinehart and Manfra, 2013.

Stephen Graham, Karen Harris, and Barbara Fink reported in a 2000 paper published in the Journal of Educational Psychology titled, *Is handwriting causally related to learning to write? Treatment of handwriting problems in beginning writers.* Studies found that handwriting instruction is an important component in "...preventing writing difficulties in primary grades." The authors also discovered that "writing speed and output increase when fine motor skills are developed in conjunction with learning handwriting skills." In a later edition (93, 488-497) research suggests that handwriting is related to writing fluency and quality for both primary and intermediate elementary students. The tendency in schools to place greater emphasis on content and process at the expense of form may well be adversely affecting the ability of beginning writers to develop handwriting and compositional skills. This trend can also have negative consequences for older students and adults regarding quality, efficiency, and effectiveness of work.

Any doubts about the importance of handwriting? Yet, many school districts are downplaying the importance of handwriting. So if your child's school is deficient in this area, the parent can help fill the void by working with their child. See some suggestions in "TIPS" below.

Doing one's best takes effort. It means taking the time to review, check, and ask for assistance if needed. It means working smarter, not harder. When students take pride in their work, they are conveying to their teacher that they are conscientious about their work. It also means learning to be "effective" as well as "efficient."

In Chapter 7, I distinguished between "effectiveness and efficiency." I described how being "efficient" could help make being "effective" easier. A key component of being efficient is "organization." I also addressed "habits." What does "organization" and "habits" have to do with "neatness," you may ask? If a person tends to be physically sloppy, there is a likelihood that this attitude or habit will also be reflected in schoolwork. There are exceptions. My Chinese exchange students, for example, have neat handwriting (due to learning Chinese script), yet they are disorganized. They study hard, but not smart. They are "effective" but "inefficient." They will study five to six hours per day to get "B's," yet if they used many of the strategies of "efficiency" presented in this book, they would make "A's" and with much less time studying. Why don't they do it then? Habits! In China, they were taught to study hard. They were not taught "how" to study. I am amazed that they will get B's on written assignments that have numerous grammatical, syntax, and punctuation errors. Why? Because the "content" is good, and their papers are neat. Although I offer to check their papers for grammar, syntax, and spelling, they are hesitant to ask me. Why? Habit! One might also term it "conditioning." In China, they are taught to work independently, thus are uncomfortable asking for help. If they did, their "B" papers would be "A's." Lessons learned—Organization, neatness, and checking work make a big difference.

Go back to Chapter 7 to review TIPS on "improving organization skills" and "changing unwanted habits." Although I have tried to show the correlation between "organization" and "neatness," this chapter is about neatness as it relates to handwriting.

There is good news! Handwriting skills can be improved for those who choose to do so. Small children, of course, must be guided and encouraged in the effort. Older students and adults should consider using a good book on handwriting skills. These will help identify writing problems and give guidance on how to improve script through strategy and practice exercises. In the meantime, consider the following TIPS to get started on enhancing handwriting skills now.

TIPS
FOR NEATER HANDWRITING

- ✓ Use a writing surface/table that allows your elbows to be at about a 90-degree angle.
- ✓ Use good writing posture. Sit straight with back and neck straight. Do not bend over the table and your paper.
- ✓ Position your paper 30 to 45 degrees to your body, top edge to the right if you are lefthanded, top corner to the left if righthanded. More importantly, however, be comfortable.
- ✓ Used lined paper to help with the height of capital and minor letters.
- ✓ Use your forearm to write, rather than your fingers and wrist. Using fingers encourages pressing too hard and fatigues the hand.
- ✓ Hold the pen between the thumb and index finger with the barrel resting on the middle finger—the most common way of holding the pen or pencil. Others hold the pen between it and the index and middle finger with the barrel resting on

the ring finger. The former is the preferred way. Lefthanders often curl the palm around the pen, making use of a fountain pen a bit harder. Just practice!

✓ Try different types of pens. Ballpoint pens will generally contribute to poor handwriting.

✓ Try fountain rollerball, gel, or fiber tip pens. Experiment and use the ones with which you are most comfortable.

✓ Do not squeeze the pen. Hold it gently.

✓ Keep all letter leanings at the same angle. //////

✓ Letters should be uniformly the same size. Capital letters should be at the same height as one another. Tall lower-case letters (b, d, h, k, l, t) should be the same height as capital letters. A-b, D-d, etc. Letters whose stem extend below the line (g, j, p, q, y) should be the same length below the line.

✓ Keep spaces between words consistent.

✓ Maintain comfort and take breaks when you begin to tire.

✓ On a lined manuscript tablet designed for writing practice start making, /'s, I, s, and large and small O's. Also, practice looping in different sizes. Do them over and over until all the circles, and lines are uniform and evenly spaced. It will take practice to achieve the desired uniformity, but do not get discouraged. Practice a little every day and soon you will notice that your lettering will become more and more uniform and consistent.

Practice letters with similar strokes, such as g, c, o, and e. Work with these letters on your manuscript paper. Try connecting them in cursive.

You are not trying to be a calligrapher. Of course, you can if you want, but that is not your goal, which is to develop handwriting that is appealing and legible. As you become more comfortable with your new handwriting abilities, it will get faster.

Older students: If you were not taught handwriting skills or your handwriting needs work, practice the "TIPS" presented above. Assist your younger siblings by working on the strategies together. It can be fun while productive for both.

Parents and guardians: If your child's teachers are not teaching handwriting, you do it! As you can see from the research, handwriting neatness will make an impact on your child's educational success.

Chapter 20
Secrets to Mega Learning
What Schools Don't Teach

Few teachers, professors, and school counselors will not tell you what I am going to reveal to you. Why? Simple! Because most educators focus on the conscious level of the mind. In other words, they strive to influence, teach, coach, tutor, assist, counsel to the conscious mind, and neglect the unconscious portion of the brain. Nearly 90 percent of the abilities of our minds lie at the subconscious level.

The power of the subconscious. I have provided you with many "tools" that, if conscientiously used, will not only help with school but will also help achieve success in life. What I have outlined in this book thus far are basic tried and true methods that can be found in "how-to" books and manuals on study strategies. If you are fortunate, some teachers will provide instruction on study and learning strategies. There are a few powerful tools that most teachers and "how-to" books on study techniques do not tell you.

Win Wenger, the co-author with Paul R. Scheele of *Genius Code: Guiding You Into the Realm of Genius* and author of *Learning Strategies* and other books on brain performance actualization techniques, explains that encephalographic (EEG) studies show that 80 percent of the area of the brain is involved with visual responses. Dr. Wenger said that "less than five percent of the part of the brain and one percent of the cells of the brain are involved in the conscious experience, the rest is unconscious." Thus, the subconscious controls most of what we do and think, 24 hours a day, seven days a week. Think of it as a super-powerful computer that is always on. How powerful is it? The best-selling author and world-famous lecturer on memory and mind-mapping, Tony Buzan, whom I introduced you to in the chapter on *Memorizing Made Easy*, describes the power of the brain with an analogy to a computer. If the world's most powerful computer were equivalent to a two-story building, the human brains potential power would equal a skyscraper ten blocks square that reaches to the moon. That's good news. The bad news is we don't tap into all that unused capacity. Why? Mainly because our brains "programmer" (our conscious self) does not know how to program it.

We are not using much of our brain for creative purposes. How then can we tap into that vast reservoir of the unconscious mind so that we can increase our potential for creativity? There are several ways to name a few: relaxation/meditation, affirmations, and hypnosis. Let's look at each.

Affirmations. Affirmations are merely positive statements repeated silently or out loud that express the desired outcome. The intent is to impress upon the subconscious mind to make the positive statement come true. Correctly used, affirmations can be a powerful tool for achieving success and for improving your life. Have you ever said to yourself, or heard another say such things as, "I can't," or "It is too hard," "I just don't have the ability to," or other such negative words? When people hear such words, or if such negativisms are said to them, the subconscious mind will believe them and, consequently, begin to act on them. The subconscious mind does not think or reason; it just "does." In other words, the subconscious accepts messages that the conscious mind sends it, accepts the message as valid, and acts on it. It does not know the difference between positive or negative, good or bad, successful, or unsuccessful. Just as a computer is programmed, so too is one's mind programmed by words and thoughts.

To prove how thoughts can influence your ability to perform a task or change, try this! While standing, stretch your arms out to your sides. Without moving your legs or feet, twist your upper body in either direction. It makes no difference in which direction you rotate. Twist as far as you can go. Note how far you twisted. Now return to your original position with your arms down by your side. With your eyes closed picture in your mind, the twisting motion, but don't do it! Visualize yourself twisting further than you did when you just actually did it. See yourself twisting far, even 360 degrees if you want. Impossible but hey, you can pretend, right? You might state to yourself, *"I will twist my upper body further than I did before."* Say it several times. Now, open your eyes stretch your arms out to your side and twist. Really twist! Were you able to now twist further than you did the first time? Most will discover that they were able to turn further. This simple exercise shows how the mind can influence how our body responds to a command given to it. Can we use positive statements to get positive results? Absolutely! By repeating positive affirmations, you create mental images in the conscious mind which are transmitted to the subconscious mind. Just as a computer programmer programs a computer, you are "programming" your subconscious. Thus, you can effectively influence your behavior, attitude, or habits to help gain what you want and reshape your life.

"Well, if this is so easy, why don't people use it?" Good question! I suppose there are many reasons. Many do not know about affirmations. They may not believe they can work or may know about them but do not take advantage of them. Many of us have developed the habit of negative thinking. You know, "It is just too hard," "I don't have the ability to," "I will never," etc. Such negative thoughts neutralize any positive affirmations you may use. To get positive results, you must rid yourself of negative thoughts. Louise Hay, a well-known inspirational teacher and best-selling author, taught that people who controlled their minds, rather than letting their minds control them, were the ones most likely to lead a successful and happy life. In her book, *The Power is Within You*; she explains that for affirmations to be useful, one must "Reprogram Old Tapes." Ms. Hay states that much of our belief systems are formed by past life experiences that influence the way we think. Regrettably, much of these beliefs tell us that we are not deserving of better things. Hence, we set up mental roadblocks that interfere with our accomplishing what we want. "When we don't believe that we deserve good," states Hay, "we will knock the pinning's out from under ourselves, which we can do in a variety of ways. We can create chaos, we can lose things, and we can hurt ourselves or have physical problems like falling or have accidents. We have to start believing that we deserve all the good things that life has to offer." In Chapter 2, I posed the question "Why Aren't You Getting What You Want?" In Chapter 3, I provided some answers to the question. To those principles for success, add Ms. Hay's teachings that affirmations are an excellent way to help change self-sabotaging beliefs. Start with these four then build on them, advises Hay:

- "I am worthwhile."
- "I am deserving of..."
- "I am loved."
- "I allow myself to be fulfilled."

Follow these affirmations with, "I will not allow negative talk to interfere with my success," or "When negative thoughts enter my mind, I will replace them with positive thoughts." See Appendix C for a list of affirmations you can use. You can make up your own if you wish. Note that the affirmations are stated in the positive to help get what you want or change. For example, you would say, "I am learning to concentrate" rather than "I will not be distracted."

How long does it take to get results? It depends on your commitment to change, your focus, and the strength of the affirmation. Change may occur right away, in a few hours, in a few days, or take weeks or longer. Just don't give up if you do not get results right away. With patience, you will soon begin to experience results.

Subliminal programming. Another method that can efficiently be used with affirmations is subliminal programming. Subliminal programming is a method by which messages bypass the conscious mind and go directly to the subconscious. Unlike the conscious mind that will discriminate and judge, the psyche will follow commands to produce change quicker and more efficiently and create long-lasting and positive results. Research indicates that subliminal messaging is most effective when subjects are first consciously aware of the messages. Thus, affirmations are presented so you can hear them, then followed with embedded subliminal messages complemented with special music selections that promote the most significant psychological influence. To make this method even more powerful, one can utilize brainwave entrainment based on binaural-beat frequency research. Binaural beat recordings are a safe, non-addictive means for stimulating the brain to release tension, boost a super-focus state, and enhance creativity. This is accomplished by stimulating the brain with specific frequencies to create altered levels of consciousness. A fully awake person is said to be at the Beta level of consciousness which is recorded at the 13Hz to 30Hz brainwave frequency. The Alpha state or meditative state of mind (often termed "In the Zone" by athletes) can be created at a brainwave frequency of 8 to 12Hz. Scientists have proven that the best level of consciousness for maximum learning is to be in a meditative or relaxed state. Since the ears can only typically hear between 20 and 20,000Hz, frequencies such as 8Hz, simply don't register. Miraculously, we can get the mind to "hear" those lower frequencies, thus can recreate such states of mind literally "on demand."

By playing two different sounds of similar frequencies in each ear, a third "binaural beat" is created in the subcortical auditory system of the brain, thus altering the state of mind. For example, using stereo headphones, a pure tone of 400Hz is presented to the right ear, and a pure tone of 410Hz is presented to the left ear. Inside the head, the difference between the two tones is realized; a third beat called a "binaural beat" of 10Hz is produced. The following chart outlines the four different wavelengths humans operate.

WAVELENGTH	STATE OF CONSCIOUSNESS	EFFECTS
Beta 13-30 Hz	The normal state of alertness.	Stress and anxiety can be experienced
Alpha 8-12 Hz	Slight meditation/ relaxation.	Learning, concentration, creativity
Theta 4-7 Hz	Deep meditation/ relaxation.	Highly focused and increased memory
Delta 1-3 Hz	Deep sleep, lucid dreaming	Relaxed

Accelerated learning can take place in the Alpha and Theta levels. Because most students have difficulty getting themselves into these levels, they often find themselves "spinning wheels" when trying to study. Now with 21st-century technology, students can quickly, safely, and effortlessly influence their state of mind to maximize study efforts. The specially developed affirmations, subliminal messages and binaural beat tones embedded in formatted programs provide a unique yet powerful tool. Thus, the student can realize the desired outcomes by merely listening to the program. Psychologists suggest that it takes about thirty days to change habits, although it is possible that benefits will start to take effect within days after beginning use. Any behavior change program should be used frequently and consistently for at least 30 days to help bring about the desired change. Periodic use will help to insure new habits are re-enforced.

There are several sites a person can access to order programs that provide subliminal programming. I like a product put out by self-development leader Bradley Thompson of *Self-Help Street* called Razor Sharp Focus. This program can accelerate study and learning by assisting with relaxation, improving concentration, problem-solving, and memory. You can also check out your search engine for different programs that will help you get "in the zone" for enhanced study and learning.

Another excellent program that utilizes subliminal programming is *Brain Power Pro* by Lee Benson. With this program, you upload affirmations on your computer. The affirmations are projected on your screen, but at a rate that your eye can not see. There are many subject areas that you can choose from and include passing exams, memory enhancement, speed reading, motivation, self-esteem, decision making, stress relief, and leadership.

Relaxation. Why is it that many students have so much difficulty getting started on their studies, or when they do get down to actual study are unable to concentrate efficiently? The answer is they have trouble getting into the proper mental state of mind that is most conducive to study. An essential element of active learning that is often overlooked by students and educators is the importance of relaxation. Proper relaxation used just before beginning study periods and during study periods. There are several ways to effectively bring one into the Alpha level of consciousness, or "the study zone." See "TIPS" below.

Nature. What does nature have to do with the ability to improve study? It has long been theorized that smell receptors respond to certain scents that affect the brains limbic system. The limbic system affects moods and emotions.

In the July 2017 issue of *Time Magazine,* an article entitled "The Healing Power of Nature" reported that Japanese researchers have discovered that when people take walks in nature, they experience measurable beneficial changes in the body. Included is a lower level of the stress hormone cortisol, resulting in a state of physiologic relaxation. (Yoshifumi Miyazaki, et al. Chiba University). Another researcher, Dr. Qing Li, Nippon Medical School, found that trees and plants emit aromatic compound called phytoncides. When breathed in, these scents created changes in the blood that help contribute to certain immunities to include cancer and high blood pressure. Other recent studies, state the *Time* article, "have linked nature to symptom relief for health issues like heart disease, depression, cancer, anxiety, and attention disorders." So if a walk in the woods can do all these things, would it not seem logical that by doing so might help a student study and recall information?

I remember that when I was in high school, my history teacher decided to conduct a class under a tree in the garden of the school. I recall enjoying the course and focusing on the lecture more than I typically did when sitting in the four-walled classroom. A few days later, when preparing for the test, I decided to study in the garden rather than my usual place in the dorm room. My score on the test was the highest I had ever scored in that class. I always presumed it was because I was able to concentrate better in the garden, which may indeed have helped, but now I wonder if the scents of nature may have also helped contribute to my high-test score.

How to quickly get into a relaxed state of mind. Relaxation is the process of allowing physical and/or mental tension to be released. To quickly get into a state of relaxation for proper study, it takes a bit of practice. I provide some strategies below. There are also many books and audio programs that can help teach effective relaxation techniques.

TIPS
For Getting Into The "Study Zone"

Think about what it feels like just as you are about to fall asleep. Although conscious, you are aware of noises and movement in the room, but your eyes are closed and very relaxed. You are somewhat indifferent or overly distracted by what is going on about you. You might note that when you are in this state of mind, although not distracted by multiple stimuli, you can easily focus on a single subject. It is this state of mind that you want to be in for the maximum benefit of study. But you cannot study when you are about to go to sleep. So how can you get into the "study zone?" Easy, here's how.

Music. The right type of music can be used for creating the right mindset before and during study. Once relaxation is achieved, relaxing music can help keep oneself in an efficient state for maximum study. The best form of music for study is Baroque Largo music. Music was used as part of a rapid learning program developed in Bulgaria by Georgi Lozanov that helped students learn entire languages in a month. This classical, instrumental music is a 40 to 60 beat-per minute rhythm that has been found to increase learning comprehension and speed. Although merely listening to music in the Baroque style does not suggest that you will be able to duplicate the learning speeds realized by Lozanov, it is probable that it can enhance your study effectiveness. When used in conjunction with other techniques described in this book, certain types of music significantly accelerate learning. By softly playing the music in the background while studying, a state of mind is created that will maximize learning. Although Baroque-style music has been shown to be very effective, if you prefer, you may try other classical styles, jazz, pop, rhythm, and blues. Just make sure it is easy listening. Avoid music with lyrics, or music that has a fast beat that can be detrimental to helping you stay "in the zone." Don't force yourself to listen to music that you do not like. Some may find that studying in silence works best for them. Ultimately, do what works best for you.

During a recent visit to Arizona, I had the opportunity to meet a Native American flute player, David "Wolfs Robe" Booher. David is an Army veteran who served in Desert Storm and Iraq. He visits Veterans Administration hospitals to play Native American tunes on the flute for patients, many of whom had Post-Traumatic Stress Disorder (PTSD). David told me that after hearing the soothing, rhythmic sounds of the flute, the patients experienced a deep sense of relaxation that helped to alleviate their stress.

Breathing. One of the quickest ways a student can relax and get into the "study zone" is to use the breath. William Atkinson in his book, *Eliminate Stress from Your Life Forever,* explains the importance of breathing in helping to reduce tension and increase relaxation. Atkinson states that most people breath in a shallow manner. In other words, we breathe from the chest. This results in quicker breathing, which can contribute to tension. It also limits the amount of oxygen we take in, thus depriving our bodies of the opportunity for increased levels of oxygen that can be gained by abdominal breathing. Breathing is far more effective when we use our diaphragms, rather than with the chest muscles.

Here is how it is done. Sit comfortably in a chair, feet on the floor. Place one hand on your chest and the other on your stomach. Take two or three reasonably large breaths. The hand on your stomach should move rather than the one on your chest. Your stomach should go in when you breathe in rather than out. Try breathing out a little more slowly and more deeply. When we exhale, we release tension in the chest muscles. Do this for two to three minutes four or five times a day. You will soon be able to change your breathing style from chest breathing to abdominal breathing resulting in the benefits of a more relaxed state of mind and less physical stress.

Affirmations combined with breathing strategies and music. While listening to music, place yourself in a comfortable position in your chair. While slowly inhaling and exhaling (try to use abdominal breathing as explained above), close your eyes and put your hands on your lap. Now, silently say to yourself:

- *I am becoming deeply relaxed so that I can completely concentrate.*
- *I will shut out all distractions.*
- *I will have a complete understanding of all the material I am about to study.*
- *I will recall all that I have studied and heard in class.*
- *I can transfer all material learned to my conscious mind when I need it.*

More affirmations at Appendix C

Practice the relaxing, breathing, and affirmation techniques several times. You will notice that you will soon be able to get into the "study zone" more and more quickly as your mind adjusts to the "training." As soon as you feel relaxed and able to concentrate, slowly open your eyes, and begin to focus on the material in front of you.

You should have your books, notes, papers, or whatever you need to be laid out on your desk in front of you.

If you become distracted. The phone rings, someone calls you from another room, little sister or brother comes running into your room, then "poof" … you are out of your study zone. No problem—quickly repeat the strategy of breathing and affirmations as provided above until you return to your relaxed study zone state.

When you are finished studying, lean back in your chair, close your eyes, place your hands in your lap, take a deep breath, then say to yourself, *"I will remember everything I just studied."* I am now becoming fully awake and aware of everything around me.*"* Now, open your eyes, stand up, and go about whatever you choose to do.

Use Nature. If possible, before a study period, take a walk in nature. If impractical, merely look at photographs of nature, forests, rolling hills, streams, etc. Use incense or aromas that stimulate concentration and help moods such as lemon, lavender, and jasmine. Listen to recorded sounds of nature.

SECTION E
Classroom Strategies of Honor Students

The difference between ordinary and
extraordinary is that little extra.

Chapter 21
The Extra Edge

Know your teacher or professor. A significant contributor to anxiety is not knowing what to expect. "How can I get to know my teacher better?" "Will getting to know my teacher better really help?" "How do I make a good impression on my teacher?" "If I meet with my teacher, will she think I am a 'brown nose'?" "I am a bit shy about asking for help, so why bother?" My eldest daughter was an excellent student. Although she practiced many of the principles provided in this book (long before the book was written), one of the strategies that helped her was getting to know her teachers and professors. Although she knew that a teacher's impression of her would not be a substitute for doing well on assignments and exams, she also figured out her final grade could be influenced by the subjective portion of the teacher's grade, such as participation and initiative. She realized that knowing her teacher well provided her with valuable insight as to how to best approach her studies for the course. In middle school and high school, the teachers knew who she was, so she did not have to introduce herself. She would find opportunities to see the teacher outside of the classroom. She might do this by a short visit after school or during the teachers' open period. My daughter would use this opportunity to ask a question or two that she was not clear on or to discuss a subject of mutual interest. She did the same in college and graduate school. If the class is large, of course, it would be a bit more of a challenge to meet a professor, but she did not let this deter her. She just made an appointment during the professor's office hours. If she had questions, she would use the opportunity to get clarification. Sometimes she would tell the professor about herself and share her academic interests. Besides getting a good idea of the teacher's preferences, expectations, and quirks, establishing a good rapport with a teacher can help find a good mentor, or even help influence a career decision. She got to know a history professor so well that he asked her to help him edit a couple of books he wrote. She later became a journalist.

She discovered that most teachers and professors appreciated feedback on how their class was going. Of course, she would not approach her teacher or professor as a self-appointed critic—that would not have been wise. She also was smart enough to not criticize a teacher, even if she felt like doing so from time to time. She reminded herself that her purpose was to sell herself as a serious student interested in learning. My daughter has passed this, and many other strategies described in this book, on to her daughter, who graduated with top honors from high school and is now a presidential scholar in college.

Getting a grasp of your teacher's likes, dislikes, and preferences can often be the extra edge you need to push your grade a bit higher. This is even more important in college than in elementary, middle, and high school. Teachers at these levels majored in education. In contrast, college professors are experts in their fields, but many (other than those in the Education Department) have never taken a single course in education and may even be weak in knowing how to teach. The same course taught by different professors can be miles apart in how they teach similar material. To respond to the diverse preferences, personalities, and teaching styles of your teachers and professors, adapt your strategies to the various quirks and styles of your teachers and professors.

TIPS
FOR GETTING TO KNOW YOUR TEACHER/PROFESSOR

Participate in class, but do so by your teacher's preferences, and class rules and boundaries. Class participation is essential, but do not dominate class discussions as this may irritate fellow classmates or even the teacher.

Meet your teacher outside of the classroom. Ask pertinent

questions. Ask what they think about something that you may have read or heard about the subject.

Ask questions that are relevant to the subject at hand. Come across as sincerely interested (even if you may not be).

If nervous about meeting with your teacher or professor, remind yourself that the teacher wants students to visit with them and ask questions.

Chapter 22
Increase Retention and Reduce Nervousness

Two significant questions students ask are, "How can I better remember what is presented in class?" and "How can I get over my nervousness when I have to make a presentation in front of the class?" The underlying emotion behind the anxiety is the fear of not doing well. If unable to give full attention to what is being presented in class, then the material will be missed. Naturally, this contributes to the conscientious student's stress. In Chapter 11, Communication Strategies to Get Ahead, I explained how vital listening skills are to understanding and retention of classroom lectures. Although active listening is essential, students must give themselves every chance to "retain" what they have heard and observed. Here are a few "TIPS" to help minimize distractions and maximize focus, which will foster a better understanding and retention. In the second part of this chapter, I will provide a few suggestions for helping to get through the jitters when you must stand up in front of the class to make a presentation.

TIPS
To Increase Attention and Promote Retention

Sit near the front, if possible. This helps you to stay focused, hear what the instructor is saying, and see the whiteboard or PowerPoint presentations.

Avoid distracting classmates.

Be comfortable in your chair, but not too much. Do this by sitting up straight, feet on the floor. In other words, no slouching, leaning back in your chair. If parts of your body begin to ache or become uncomfortable, change positions a bit to keep your mind from focusing on the discomfort.

Actively participate in class. Some students are anxious about raising their hand to ask questions or contribute to class discussion. The best way to deal with such feelings is to face up to your fears and just do it. You have a choice. Give in to the fear, in which case you will not overcome it, or acknowledge it, take a deep breath or two and raise your hand. Do this a few times, and the fear will go away. Remember, most teachers grade, in part anyway, based on class participation. So keep in mind the benefits.

Listen with a purpose. When listening with a purpose, you tend to listen more closely. Watch and listen for clues the teacher or professor may give that can help with exam questions. Sometimes they tell you questions that will be on the test. Listen for key terms and write them down. Many, if not most, exams test a student's knowledge of terms. Identify the lecturer's main topic, then write down the most important pieces of information that relate to the main topic. Write in your notes, answers to the questions: "who, when, where, what, why, and how." Distinguish between the main topic and subtopics, which generally are facts and events that led up to support, exemplify, or illustrate the main topic. Put another way, when you grasp the big picture, the details will be easier to understand and memorize.

Pay attention to the beginning and end of a lecture where main points are emphasized.

TIPS
WHEN YOU HAVE TO SPEAK IN FRONT OF A GROUP

Every student starting in second grade through graduate school will be required to give a presentation in front of the class or group from time to time. This requirement often causes a great deal of anxiety in most students.

In all the "how to study" publications I have reviewed, not one addressed the subject of how to make effective presentations. Getting up in front of a class, or any other group, to give a presentation can cause one or more of such symptoms as butterflies, cold sweat, feeling nauseous, hands or knees shake, or rapid breathing. Such feelings are perfectly normal for a person who is not accustomed to getting in front of a group. Almost everyone has experienced some anxiety before making a presentation. But there is good news. "Right," you may be thinking, "how can such uncomfortable feelings do any good"? There is a term I introduced in Chapter 6 called "creative tension." When a former supervisor used it, I didn't like it. I thought to myself, "Who likes tension? It's just another word for anxiety or stress," as far as I was concerned. I soon learned, however, that he was correct. A little of tension can help the body work for you. It is the body's way of saying to itself, "OK body, let's call upon our reserve forces so we can perform better." Put another way; it is kind of like tapping into the other fuel sources our body stores up for special situations. Athletes commonly get butterflies before a game or match. Their adrenal glands are pumping extra energy to the body"—creative tension! Too much stress, however, can be counterproductive. So, what can we do to minimize anxiety before getting in front of a group? The following "TIPS" provide ways to help reduce "stage fright" as well as significantly improve presentation and public speaking skills. An excellent book is *Public Speaking Secrets... 52 Proven Ways to Increase Your Impact Every Time You Speak"* by Dr. Michael Hudson. Dr. Hudson provides easy to read, practical suggestions anyone can use to deliver great presentations. The book is available in both e-book and print. At the Delaware State Fair, Hudson told a group of Delaware 4-H Public Speaking finalists, ages 8 to 18, that many speeches were as good as, and many even better than, adult professionals whom he has coached. Quite a testament from a man who has provided consultative guidance to over 3,000 organizations.

My granddaughter has won several blue ribbons at the county and state levels for 4-H Public Speaking. At the age of 9, she stood in the front of church congregations and civic groups delivering an appeal for soap donations to help combat the cholera epidemic in Haiti. She was able to do this by using the strategies listed below. Her little sister, age 7, recently volunteered to get up in front of an audience of 60 to sing a song. Afterwards, she told her father that she was nervous, but she went on to say, "I just felt the fear and went ahead and did it. It was not as bad as I thought it was going to be. I would like to do it again sometime." Her courage to face her stage fright helped her to overcome it, just as it had done for her sister. My other three granddaughters also perform in front of audiences and deal with butterflies in the same manner. They do not give in to their fears and avoid uncomfortable situations. Instead, they realize that the "stage fright" is only temporary and will go away once the performance begins. The same principle goes for presentations made in front of small groups such as a classroom.

TIPS

To Deliver an Oral Presentation
with Impact and Fewer Jitters

Even the most experienced public speakers get nervous before standing in front of a group. So, don't feel alone when you must do it. Here are a few TIPS to help deal with the jitters.

Prepare! The best thing one can do is to be prepared for the presentation. This includes not only being thoroughly knowledgeable about the subject you are to present but also includes organizing the material in a manner that you are most comfortable. Some presenters use notes, cards, some use outlines, and some memorize. Unless the assignment calls for the presentation to be memorized, I would not suggest doing so, unless you are an excellent memorizer. The audience is more interested in what you have to say, not if you have memorized your presentation. Besides, if you should forget a line or two, this can be very distracting to your audience, not to mention a distraction for you. Start by stating your "objective" or purpose. Then develop your objective by adding main ideas and sub-ideas. Consider giving interesting examples to support your thoughts. Conclude by stating the benefits and summarize the main thoughts. Caution: If you use a written paper rather than notes or cue cards, you will be tempted to read your presentation. Doing so will tempt you to look at your paper instead of your audience, resulting in a much less effective presentation. When turning pages, the paper makes noise, which can be distracting. Notecards, on the other hand, are easier to handle and make no noise.

Rehearse out loud to yourself or in front of others. Have them give you suggestions. Don't be shy, your friends or family want to help, and believe me most have been there themselves, so they know what you are feeling. Another good strategy is to video yourself. The more you rehearse, the better your presentation will be. With much practice, you will increase your comfort level.

Mentally prepare by visualizing yourself, giving the presentation. Picture in your mind's eye standing in front of the group and giving the presentation. See your audience and you standing in front of them fully confident. Picture them looking at you and listening to what you have to say. By the way, if any of your classmates are not listening, it may be that they are thinking about their own presentation. Don't allow these persons to distract you. Others are listening. Here is a strategy I once heard that I thought was rather clever. If you are anxious before you make your presentation, picture something ridiculous happening, such as all your notes flying out the window. Of course, that will not happen, so knowing that will help you realize nothing worse will happen. The humor in it can help relieve a bit of tension.

Focus on only a few people. When I was a novice at public speaking a strategy I used to pick out one or two people in the audience (preferable people that I already knew) and direct my speaking to them. Why would one want to do this when we know that there is a bunch of folks out there? In our ordinary conversation, we speak to only one or a few people at a time. We have no problem speaking in this situation, do we? Yet, when we must talk to lots of people, we become anxious, and in some cases, down-right petrified. Think about it, though! Is not a group of people just a bunch of individuals? So why the butterflies? Because we are not accustomed to speaking to more than one or a few people at one time. By focusing on one or two in the audience, we are, in effect, tricking our mind to that which it is accustomed. I usually found that after a few moments of "pretending" to speak to one or only a few folks, I became more comfortable and was able to begin looking at others in the audience. In other words, I used the focus on a few people trick to help get over my initial butterflies. With practice and experience, I found that I soon did not need to use this strategy. But for those new to having to get up in front of a group, this can be an excellent strategy to help calm nervousness.

Distractors. Be aware that jingling of coins or keys in your pocket or repetitive movements such as rocking back and forth, scuffling of feet, may help calm your nerves but it can be very distractive to your audience. Repetitive verbal sounds, such as "uh," "you know," and "like" should be avoided.

Physiological stress relievers. Some speakers will use an object to help relieve tension. An example might be a smooth or soft object held in your hand or in your pocket. Simply rubbing the object with your thumb and forefinger can help. But be careful! Use this technique only if it does not distract you from your speech. Also, it must not be noticeable to your audience.

Relax and breath. Stand with your feet about shoulders width. Relax your shoulders. Take a few deep breaths. Clear your mind, then as you inhale, say to yourself, "I am relaxed." You may say this several times to yourself.

Dr. Michael Hudson, whom I mentioned above, provides these techniques to help ease nervousness.

- Before getting in front of the group, while sitting quietly, place your hands together and lay them on your lap. Gently squeeze the right thumb of your right hand against the palm of your left hand. By doing this, you are massaging the ulna point closest to your heart via the circulatory system, helping to calm nerves.

- While sitting or standing role gently up on the balls of your feet, then roll back to heels while lifting your toes off the floor.
- Mistakes will happen but don't them let throw you off. The audience will not even notice most of them, and if they do, they are not sitting back wishing to see the speaker flub up. They are on your side and become uncomfortable when they think the speaker is. So, if a mistake is made that you think the audience notices, a good strategy is to acknowledge it and maybe even joke about it. Doing so will help ease you, as well as the audience.

Chapter 23
Getting the Most From Pre-Class
Prep and After-Class Review

The willingness to prepare for class and then review after class are essential strategies that distinguish between the average and honor students. Pre-class preparation and after-class review requires minimal time and effort yet are potent strategies used by highly successful students. Here are the strategies that will make you an honor student.

TIPS
FOR CLASS PREPARATION AND REVIEW

Be prepared. Before class, make sure you have everything you need, such as a notebook, pen or pencil (with extra), textbook, and anything else required for the class. You would be surprised how many students arrive in class, having forgotten something necessary.

Organize. Make sure your notebook is neat, organized so that you can quickly find notes and handouts. Three-ring binders are easier to organize than bound notebooks. Avoid folding papers and sticking them in your notebook, which is an easy way to lose important documents. Stock your locker with extra supplies you may need.

Arrive to class on time—always!

Review previous class notes. Doing so will mentally prepare you for the subsequent class. It will also help point to content you may have questions.

Read. If the teacher tells you to read something (text, handouts, articles, etc.), do it! Reading the material not only prepares you for the lecture, but it can also be embarrassing if the teacher asks you a question about the reading assignment. Reading familiarizes you with the material, so you are better prepared for the class lecture and provides an opportunity to identify questions you may want to ask. Examine the textbook guides when reading textbooks. Most modern textbooks are well organized to help students understand and learn the content. Examples include section assessments, chapter/section preview and synopsis, and practice questions, and study strategy hints. Many textbooks provide summaries of main ideas, terms, and explanations of "why it matters." Pay attention to and use timelines, maps, charts, guides, figures, photographs, vocabulary lists, glossary, appendix, and sources. In effect, most authors have taken the guesswork out by laying all the essential facts out in a straightforward, easy to study format

Complete all assignments. This may seem obvious, but a sure way to lose points is to not turn in homework and assignments completed and on time. Even if the work does not have to be turned in, or checked, homework is essential to maximize understanding of class instruction. If unable to finish because you don't understand, meet with your teacher and ask for assistance. Do not make excuses! The teacher or professor will usually see through any attempt to make excuses; besides, they appreciate honesty.

Have questions ready to ask in class. As you study, when you have questions, write them down. If clarification is not made during the teacher's lectures, then ask for it. The probability is that a few of your classmates have the same question on their minds.

Get at least eight hours of sleep on school nights. Staying up late and getting insufficient sleep is one of the best ways to miss important information that is provided in class. If, for whatever reason, you find yourself sleepy during the school day, try doing some stretching and deep breathing before class. Try not to get too comfortable while sitting in your chair. Sit up straight. Do not slouch. Move feet, wiggle toes. If you still can't keep your eyes open or having difficulty focusing, you might tell the teacher you are having trouble paying attention and ask him/her if it would be OK if you stood during the class. The teacher will appreciate your honesty, regardless if he/she allows you to stand.

After class. Review notes as soon as possible. Re-write them, if necessary. Make sure you have recorded in your planner all upcoming assignments, quiz dates, test dates, project due dates, etc. A way that students lose points is missing suspense dates on assignments and walking into class only to discover they are having a quiz or (horrors) an examination.

In conclusion, all of this may seem intuitive, but you would be surprised how many students do not practice these critical strategies. If you struggle with the self-discipline, take a few moments, and review Chapters 2 and 3.

SECTION F
Roadblocks in the Road

If a man harbors any sort of fear, it percolates through all thinking, damages his personality, and makes him a landlord to a ghost.
Lloyd Douglas

Chapter 24
Obstacles to Achievement (And What to Do About Them)

In this chapter, I will identify some major issues that interfere with effective learning and success. Many of the "roadblocks" create negative emotions and outcomes for students and families. Although I provide some guidance as to how to respond to such obstacles, I cannot address all possible ways to address such issues, nor am I qualified to do so. I hope that students and the parents of students who are experiencing life challenges may be able to identify one or more of these roadblocks and thus better able to appropriately act to address these demons. If you have concerns, seek out professional help!

The adolescent years are a time of significant change and challenge. The period from 12 to about 24 is a time in which the body and mind go through many adjustments. Although negative emotions from time to time are perfectly normal, continued expression of negativity can be a signal of deeper-seated problems. For some, adjustments to adolescence can be so overwhelming that feelings of anger, depression, or anxiety can result. Underlying negative emotions give rise to outward manifestations such as withdrawal, sarcasm, blame, avoidance, excuse-making, dishonesty, and disobedience, to name a few. Such emotions can lead to low self-esteem, poor interpersonal relations, drug and alcohol abuse and assuredly, poor performance in school. Let's look at some negative emotions that affect school, life success, and happiness.

Fear and Worry

One of the most common causes of poor school performance is "fear." Fear generates from the subconscious. Reaction to that fear results in destructive outcomes. Just as fear can rob us of the chance of fulfilling our dreams, so too can positive thoughts help to achieve desired outcomes. The famous evangelist and philosopher Norman Vincent Peale stated that "if you think in negative terms you will get negative results. If you think positively, you will get positive results." Loss, illness, unhappiness, failure, or any other undesirable event, are indeed challenging to a persons ability to think positive. If, however, such emotions become obsessive, then they can serve as a barrier to creating positive outcomes in one's life.

A student who has convinced him or herself that they cannot do well in math will, probably, not do well in math. However, even if math is not a student's strongest subject, if this student imprints in his/her subconscious that they can do well in math, he/she has a higher chance of success. Studies have shown that parents were surprised to learn that their children had more fear of doing poorly in school than they did of going to the dentist, getting lost, or even being seriously hurt. Most school-age children are so concerned about what other kids think of them that even the appearance of being unattractive or stupid is enough to give rise to fears and anxiety.

Worry is often synonymous with "fear," although there are differences. A student may not fear the challenge of a subject or situation, but they could worry that they may not complete an assignment on time, do the assignment well, forget their material or not do well on an exam. Many students waste a lot of time fretting over schoolwork. Worry, as well as fear, can be stagnating. To be "concerned," on the other hand, is appropriate and not as destructive. It can help motivate one to accomplish.

Conversely, worry, and fear can de-motivate. Such emotions can be the result of actual experiences. Children who have been or are currently experiencing physical, sexual or emotional abuse are very susceptible to negative emotions. These days there is much focus on bullying. Bullying is showing disrespect toward another. Despite the focus by schools to bring increased awareness about bullying, some kids persist on teasing and bullying others. Disrespect of others occurs at all levels in school—pre-school through college.

Being a bully, which includes teasing at the expense of another's emotional or physical wellbeing, is harmful to both the victim and the bully. Bullying can be verbal or physical. Students subjected to such inappropriate conduct can cause fear and worry to the point of not wanting to go to school, or not do schoolwork. Victims of bullying can experience social and emotional issues to include depression and even self-destructive behavior. Some have committed suicide as the result of being bullied.

If bullying is suspected, take immediate action to report it. Given the attention to this subject today, it is unlikely that school officials will not take the allegation seriously (although, unfortunately, I have heard of some that do not). For both the victim and the bully, unless stopped, can lead to difficulties with academics, social, emotional, and legal issues. If you are doing the bullying, you may be doing it to show off to your friends or maybe because you are suffering from abuse yourself. Taking out your frustrations on others is not being tough, instead is weak. Acknowledge the mistake and have the self-fortitude (meaning, guts) to stop, apologize, and if necessary, seek guidance on why you have been inclined to do it. Remember, laughing WITH someone is OK. Laughing AT another is not OK.

If you are the one who has been bullied, tell your teachers, counselor, and parents. Do not be ashamed! You are not to blame. The bully is at fault, not you. The best way to deal with a bully is to ignore them. Remember, they are doing it for attention. Just don't give it to them. If the bully persists even after you try to ignore them, you may have to be assertive by telling them to leave you alone. Refrain from getting into a physical altercation. Many schools will punish both. When possible, stay in the company of others. Bullies will usually shy away from groups.

Stress

Many factors can interfere with effective study and learning. One of the major issues is "stress" and its effect on school expectations, family harmony, and personal happiness. A survey conducted in

August 2013 by Harris Interactive, for the American Psychological Association on Stress and reported by Sharon Johnson in "USA Today," (February 2014), said "that more than 27 percent experienced "extreme stress" during the school year, and 34 percent anticipated that their stress level would increase during the coming year."

Sometimes we use the term stress and tension interchangeably, although there are slight differences. For the purpose of this book, I use the term "stress" to refer to any psychological and physical strain resulting in unhappiness and difficulty to deal with school, social, and home life.

Stress is defined as the body's response to a situation, whereas tension is caused by pressure on the nervous system after the stress. Some symptoms include fear, anger, feeling helpless, and paranoia. Tension can cause pressure on the body. Have you heard of a "tension headache?" Have you felt muscles tighten up or stomach aches because of something that has happened, or you expect to happen? If the tension becomes too severe, it can cause anger, tantrums, violence, and possibly a total collapse.

The suggestions provided in this book can help with both stress and tension. If symptoms persist, professional counselors can help.

Stress can be either constructive or destructive. Constructive stress (sometimes referred to as "tension") can be the motivation behind learning a new task. Do you recall your feelings just before you rose to the challenge of doing something for the first time, such as riding a bike, driving a car, or learning to swim? Once you faced up to the new experience, the feelings of anxiety or stress disappeared. When you overcame such feelings, you probably felt pretty good about yourself. Some people work better when they know a deadline is approaching. Some call this "creative tension." The tension they feel serves as a motivator to get moving. Stress causes a surge in adrenaline that helps your body to prepare for action. Thrill seekers get a natural high from stress related to doing an activity that is dangerous and, in some cases, even life-threatening. Destructive stress, on the other hand, will not only block task accomplishment but can result in adverse mental and physical consequences. Destructive stress can be caused by problems at home, with peers, or in school. If appropriate coping skills are not used, stress-related responses can result, such as sleep interference, lack of exercise, and poor eating habits. If current life circumstances are such a degree that stress is consistently interfering with happiness and productivity, then it is imperative to address the contributing issues immediately. Failure to do so will assuredly interfere with health, happiness, and success in and out of school.

Stressors can be identified as things we can control, such as tasks that must be done, or things that we do not have control, such as the weather or world events. How do we stop stressing about things we can or cannot control? I will tell you how in the TIPS section of this chapter.

The Blues

We may have emotions called the "blues" when we experience a life event that makes us sad. Everyone has ups and downs in life. It is kind of like riding a roller coaster. Just as we feel the thrill, fright, anticipation, or other emotions typical of a ride on a roller coaster, we experience similar feelings in our daily lives. The intense emotions of a roller coaster ride go away when the ride is over.

Similarly, the emotions we feel in our daily lives will also not last. The "blues" do not result in feelings that cause one to have difficulty in dealing with day to day events and responsibilities. Although feeling "blue" is a normal and temporary emotion, there are simple and effective ways to deal with the feeling to help shorten the uncomfortable feeling and quickly get back on track. See "TIPS for Emotional Issues" below for suggestions as to how to deal with stress and the blues.

Depression and Related Disorders

When sadness lingers or becomes so excessive, it can result in such symptoms as abnormal sleep patterns, unusual weight gain or loss, fatigue, guilt, hopelessness, relationship, or work-related problems. Persistence of such symptoms suggests possible depression, a condition that goes beyond the ordinary ups and downs of the blues, worry or moments of anxiousness. Depression is a serious medical condition and should not be taken lightly.

According to *Facts for Families*, suicide is the third leading cause of death for 15- to 24-year-olds. People suffering from a learning disability or other mental or physical challenges are especially susceptible to depression. Dr. Les Carter, the author of *The Anger Workbook* and Dr. Frank Mirth, author of *Happiness is a Choice*, have co-authored a book, The *Freedom from Depression Workbook*. The Workbook provides a 12-section interactive program that helps to identify the causes of depression and how to deal with it. It is an unfortunate fact that depression will afflict one in four persons at some point in their lives, so state Doctors Carter and Mirth. They define depression as "feelings of sadness and dejection, resulting in an increasingly pessimistic outlook on life." Naturally, such manifestations are not conducive to happiness, much less academic success.

There are several types of depression. A woman who has just delivered a baby may experience the blues, but if such feelings linger over an extended period, she may be suffering postpartum depression. Postpartum depression is thought to be triggered by the hormonal changes following childbirth. When a person experiences or witnesses a traumatic event, they can become depressed. One of the most common disorders of traumatic induced depression is Post Traumatic Disorder or PTSD. The *Diagnostic and Statistical Manual of Mental Disorders (DSM-5)*, defines several other disorders, any of which can adversely affect daily living. Included are acute distress disorder, anxiety disorder, obsessive-compulsive disorder (OCD), personality disorder, traumatic brain injury, and conversion disorder (physical symptoms with no known physical condition).

If you or a family member, or anyone you know is experiencing lingering feelings that affect motivation, difficulty in concentrating, ability to reason, unusual sleep, eating, or relationship patterns, seek professional help! **DO NOT try to deal with depression or other emotional issues on your own, and NEVER, NEVER try to deal with it by self-medicating with alcohol, drugs, or non-doctor prescribed medication.** Doing so is both dangerous and often leads to full-blown addiction. It will sabotage any chance for success, and for many— DEATH. Do not ignore symptoms, nor think that they will go away on their own. Many personal, family, job, and school-related failures are the result of emotional issues gone untreated. Such conditions are treatable!

TIPS
FOR EMOTIONAL ISSUES

Identify issues that are causing negative emotions (fear, anger, and resentment). Notice negative thoughts and feelings such as worry about things in the past or the future. When we fixate on problems, we are nor focusing on solutions. How can we make ourselves feel better? By taking steps with one or more of the techniques described below.

Know that our "Defense Mechanisms" (avoidance, suppression, repressions, etc.) help us to avoid pain, but do not typically get rid of the underlying cause. It is like sweeping dirt under a rug. You can't see the dust, but it is still there. If we do not challenge negative thoughts, our minds will begin to accept them as fact, and soon our bodies will react to them. Understand that it is your belief about an event or situation that triggers feelings of sadness. When one alters a belief, feelings can likewise be changed. Here are a few strategies you can use to help alter your beliefs.

- It is essential to recognize what is causing your fears, worry, stress, or anxiety. Is it an up-coming exam? Issues with other students? Arguments with friends or family? Too many tasks at once? Once you realize the source, do not ignore it. Address the issue!

- Identify what is in your control and what is not. Fretting about that which you have no control wastes energy. The past is the past, and we have no control over what was. We also worry about the future. Too much worry about what has yet to come can cause negative stress.
- Focus on the present. We can do something in the present.
- Taking action deflects the tendency to stew on the problem and helps the feelings subside. It is like having a minor open wound. Instead of doing nothing and possibly causing it to worsen, by treating it with an antiseptic, it promotes healing.
- Set goals and have a plan to reach them.
- Maintain a regular daily routine.
- Get at least eight to nine hours of sleep daily.
- Use soothing music while relaxing. Avoid music with negative messages. Fast tempo music as is typical with much hip-hop, hard rock, or rap do little to help place one in a relaxed state of mind. Save this genre for when you do not need to relax.
- Read books and television shows that are uplifting and give positive messages. Avoid media that elicit fear, anger, or anxiety. Seek out and encourage support groups that promote positive ideals (clubs, church, family, friends, AA/ NA/ALANON/ALATEEN).
- Choose and participate in hobbies and extracurricular activities that provide joy.
- Use positive affirmations (See Chapter 20 and Appendix C).
- Meditate.
- Eat well-balanced meals three times a day. Eat lots of complex carbohydrates such as fruits, vegetables, beans, and whole grains. Drink at least six glasses of water daily. Speak to your doctor or a dietician for specific advice.

Exercise!

Dr. Andrew Weil, the founder of the University of Arizona Center for Integrative Medicine, states, "In my experience, the last thing depressed people want to do is move. Regular exercise can be a highly effective way to improve mood because exercise increases certain neurotransmitters that affect body chemistry." Dr. Weil also advocates breathing exercises to reduce stress and improve health. In fact, Dr. Weil states that "If I had to limit my advice on healthier living to just one tip, it would be simply to learn how to breathe correctly." His audiobook, *Breathing: The Master Key to Self-Healing,* can be found at www.soundstrue.com/store/breathing.

• Take a nature walk.
• If the sun is shining, go outside! Sunshine will help to raise spirits.
• Get regular medical check-ups with your doctor and dentist. Address medical issues while they are minor. Follow your doctor's advice.
• **If stress persists and begins to interfere with routine daily activities, seek professional help!**

Lethargy.

Some may call this laziness, or it may just be a lack of interest or incentive. It could also be a symptom of depression. Whatever you want to call it, it is manifested by lack of motivation. It may start with one or two subjects, but if allowed to become a habit, it can spread, resulting in a failure in school and professionally. If you feel unmotivated, review the principles below.

TIPS
To Get Motivated

Having goals and a commitment to achieving those goals serves as one of the key motivators in overcoming lethargy.

Also, having a "purpose" can have a powerful effect on creating motivation. See Chapters 4 and 5.

It is essential to care about what you are studying. Even if no matter how hard you try, you cannot develop a real interest in the subject, it is still essential to want to do well. In other words, you need to at least care. A lack of caring can be attributed to many factors: negative emotions, avoidance of pain, negative peer or family relationships, insufficient sleep, poor diet, or lack of proper exercise are a few causes. If you have difficulty getting things done because of lack of interest, use the TIPS under "Emotional Issues" above, and principles outlined in SECTION's B and C.

Many college students do not do well because they are not committed to being there in the first place. If you are a college student and find yourself often skipping classes, missing assignment deadlines or unable to stay on top of your studies, it is essential to carefully examine why you are in college and honestly decide if you should be there. It may be to your advantage, and to whoever is paying the bills, to postpone your college education until you are sufficiently motivated. To make the right decision, seek assistance from family, friends, faculty, clergy or counselors, or health care providers. You may want to consider a "gap year" as explained in Chapter 25C.

Relationships

As a rule, students who have supportive families and friends do better in school than those who do not. Students who hang around with others who do not place a high value on school and grades will have a more difficult time achieving top grades. Negative influence result in negative outcomes. Positive relationships translate into positive outcomes. Sadly, in some communities, peer pressure is exerted on the child NOT to do well. Some call this the "crab syndrome." Just as a crab in a bucket tries to crawl out, other crabs will pull them back in the bucket. So too will poor students try to lure students who are striving to do well, down with them. Misery loves company. If you wish to be a good student, avoid those who do not care about school or their future success. If the friends you have are not contributing to your success goals, make new friends. If making new friends causes you a bit of anxiety, know that for many, this is a normal emotion. A great way to find new acquaintances with common interests is to join clubs and organizations. With time and patience, every student can develop friendships with persons who can be a positive influence.

When problems in relationships arise, it is normal for people to spend an excessive amount of time involved in trying to resolve the issues. Worry and stress over negative associations are a significant distraction. Ask friends and family for their support, such as allowing time and space to study without unnecessary distraction. If the home or dorm has distractions and it is impossible to get quiet study time, plan around the distractions. Go to the library, or plan study time when the distractions are not present. Do not try to compete with distractions! Serious students must take their relationships and environment into account and plan accordingly.

TIPS
To Improve Relationships

Choose your friends wisely. Be kind to others, and they will be kind in return. Show interest in others, especially if you would like to get to know them or get to know them better. If they do not respond, seek out someone else.

Keep in mind that others wish to be liked. The best way to be liked is to be "likable." How do you do that? Treat others the way you want to be treated. Avoid pettiness, gossip, bullying, jealousy, and any other behavior that you do not like to witness displayed by others. If you do not care to see the negative behaviors of others, then why would they want to see it in you?

Participate in clubs and organizations that promote positive social human relations skills and develop character.

If others are interfering with your ability to study, ask for their cooperation.

Over-extension

Friends, significant others, hobbies, television, music, work, extra-curricular activities-there are so many activities that students can get involved in today. This is wonderful, and students should indeed take advantage of such opportunities. However, if a student tries to do too much, they will quickly become overextended, overwhelmed, and stressed. Hardly a situation conducive to making good grades. **The key is "balance." The best time managers, generally, are those who are the most successful.**

TIPS
To Avoid Over-extension

Don't take on more than you can efficiently handle. If you find yourself being challenged in your ability to stay on top of your studies, you may well be overextending yourself. If you are feeling overwhelmed before you take on a new project or activity, commit to yourself to drop an old one before taking on the new one.

Set clear goals and priorities. Doing so helps to maintain focus. The proper use of goal setting and prioritization is one of the most effective tools a person can use for enhancing efficiency and minimizing stress. See Chapter 4 for guidance on how to effectively set and use goals.

Manage time wisely. "I just don't have enough time," is a common complaint many students have. Everyone can feel overwhelmed with all that is required of us every day. Why is it though that some seem to get things done and done on time, yet others do not? The answer is in how people manage their time. If you have ever felt that there are just not enough hours in the day to get all the things done that you need to get done, then here are a few things that will significantly help. First, take a hard look at how you currently use your time. Be honest with yourself! Try answering these questions!

- Do I tend to put things off?
- Do I have more than three projects started and yet unfinished?
- Do I often find myself trying to meet deadlines at the last minute?
- Do I sometimes turn in work late (or not at all)?
- Do I often feel stressed or worry because of all the things I must do?
- Do others remark to me (or about me) because of something that they counted on me to do, yet was not done, or done when expected?
- Do I often rush to meet deadlines, or to arrive on time to places I am supposed to be?

If you answered "yes" to one or more of these questions, you are not alone. Let's look at why we fall victim to one or more of these frustrations and some neat tricks that can be done to help overcome them.

There is a common saying that "People do not plan to fail; they fail to plan." Those who plan the use of their time are seldom controlled by time. According to a September 2014 *Time* magazine article, in 2012 the average workweek for employed people ages 25 to 54 was about 48 hours; Sleep—56 hours; eating—7 hours; household chores—10 hours; caring for others, e.g., children—14 hours; and 7 hours for other commitments. For students, we can replace school for work hours. Thus, in a 168-hour week that leaves 26 hours for other activities. Yet, many complain they don't have enough time to work toward daily goals. Why? Poor time management is often a result of *habit*.

Being Victim to "Time Wasters."

We can divide the use of our time into two general categories— that which we cannot control and that which we can. For example, we usually have little control over the time that is imposed upon us, such as classroom time, extracurricular activities, family time, and commute time. However, we can control the self-imposed time. It is in the self-controlled category that we waste the most time.

Being aware of forces that gobble up time can go a long way to opening opportunities for increased use of time efficiency and, ultimately, more productivity and improvement.

TIPS
To Improve Time Management

Use this strategy to get a good grasp on how you use your time. Record everything you do from the time you awaken until you go to bed. Note the number of minutes you spend on each task. If you spend thirty minutes getting ready for school in the morning, write it down! Twenty minutes to eat breakfast, write it down! Record your commute time to and from school, time at school, after-school activities, TV time, time on the phone, chores, homework, visiting with friends, talking to family members, etc. Be honest! This exercise is to help you to meet the goals you have set for yourself. Fudging will give you an inaccurate picture and less latitude to adjust. Once you have completed the task, note the time over which you had no control and time over which you had control. How many minutes were spent on activities that did not help contribute to your goals and priorities? You may be surprised to note that the number of hours you have each day on "self-controlled" time is much more than you may have initially thought. It is the use or misuse of self-controlled time that has a significant influence on our success or failure in meeting our desired goals.

- **Set clear, achievable goals.** See Chapter 4.
- **Have a daily, weekly, and monthly planner.** See Chapter 7.
- **Prioritize your tasks.** Again, see Chapter 7. This simple but powerful little system for prioritizing will not only help you do the most important things first, but it will also provide an incentive for you to get things done. By the way, although I

used only three priorities in the example, you can add more. Remember, establish set daily times for specified tasks, such as study time, and stick to it!

- **Use timers for keeping track of non-productive time.** If taking a 15-minute break from homework, for example, set the timer! When the timer goes off, get back to your homework without delay.
- **Ask for support.** Inform friends and family the times you will be occupied and ask them to not to interrupt you while you are busy. Let them know when you will be free. This way, they will be less inclined to interrupt you during what should be your most productive time.
- **Limit phone, leisure, TV, and computer or other activities that do not help you accomplish your goals and priorities.** Turn off the cell phone, e-mail, texting, social networks, and anything else that may interrupt you during study time. Electronic devices are a huge distraction! Remember the fewer interruptions and distractions, the better you will manage your time and the sooner you will achieve your goals.

Procrastination

Everyone will procrastinate from time to time. Repeated postponement, however, can have serious consequences. Excessive procrastination results in loss of valuable time, incomplete tasks, inefficiency, and frustration by others towards you and ultimately a poor self-image. With such negative consequences, why do people procrastinate? Fear or anxiety, lack of interest, no motivation, and fear of failure are a few causes. For others, it just may be a habit that has developed over the years. So, what can one do to break the procrastination habit? It takes about 30 days of concentrated effort to change a pattern. Use the following steps to replace undesired habits with desired ones.

TIPS
To Help Avoid Procrastination

First, admit that you have been procrastinating and acknowledge to yourself that you want to change.

Next, write down the reasons or excuses you use to keep from starting or following through on a task. For each, write down why you think your reasons or excuses may not be realistic. For example, your reason/excuse may be, "I often put off doing my math homework because I don't like to do it." Your realistic response may be, "I may not like it, but if I don't do it, I will not learn it, which in turn will further contribute to my dislike of the subject and will result in me getting a 0."

Positive thinking is essential to changing habits and success. If you are inclined to think negatively or have defeatist attitudes, STOP!! Replace such thoughts with positive affirmations. I go into more detail about the power of positive thinking and how you can use your subconscious mind to create positive change in Chapter 20.

Feeling Stuck

Sometimes we get stuck. It is as we are traveling along the road of life and we come to a Stop sign. We look to the left, then to the right. No cars in either direction, but we cannot move. Suddenly, we feel immobilized. What causes this? Fear! But where does this fear come from? As explained in Chapter 20, the subconscious. How does fear get planted into our subconscious? One way it could have been put there due to early life experiences. For example, a child is riding his tricycle. She hits a bump and the bicycle tips over. The child falls off the bicycle, and she hits her head on the sidewalk. Just then, the child hears a police car siren. The child's mind subconsciously records the banged head with the siren. Years later, she hears a siren, and her mind associates the pain of her injured head with the siren. Her body then responds with fear. As the little girl grows older, her mind holds on to the fear, although she has no recollection of the event that caused the fear of sirens. In effect, your mind has been "programmed" to the association of the event (the banged head) with the sound of the siren. This stimulus-response type event can happen with many types of stimuli. Trauma, ridicule, abuse, rejection, to name a few. Such traumatic experiences can cause symptoms later in life of which we have no conscious recollection of the underlying cause. Also, when we tell ourselves such things as "I can't," "it is too hard," "I will never," "I am not smart," etc. we are programming our mind to believe it. Can negative thoughts interfere with learning? Yes! How? Because they are a distraction to your concentration. Although a siren may not interfere with learning, ridicule of a young child can well set up a child's belief that they "can't" perform a task or a fear of a subject or task. Can we change such negative beliefs? Again, Yes!

TIPS
To Help Get Out of Feeling "Stuck"

First, recognize the limiting or negative thought, such as what you may be fearful.

Second, admit that such thoughts are not based on valid reasons.

Third, affirm to yourself that you can achieve anything that you are willing to work for.

Fourth, establish goals, then develop a plan to meet those goals.

Fifth, use the strategies presented in Chapter 20 to re-program your subconscious to move from your "stuck" state to get what you want.

If you are not making progress? Seek out a professional counselor!

Drugs and Alcohol

There are few families today who have not been personally affected or know of other families who have not been adversely affected by drug and alcohol abuse resulting in broken families, lost opportunities, illness, and death. The National Institute of Drug Abuse (NIDA) reports that the economic cost of substance abuse in the United States exceeds $414 billion, with healthcare costs attributed to substance abuse estimated at more than $114 billion. By the 8th grade, 52 percent of adolescents have consumed alcohol, 41 percent have smoked tobacco, and 20 percent have smoked marijuana. By age 12, an estimated 4 million Americans used prescription pain relievers, sedatives and stimulants for "nonmedical" reasons. Most young nicotine addictions start when they are in early teen years and some even pre-teens.

In 2017, according to the National Center of Health Statistics of the CDC, over 70,000 people died because of a drug overdose, both illicit and prescription drugs. Opioids were involved in 47,600 deaths. More than 88,000 individuals died of alcohol-related causes in 2017 according to the National Center on Alcohol Abuse. This is twice as many killed during the Korean War (Americans), which lasted three years. Illicit drug use is especially prevalent among 15 to 24 years olds, according to the Canadian Centre on Substance Abuse. Young people, as young as 8 and 9, have been known to use drugs and alcohol.

Often mind-altering drugs are first used for amusement or at the urging of peers. Sometimes it is used to help alleviate uncomfortable feelings associated with stress, anxiety, depression, or some other underlying psychological issue. Even though warned that the use of drugs and alcohol could, and frequently does lead to more severe problems, warnings are often ignored by young people. The result is destructive effects on body metabolism, addictions, and even death. It probably is safe to say that drug and alcohol abuse has resulted in more academic and life failures than any other single cause in modern-day history. The Federal government and state governments have acknowledged that illicit drug use is an epidemic. With a few exceptions, most communities and countries expend far too little energy and resources to drug education. When was the last time you saw an anti-drug or anti-alcohol spot in your school, the television, or any other media source? As of this writing, our culture, led by the movie, television and the music industries, expends more effort in glorifying the use of drugs and alcohol than educating the public about the actual dangers of drug and alcohol use. Even though our schools try to devote some time and resources to educating young people about the real risks of drug and alcohol use, it is far too little. So, when it comes to the prevention of the epidemic of drug and alcohol abuse, our society is failing.

It is up to you to make wise choices before you yield to the peer pressure and the temptation to try a drug. I know, the initial thinking of most young people when offered the opportunity to try a drug, is "It will not hurt to try it once or twice," or "This will not cause me to get addicted." If this thinking is correct, then ask yourself, "Why are so many people addicted to drugs and alcohol?" I know many addicts, and every one of them started with the same thinking. According to my friend Lewes Meltzer, Psychologist for the Pennsylvania, Delaware County Juvenile Detention Center, "Teens do not intend to die; they are just plain ignorant to the effects that drugs and alcohol can have on their bodies. Many teens die because they mix alcohol or heroin with prescription pills often retrieved from their parents' medicine cabinet."

So, a word to the wise, don't try to pull the wool over your parents' eyes. They know more than you may think they do. More importantly, don't lie to yourself that drugs will not hurt you. They will! Here are the warning signs of possible drug or alcohol abuse. These indicators are also listed in PART TWO, which is for parents and guardians.

- Mood swings, easily irritated, quick to anger.
- Poor hygiene, organization, and eating habits.
- Unexplained weight loss.

211

- An unusual drop in body temperature (they are cold when most others are comfortable).
- Indifference or withdrawal from family.
- Poor academic and extracurricular performance.
- Change in normal sleep routines.
- Dishonesty/stealing/excuses.
- Scratching.
- Bloodshot or glassy eyes.
- Drowsiness or drifting off when others are speaking.
- Poor judgment, irrational.
- Forgetfulness.
- Delayed motor skills/reflexes.

TIPS
TO HELP ADDRESS DRUGS AND/OR ALCOHOL ABUSE

Once a person begins to rely on drugs and alcohol to help resolve issues in their lives, not only will their problems not be solved, things will get worse—much worse. It is also essential to realize that you are not alone. Seek out the assistance of professionals, friends, and family, or support groups. Search the internet for teen recovery programs. There are many. Use of non-physician prescribed medications (and even physician prescribed) may help relieve you of any issues you may be having, but the benefits will be replaced by negatives that will far exceed any temporary relief the drug will give you. So, if you find yourself beginning to rely on drugs or alcohol, STOP!! Once addicted, it is tough to break the addiction cycle. Many don't, and the price they pay is enormous, to include lost opportunities, broken relationships, disease, and premature death. So, before you get to this point, seek out assistance in helping to resolve any concerns or issues you are experiencing before the leech gets control. If you don't get the support you expect, keep searching until you do. Also, I implore you not to allow pride or embarrassment to deter you. Most people recognize that drugs and alcohol abuse by young people is a huge problem that can and does affect families regardless of race, creed, or socioeconomic status. They will respect your initiative in wanting to get help. They will not respect you if you do not. If already addicted and you are fortunate enough to receive professional help, great! But I implore you not to presume that once you have completed your treatment that all be well. Sad to say, relapse is probable. To help avoid relapse, I strongly urge you to attend Alcoholics Anonymous or Narcotics Anonymous meetings. If you have not become addicted but feel you might, participate in open AA or NA meetings to help encourage you to address the issue before you become a full-blown addict. AA and NA follow the 12-Step Program. I have done much research on addictions and am convinced that the 12-Step Program to be highly effective for long-term recovery. Another excellent resource is "Celebrate Recovery," which is presented by many churches. Celebrate Recovery follows the 12-Step Program but relates the recovery process to Christian principles. Celebrate Recovery is not limited just to substance addictions, rather to anyone suffering from other addictions, unwanted habits, internal conflict, or emotional pain. Addictions are also addressed in Chapter 6.

Family and friends can gain essential insight about addictions and how to best cope with a loved one's addictions by attending Al-Anon or Alateen meetings. These groups follow the highly effective 12-Step Program.

All the programs cited above are free!

Tobacco Addiction

"More deaths are caused each year by tobacco use than by human immunodeficiency virus (HIV), illegal drug use, alcohol, motor vehicle injuries, suicides, and murders combined," according to the U.S. Department of Health and Human Services. (2014). *The Health Consequences of Smoking—50 Years of Progress: A Report of the Surgeon General.* In Chapter 8, I spoke about the importance of physical health as one of the "five essential columns." In that chapter, I did not speak to the use of tobacco products by young people and the effects on health and productivity. So, I do it now.

"So, what is the big deal about trying a cigarette? If I try one or two, I won't get addicted to cigs. How about e-cigarettes, they are harmless, right?" Well, if you dare, let's look at the facts.

"Some people smoke to try to deal with stress. When they quit smoking, they may replace it with other unhealthy behaviors that do not address the source of stress and may even make stress worse. This can make quitting harder. Understand the connection between stress and smoking, and plan to find better ways to deal with stress." See *Handling Stress* at https://www.matrix.edu.au/coping-with-stress-how-maintain-your-mental-health-during-hsc/

In a University of Michigan report *Overview, key findings on adolescent drug use; Monitoring the Future National Survey Results on Drug Use, (1975-2016),* the authors state, "Although tobacco use by adolescents and young adults has declined substantially in the last 40 years, in 2016, almost one in 20 high school seniors was a daily smoker, and almost one in 10 had smoked within the last 30 days." Furthermore, adolescent's use of smoking products is evolving. In 2014, and for the first time in history, more pre-teens and teenagers used electronic cigarettes (or e-cigarettes) than smoked tobacco cigarettes.

Tobacco use remains the number one cause of preventable deaths in the United States. On average, smokers die at least ten years earlier than non-smokers and, every day more than 1,200 people in the United States die from smoking-related causes such as lung cancer, emphysema, chronic bronchitis, coronary heart disease stroke, chronic obstructive pulmonary disease. Smoking also results in a reduction of quality of life caused by diseases such as chronic obstructive pulmonary disease, stroke, asthma, ectopic pregnancy, reduced fertility, premature births, increased chance of type 2 diabetes, eye diseases, and suffering from many types of cancer. In a 2016 the Centers for Disease Control and Prevention published a report titled *Smoking and Tobacco use: Tobacco Industry Marketing.* The investigators wrote that almost 90 percent of those who die from smoking-related causes began using tobacco products at or before age 18.

TIPS
To Help Avoid the Smoking Habit

If you have not yet tried smoking, then don't! I know that is easier said than done. For many, it is just too hard not to try, especially when your friends are doing it. Breaking the nicotine addiction is extremely hard. Don't believe me? Ask any former smoker. Why is quitting so hard? Because nicotine is the main ingredient in tobacco, and nicotine is highly addictive. Nicotine isn't the only chemical in cigarettes. There are thousands of chemicals in cigarettes. Many who stop smoking experience such withdrawal symptoms as headaches, lethargy, dizziness, irritability, diarrhea, or constipation. Fortunately, such symptoms will subside after a few days and go away completely with time.

Incentivize yourself. I have a friend who, at about the age of 13, noticed how much money his friends were spending on cigarettes. He decided to save money he would have spent on cigarettes (had he taken up the habit) to buy himself his favorite car, a Corvette. I do not know how much he saved, or for how long, but I do know that, combined with money he earned from his part-time job, he met his goal and was able to buy a pre-owned shiny red Corvette by the time he was 18. In 2018, the average price of a pack of cigarettes ranged from $5.72 in Kentucky to $13.95 in New York City. So, if a teen, aged 13 started saving $5.72 a week for five years (age 13 to 18), she would have saved $1,393. A kid from New York City would save over $3,438. This does not include interest if the savings were to be put in an interest-bearing account. Maybe not enough to buy a car, but enough for a down payment or something else you may desire. You get the idea.

Think about the following facts:

- Ever kissed a person with a smoker's breath? Yuck!
- Most people do not smoke, nor do they like others smoking near them.
- Smoking makes our clothes stink.
- You must go outside to smoke, even in the heat, rain, and cold.

- It is unhealthy for you, and those around you. This includes small children and pets.
- Smokers do not have as much energy as non-smokers.
- According to the American Lung Association, there are more than 7,000 chemicals in cigarettes when burned. At least 69 are poisonous and are known to cause significant health issues, to include cancer.
- Smoking is expensive. Besides the cost to buy cigarettes, smokers pay higher premiums for health insurance, life insurance, and generally have more medical bills.
- On average, smokers die sooner than non-smokers.

TIPS
To Quit Smoking

- Have a plan! Start a notebook. Title it "How I will quit," or something similar. Write in your journal the reason you want to quit and your plans for doing so. Record the date and time you smoke a cigarette.
- Set goals and reward yourself for every milestone reached. Goals should include a gradual reduction.
- Substitute cigarettes with gum, mints, or something similar.
- Ask for help! Friends, family, family doctor, professional counselors. Check out the websites at https://smokefree.gov/tools-TIPS/text-programs/faqs)SmokeFreeTeen and NIDA for Teens.
- Avoid situations (triggers) that can tempt you to want to smoke.
- Associate with non-smokers.
- Join with a friend or friends who also want to quit.
- Exercise and stay busy with enjoyable activities.
- Try meditative exercises such as Yoga.
- Try hypnosis.

This book provides many guidelines on how to deal with stress. Use them!

It takes weeks and even months for the cravings to subside. Be persistent! "Hold On"! Be patient with yourself!

Gaming Disorder

A very intelligent Chinese student whom I was acquainted become so fixated on gaming that she started missing school. Despite the pleas of her friends, host family, and agency staff, she continued playing video games. The school placed her on academic probation. The agency counselors and executives advised her natural parents that their financial commitment to their daughter was being squandered and suggested that she return to China. This was a huge disappointment to her parents, who had sacrificed so much to help provide a coveted academic opportunity for their daughter. She was pleasant, intelligent, and had good potential. Unfortunately, she had a great fear of failing. Rather than addressing her studies and her methods of study (she was working harder, not smarter), she found solace by escaping to the fantasy world of playing video games. This would have been OK if she used the video games as a temporary "recess" from homework. Instead, her playing became an obsession to the exclusion of all else.

The World Health Organization (WHO) has recently defined "gaming disorder," sometimes called "digital-gaming," or "video-gaming," as "impaired control over gaming takes precedence over other interests and daily activities despite the occurrence of negative consequences."

A PBS radio special that aired on August 8, 2018, reported that many studies had been conducted on the subject. No conclusive evidence has been established as to how prevalent the disorder is. In other words, the percentage of persons who play video games to such an extent that it results in the disorder has been inconclusive. In fact, for many, gaming can be a constructive way to provide temporary relief from anxiety or depression or social pressures. (Granic, Isabela, et al. *The Benefits of Playing Video Games.* Vasterling, Jennifer, et al. *Can Video-games Be Good for Your Health?*). If gaming becomes so excessive that it starts to interfere with more important activities, such as schoolwork, chores, family, social and extracurricular activities, then the amber light is "on." In the early stages, the interest may be a compulsion rather than an addiction. At this stage, it is easier to regain control. If unchecked, however, gaming can evolve into an addiction, and addictions are much more challenging to change. Here are a few TIPS to help recognize when gaming is becoming a problem and how to respond to it.\

TIPS
To Recognize and Respond to
Possible Gaming Disorder

The WHO advises people who partake in gaming should be alert to the amount of time they spend on video game activities, mainly when it is to the exclusion of other daily activities. Be aware of any changes in physical or psychological health and social functioning. These may be symptoms of gaming disorder.

Be alert to the possibility that a fixation on video gaming may be related to association with psychological issues such as stress, loneliness, anxiety, depression, attention deficit hyperactivity disorder, or obsessive-compulsive symptoms, Professional counseling is appropriate and often useful. When indicated research (King and Delfabbro, 2014) suggests that psychological or pharmacological treatments can also be helpful.

In many countries, treatment is only reimbursed when the condition is officially recognized as a disorder. Fortunately, Gaming Disorder has been recently added to the International Classification of Diseases manual ICD 11th edition. This classification allows practitioners to submit for reimbursement to medical insurers. Be advised, however, that approval for treatment may vary by insurance and the type of therapist and whether the provider participates with the payer.

Social Media

Jane Twenge, a professor of psychology at San Diego State University and author of *iGen: Why Today's Super-Connected Kids Are Growing up Less Rebellious, More Tolerant, Less Happy and Completely Unprepared for Adulthood stated:* "Since 2012, there's been a pronounced rise in unhappiness, depression, suicide attempts and suicide among adolescents and young people." Studies indicate that associations between social-media use and happiness among adolescents found that as use of social-media increases also negative feelings. The reason for this points to increased social isolation and a tendency to compare ourselves with others on such media as Facebook, Instagram, and Snapchat. On the positive side, for many social media provides adolescents with increased opportunity for social contact. Twenge said that studies show that when the use of social media becomes excessive, the negative outcomes begin to show up.

TIPS
To Avoid Negative Consequences of Social Media Use

Moderation! To not use any social media would be challenging. It would also deprive users of the benefits. On the other hand, spending countless hours with eyes focused on a screen is not only taking one away from other more important activities, it is stressful on the eyes and brain. Instead, take time to talk to others face to face or on the phone, read, study, play games, watch TV, do a hobby, or anything else, but stay off the cell phone or computer at least for most of the time. Doing so will help contribute to your life-balance and success.

A few final thoughts on dealing with "Roadblocks to Achievement."

You have the power to change the way you think. Focus on what is going right. Because a few things may not be going right does not mean all is bad. When you change your negative thoughts to positive ones, your attitude changes, and thus, your experiences change for the better. So how do we turn a negative situation and negative thinking around? If you are experiencing negative emotions such as stress, anxiety, worry, sadness, loneliness, envy, and insecurity, to name a few, try to recognize the underlying feeling behind the thought. Often it is "fear." This may be hard but try to uncover what it is you are fearful. If you cannot readily identify your fears, you may need professional assistance. Don't be timid about getting help. You are not unique. Everyone has something that they are afraid of. The benefits to be gained by getting a good handle on our emotions far outweighs the negatives of holding on to old beliefs.

When you give out positive, you get positive in return. Philosophers, scholars, and theologians don't know why this is true, but all agree that it is. One does not know when or how the positive or negative comes back to you, but it will. A loving person lives in a world of harmony. A negative person lives in a world of disharmony. I have stated this point several times throughout this book. I have done so because I sincerely believe it is such a powerful truth, so needs repeating.

Use the power of positive thinking. It takes some practice, but it can be achieved by anyone willing to devote to it. First, choose by asking yourself the question, "Do I choose to hang onto my troubles, or let them move onto my greatest good?"

Although I have reviewed some common roadblocks that students encounter, I only touched on some strategies to help meet such challenges. If I did try to address all possible obstacles and resolutions to them (even if I was able and qualified), this book would end up being thousands of pages, and we don't want that! However, I sincerely hope that the skills, strategies, and tools provided will help to avoid or overcome obstacles in your journey and you to realize your goals and dreams. You are the master of your life. Happiness will come to you when it comes from you.

SECTION G
After High School, Now What?

Look for opportunity, not guarantees.

Chapter 25
Options and Decisions

A. Choosing a Career. Most high schools have Career Days in which guests tell about their professions. Many high school counselors try hard to make such events worthwhile but usually will not provide enough information for a student to make an informed decision. Look upon Career Days as merely a brief introduction to various career options. Start thinking about career options early! How might you do this? Observe what adults do when watching a television show, when reading books, or when listening to adults speak about what they do on the job. Ask questions! Don't be timid about this. People like to share their experiences. When allowed to go to with a parent, relative or friend to their workplace, do it! It is a great way to get a good feel for what a specific job is like.

A college major usually does not have to be chosen until the second year of college. Caution, however! The National Center on Education Statistics reports that for years 2010 through 2016 only 60 percent of students completed a bachelor's degree at the same institution where they started. Changing majors, transferring schools, or taking courses that do not count towards the degree they are aspiring are causes for the extended college experience, resulting in extra costs and higher debt. When a high school student has a pretty good idea of what they would like to do for a career, it can make choosing a college and major much easier.

B. College or Not? College may not be your choice. Many feel they must go to college to be successful. From a financial standpoint, this may be true for many occupations. According to the U.S. Census Bureau data, 19 percent of Americans hold a bachelor's degrees, while approximately 31 percent have a high school diploma. Census data also shows that the mean income for a college graduate is about 31 percent more than that of a high school graduate. This does not mean that you cannot earn a sizeable paycheck if you do not have a college degree. Many jobs that do not require a degree, seek persons with specialized skills. Many employers also value experience over a degree. There are lots of good-paying jobs which require an advanced college degree, particularly those in the professional fields (doctors, lawyers, social workers, pharmacists, physical therapists, etc.). Let's take a brief look at different approximate salaries. But first, let's look at what it costs on average, to earn a degree. These are ballpark, as costs can vary widely according to location, the educational institution, and financial aid.

Associate degree, $5,000
Bachelor's degree, $110,000
Master's degree, $160,000
Professional degree, $250,000

Quite a difference! So what is the return on investment (ROI)? That is, after factoring in costs, what will be the return for you? There are two types of expenses; quantifiable and non-quantifiable. Quantifiable costs can be measured, such as tuition (after deducting grants, aid and scholarship amounts), and the costs associated with the degree earned. Then there are the non-quantifiable returns, such as job satisfaction. Also, many graduates will end up working in a field other than in which they earned their degree, thus making it difficult to determine actual ROI. Tuition, quality of education, and how marketable graduates are, vary considerably. Therefore, to ascertain true value or ROI can be challenging. Only you, the student can determine the "non-quantifiable" as this is more about personal preferences and the value you place on various academic majors and career aspirations.

Since college is a considerable investment of time and money, it is well worth it to examine the long-term payoff. PayScale.com, an online compensation company ranks U.S. colleges and universities to determine the potential financial return of attending each school given the cost of tuition and the payoff in median lifetime earnings associated with each school Many college degrees don't have significant income potential. According to PayScale.com college degrees that tend to pay lower are those in the public sector, education, and services career fields. Examples include drama, fine arts, hospitality and tourism, music, theology, horticulture, education, and social work. Keep in mind that other factors than salary must be given due consideration, to include the potential for job growth, personal satisfaction, and location. A social worker can become certified in a variety of specialties, such as a family therapist or drug and alcohol counselor. The National Association of Social Workers and the U.S. Department of Labor's Bureau of Labor Statistics report that social work is one of the fastest-growing careers in the United States. Teachers may not start at the higher salary levels, but benefits (worth about 30 percent of base salary) are often quite respectable. There is another and more significant factor. Those who choose a career field such as education, theology, military, police and fire, ancillary medical, and therapeutic support see such careers as a "calling." They choose such careers because they have a passion for it rather than how much money can be earned.

The highest-paying jobs for bachelor's degrees include mechanical, nuclear, chemical, petroleum and electrical engineers, computer science, and physics. Of course, there are exceptions. Some of the wealthiest career fields are in business, music, theater, and sports, but persons who rise to the top income in these occupations represent a small minority.

Reflecting on the traits listed in SECTIONS A and B, you might note that "money" is not cited as a primary factor for success or happiness. Thus, salary should not be the primary factor in deciding career aspirations. Many highly paid people are unhappy in their fields. Go after what you are passionate about, the money will follow! If your career choice does not provide an adequate income, and you are not excited about your first choice, reevaluate your career choices. Also, see if there is a way you can supplement your income through other means, such as a job in an area that you enjoy. Consider a hobby that can generate income.

In the television show "60 Minutes," Charlie Rose interviewed Tim Cook, CEO of Apple. Cook pointed out that the United States over the past several decades has de-emphasized vocational skill training. China, on the other hand, has placed a high priority on teaching vocational skills. This combined with lower costs in China are significant factors in contributing to the fact that so many consumer products purchased in the United States and Europe are made in China. It can be anticipated that low-employee wages in China will not continue. Changes expected in world economics may result in increased demand in the U.S. for technically trained skills. I recently spoke to a manager at an auto body shop who told me that there is a shortage of auto body technicians in the country. He stated that auto body technicians would never have to worry about employment. He also said that the trade pays well, sometime in the six figures. So those who do not aspire to a college education can still look forward with optimism to finding a career that can be fulfilling and financially sound.

If you have a high school or GED diploma and are not inclined to go to a four-year college or university, or don't have the money or time, consider a two-year junior college program, a technical school, or a career field that does not require a degree or certificate. Here are some career fields that a four-year college degree is not needed. Technical trades often require training from a vocational training program, a junior college, or on the job apprentice training. For current approximate salaries consult CareerBuilder.com.

Automotive service technicians
Carpenters
Customer service representatives
Dental assistants
Electricians
Fitness trainers
General maintenance and repair workers
Home health aides
Interpreters and translators

Manicurists and Pedicurists
Manufacturing
Mechanical designers
Medical assistants
Office clerk
Pharmacy technicians
Restaurant cooks
Retail salesperson
Telecommunications technicians
Truck drivers, heavy equipment and tractor-trailer operators

    C. "Gap "Year—The Pros and Cons. What is a "Gap Year"? It is a period of up to a year between graduation from high school and the start of post-high school training or college. Typically, this has been more popular in Europe than in the United States but is beginning to catch on. What are the advantages and disadvantages of taking a year off between high school graduation and starting college?

Pros

    Allows for a year in which the student can gain a little more life experience before starting college. This can be achieved by working a job, doing volunteer work, or traveling. It can be a time for self-discovery and possibly to gain more insight into potential college majors and career preferences. According to the American Gap Association (AGA) out of Portland, Oregon, over 90 percent of Gap Year students report that the experience helped them to mature, gain self-confidence, and improve communication skills. Seventy-seven percent reported that it helped them find a purpose in life (see Chapter 2). Over half said that their experience helped them choose what courses to take in college.

    A Gap Year can allow young people to gain experience in managing personal finances that includes an appreciation for earning and spending money.

Many students who take a Gap Year report that they are better prepared for the challenges of college academics and the new independence of living away from home.

Some Gap Year students can help defray college costs by saving wages earned by securing scholarships or tuition assistance. For example, AmeriCorps places volunteers in communities throughout the country. In the Fiscal Year 2017, AmeriCorps offered up to $5,815 in scholarship money. Some colleges will match a portion of the award. Military Reserve and National Guard offer substantial tuition assistance programs.

Experiences can be a positive addition to job applications and college applications. Many use the experience as a topic on college essays.

Many colleges view a Gap Year positively and will hold an applicant's spot after being accepted. It is a good idea to apply for the college of your choice before taking a Gap Year. Speak to the Admission Counselors so that admission expectations are well understood. Often colleges are receptive when a student can clearly explain his/her goals when considering taking a Gap Year. Colleges also like the fact that many Gap Year students can access merit-based aid to help pay tuition costs.

Cons

Some students feel that taking time off between high school and college will result in losing momentum. In other words, they think that a break in study will make it more challenging to back into the study groove.

A Gap Year may result in a year delay in salary earnings after graduating from college. But this is assuming the graduate can land a decent salaried position right after college.

Some who choose a Gap Year squander the opportunity doing non-productive tasks such as playing video games, watching television, lying around, or with some other activity that does not contribute to future aspirations.

D. If You Choose to Go to College. The Search and Admission Process.

If college is your choice, you must adequately prepare! There are many things to consider if college is your goal. To name a few:

- Prerequisites (high school courses, grade point average, class standing, extra-curricular activities, college admission test scores).
- Application procedures
- Location, size, campus offerings, your personal preferences
- Courses and majors offered
- Cost

Making it easier. All these things may seem overwhelming, but when broken down and developing a plan, the entire process will be much less daunting. The following TIPS can help you with college preparation, planning, and admission. Sit down with your parents and review the TIPS provided. Remember the points presented in Chapter 4, "The Miracle of Goal Setting"? A great way to facilitate the process is to develop the criteria described below to short and long-range planning.

TIPS
To Facilitate the College Search and Admission Process

Proper planning and organization will do a lot to help de-stress the college search and application process and help maximize the best outcome for you. For many students, this can be a challenge. Admission to junior, community, vocational schools, and some four-year public colleges is not competitive. However, gaining admission to many four-year colleges or universities can be difficult. So if it is your choice to gain acceptance to a competitive college, here is some guidance on how to maneuver the college admissions process.

Grades count—but they are not the only things that matter. Grades, extra-curricular activities, and college admissions tests are the three most essential criteria that colleges use to choose who will be admitted. As such, grades and extra-curricular activities must be focus areas throughout a student's high school years. To find out what a college admission criterion is, check out the following sources: the college or universities website, *"U.S. News and World Report's"* annual publication on *Best Colleges, Private Colleges.com, Fiske Guide to Colleges*, or Princeton Review *The Best 380 Colleges,"* and NICHE, to name just a few sources. Terri Akman, a staff writer for Metro Kids, writes in her article *What Colleges Want, Cracking the College Admissions Code* (November 2015), college applicants must focus on several areas. She has spoken to several college admissions directors and passes on their advice. Douglas Zander, Director of Admission at the University of Delaware, urges students to take a rigorous high school curriculum. Courtney McAnuff, Vice President for Enrollment and Management at Rutgers University in New Brunswick, NJ, says that the best indicator of potential is what the student has already accomplished. "Grades, commendations, and other indicators of success," are what we look at. Students should choose extra-curricular activities that they enjoy, rather than an extra-curricular activity just because it may be popular. It is more important to demonstrate a commitment to the selected activity and reflects the student's attributes of leadership, responsibility, and persistence.

Anyone who wants to go to college—can. Although some colleges and universities are competitive, many higher learning institutions are not selective and provide an excellent education. Some, such as Kaplan University and the University of Phoenix have relatively liberal admissions policies, but then expect steady progress once coursework is undertaken. Most junior and community colleges are less selective, cost less, and provide an excellent steppingstone for transfer to a four-year university at the junior level. Many four-year colleges and universities have partnerships with two-year colleges by allowing students who earn an associate degree, then matriculate to the four-year institution. Frequently this is less costly and sometimes allows a student to gain admittance to a more competitive four-year college. It is kind of like sneaking in the back door.

Do you need to go to a top-tier college to be successful? Although attending and graduating from an elite college can open doors in the job market, it is not essential. Consider the successful people you may be acquainted. How many went to Harvard, Yale, or Princeton? Success in life has more to do with your personal qualities, effort, and life experiences than what college you attend. Although attendance at a prestigious college may give "bragging rights," not attending a top-level college does not mean you cannot get a good education. Ultimately it is what you put into it that counts.

Employers and graduate schools are looking for outstanding skills, experience, and potential. As you search for colleges, ask about student outcomes. You will find many colleges outperform many elite schools in specific areas. Visit the National Survey of Student Engagement (NSSE) website at http://nsse.indiana.edu/ for help in sorting through the information and for great questions to ask when visiting and choosing a college.

Two essential things you must do. The planning process for college is a time-consuming process that can be made simple by advance planning and being organized. By using these two essential elements, the process will relieve you of a great deal of potential stress.

Advance planning! I cannot emphasize this enough. Many students do not gain admission to their preferred college or secure tuition assistance because they miss deadlines. Get started early. The time to start college preparation is not a few months before high school graduation, but years before you graduate from high school. Start by selecting appropriate college prep courses when in 9th grade. Your high school counselor will help with this. Be involved in extra-curricular activities. Strive to be a leader in these organizations, if possible. College applications will not only ask what you have been involved in but what you accomplished.

Be organized. When starting the college selection process (the beginning of your 11th grade year is a good time), make a notebook to record the necessary information. Write down your:

- **Interests:** Major career, extra-curricular.
- **Preferences:** Location, large/small, city/urban, college reputation, courses/majors offered, amenities, student support services,
- **Feelings**: What are your opinions about the school? After visiting, does the college seem like a place you can feel comfortable for four years out of your life

For each college list the following essential facts.

- **Academic, extra-curricular and college admission test score requirements**: For each college you have an interest, record the mean grade point average, standardized test scores (SAT and ACT), and high school rank. Does the college emphasize extra-curricular activities? Be advised that more and more colleges do not require entrance exams, or if they do, they are placing less emphasis on them than they do other criteria, such as leadership and community service. On the other hand, some colleges give little or no concern to extra-curricular participation; instead, place their admissions criteria almost exclusively on grade point average and entrance exams. It pays to do your "homework."
- **Application procedures**: What are expectations, deadlines, and fees? Do they offer early decision opportunities or pre-college prep classes?
- **Majors and other course offerings**: Does the college offer majors in your interest areas? Also, if relevant to you, consider such things as international programs and affiliations, and pre-professional programs.
- **Class size** and professor-to-student ratio.
- **Student services**: Consider such services as residence hall requirements and availability, assistance programs for special

needs, international student support, philosophies, and programs supporting diversity and multi-cultural students, religious preferences and tolerance, student assistance for academics, health services, and career placement.

- **Costs:** College can be expensive. According to data maintained by Student Loan Hero (https://studentloanhero.com) in 2016, the average college graduate owed $37,172 in college loans. Even those who receive scholarships can expect federal students loan debts from $10,000 to $15,000. Tuition and books alone can range from $3,000 per year for community colleges (if you commute) to over $50,000 per year for private colleges (includes tuition, room, and board). Jenny, a 32-year-old guidance counselor, has over $70,000 student debt which provided for expenses incurred for both her graduate and undergraduate degrees. Karen anticipates that she and her husband will be in their 50s before the debt is paid. Karen regrets that she did not take cost-cutting initiatives, such as living with her parents, deferring loan payments, and not paying interest. I am not trying to discourage you from going to college; I am merely trying to caution you to consider all options before you commit to a specific college or university. If your parents are paying the bill, in whole or in part, you and your parents can work with financial counselors to get the best value for your education. More detailed guidance on ways to pay for college is provided in Chapter 35.

College entrance examinations, essays, campus visits, and interviews.

In the United States, two agencies administer college entrance examinations, also termed "standardized tests." The ACT and the SAT. The ACT is designed to test concepts, whereas the SAT focuses more on analytical skills. There are also Advanced Placement (AP) tests and SAT Subject Tests. I will briefly describe each here but not attempt to tell you how to take the exams. Gaining a familiarization with the exam structure and content is highly recommended and can be achieved through DVD and online tutorials, prep classes, and test preparation books. Unlike typical examinations, whereby you study for the subject presented in class over a relatively brief period, college achievement tests are designed to test knowledge acquired over your entire academic experience. Focus areas include English, Math, and Reading. AP and SAT subject tests cover more subjects. Let's look at each.

The **ACT** includes sections on English, Math, Reading, and Science. The written portion is optional. Usually, students take the exam in the junior year or the fall of the senior year. The exam takes about four hours to complete. The writing portion is about 3 ½ hours long. Visit www.actstudent.org/regist/dates.html

The **SAT** is composed of Math, Verbal, and Writing sections. It is offered during October through January, March, May, and June. The test takes about three to four hours. As is the case with the ACT, students take the test in the spring of the junior year or fall of the senior year. Visit www.collgeboard.org for details.

Advanced Placement Tests are an option that can be taken for students who take AP classes and measure the ability of a student to do college-level work in over 30 subject areas. Many colleges will give credit for AP classes and AP test scores, but this varies so check the college requirements. AP tests are administered in May. AP tests are designed and administered by the College Board, so go to www. collgeboard.org for more information.

SAT Subject Tests offers exams in 20 areas, to include nine languages. A few schools, especially the most selective, require SAT Subject Tests. Others do not require them but will accept Subject Tests as added criteria for admissions consideration. Tests are offered six times a year, October through January, May, and June. Like the AP test, some colleges and universities will award credit towards college courses for Subject Tests.

Score Choice feature: Unlike years past, today's students can take the SAT and ACT many times. If scores are higher, students can send the re-take to the colleges of their choice. Since SAT scores for all tests are sent on one sheet, colleges will see all test results. Score Choice is an option that allows students to send scores by date and subject. If not selected, the Board will send all scores to all designated colleges. Options can be selected on the College Board.org website. For ACT test scores, you must submit the highest test score. This is an advantage of the ACT. Most schools will accept both the SAT and ACT, although the weight given to each test will differ from school to school.

Many colleges and universities are placing less emphasis on standardized tests. As of this writing SAT and ACT tests are either not required or are de-emphasized by over 1,000 colleges and universities, according to the National Center for Fair and Open Testing (https://www.fairtest.org). These schools prefer to select students on performance during high school years, and other factors rather than test scores, which many argue are not a valid measure of a student's potential. So if you are a good student but may not test well, do not fret! There are many options for you. I know of many students, myself included, who struggled with standardized tests, yet did quite well professionally. College requirements, regarding standardized test requirements, vary widely, so check for the specific requirements for each college.

Interestingly, the Provost for the University of Delaware announced that they are piloting SAT/ACT optional admissions for in-state students. A few other well-known universities that do not place emphasis on SAT or ACT scores include: The American University, Arizona State University, Brandeis University, George Mason University, George Washington University, Franklin and Marshall University, Temple University, Widener University, Texas A&M University, University of Arizona, University of Alaska, and the University of Texas. This is just a sprinkling of schools that place less emphasis on standardized tests. For a complete list, go to the website for The National Center for Fair and Open Testing at www. fairtest.org. Keep in mind schools that use SAT and ACT scores as optional or less essential will put greater emphasis on high school grades and participation in extra-curricular activities.

How can you best prepare for college admission examinations? If you receive advice that you cannot study for SAT and ACT tests, IGNORE THE ADVICE! Although these exams indeed test knowledge that should have been acquired over one's entire education experience, it does not mean you cannot prepare for them. Numerous tutorials can help learn strategies for taking the ACT and SAT. Knowing the strategy can significantly help increase the odds of getting a question correct, even when you might not know the actual answer. There are too many resources for test preparation for me to list but check out internet sources such as Amazon.com for books, and programs on the subject.

Essays. Many colleges and universities require an essay to be submitted in conjunction with the application. Essays provide the admissions office with a snapshot of the students writing ability. It is also an opportunity for the applicant to provide some insight as to their interests, goals, or how they may have dealt with life challenges.

Make sure that you read and follow the guidance provided in Chapter 15, "Awesome Papers." Spelling, punctuation, syntax, format, and proper English must be letter-perfect. A few admissions counselors have told me that they are amazed at the number of essays that are submitted with numerous errors. Some colleges will provide the subject while others allow the applicant to choose their theme. Here is a tip to help you decide on an essay topic. Essays should provide insight as to who you are, and what are your academic aspirations. Cite your goals and what you may have done, or are you doing to help you reach your goals. If you have discovered your "purpose" (see Chapter 8), state it, and explain how and why you arrived at this conclusion. If you have overcome some life challenges, tell about them!

Campus visits. The college you choose will be your home for four years, maybe longer. As such, how you "feel" about the campus, services, and offerings can have a significant impact on your comfort level. The best way to gain an appreciation for the differences is with an actual visit. Many students have chosen a college by the website, photos, what they have read or heard, only to be disappointed when they arrive. Be prepared to ask questions during your visit. Do not be shy about this! When a college is visited, the choice is made more comfortable. Here are a few TIPS to help make a college trip most productive.

Most high schools will allow an excused absence for college visits, but there will be conditions, so check with your guidance counselor for school policies. Before you start, make a list of questions. Your high school counselor can help with this. Also, check with friends and relatives who have recently attended college.

Colleges have visitation days for prospective students. They provide campus tours, an overview of academic offerings, and support services. There is always an opportunity to ask questions. Often the tours are conducted by students, thus providing a student's perspective. Take advantage of visitation days whenever possible.

You can walk around campus on your own if you want, but the best experience can be gained when combined with an official tour. If a tour is not scheduled when convenient for you, make an appointment. The admissions office will help set up meetings or at least provide guidance on how to set up appointments with specific interests. Examples are the office of the major you may be interested, the financial aid office, housing, and support services such as special needs or international student support.

Interviews. Some colleges ask for an interview while others do not. Even if the school you are interested in does not request for an interview, try to schedule one anyway. Why? When selecting students for admission, colleges rely on high school transcripts, grade point averages, extra-curricular activities, letters of recommendations, and essays (if required). These may not provide a clear picture of who you are. A face-to-face meeting can help the admission staff get to know essential characteristics about you that all the documents may not adequately do. I know many young people who had outstanding credentials but had weak social skills, or even mediocre etiquette knowledge. Some students are not real strong on paper but have

239

strong personal characteristics. One of my sons was on the edge of being offered acceptance to a college he was particularly interested but was accepted based on a persuasive essay and interview. Now, I know that the idea of a meeting may be scary, but don't fret. You can overcome your fears with a bit of preparation. Here are a few TIPS to help make you an impressive interviewee.

First, keep in mind your purpose is to convey a positive impression. You want to let the interviewer know a bit about your strengths that may not be well reflected on paper. Strive to answer questions that the application did not. The interview can also help emphasize or complement points that you may have made in your essay. Everyone has unique characteristics and strengths. Express yourself with confidence, pride, and enthusiasm, but not conceited. A good strategy is to use what some call the **STAR** method that briefly describes a **S**ituation or **T**ask, **A**ction, and **R**esult. An effective strategy is to speak to failures and how you responded to and learned from them. Keep your responses short. A rule of thumb is less than two minutes.

Ask questions! Make sure the questions you ask are well thought out beforehand. I had a friend who was very well qualified for a job but managed to talk himself out of an offer by asking questions that had no relevance to the job he was applying. So the first rule of thumb is to ask relevant questions. Do a little research about the school so you can demonstrate that you are knowledgeable about the school, but still have a few questions. Arm yourself with a few statistics and national averages of the school. Graduation rates and majors that best help graduates find employment are two examples. Being informed about the school demonstrates your sincere interest. Asking relevant questions shows you want to learn more.

The best way to be prepared is to practice. First list on paper the qualities about yourself that you would like the college to know about you. Think of examples, such as experiences, hobbies, specific interests, people who may have influenced you, etc. that help to define who you are, how you became who you are, and is helping to determine the direction you are going in life. Sit down with family and friends and conduct a mock interview. Be open to constructive criticism.

Remember, the interviewer wants the interview to go well, just as you do. Their job is to gain qualified students. Your goal is to find an institution worthy of having you. So you are interviewing one another. Although every interview may be a bit different, ultimately, they all have one main goal in mind. That is to gain a better understanding of your characteristics and personality. To give them the most favorable impression of you, 1) be yourself, 2) prepare adequately, and 3) practice. The more prepared you are, the more relaxed you will be. And the more comfortable you are, the better the interview will be.

After the interview, follow up with a brief "thank you" note. It is not only a courteous thing to do; it shows you know proper etiquette and helps to re-enforce the interview. Remember, the interviewer is speaking to many students, and anything you can do to help you stand out. A follow-up letter is one more tool to help do this.

Have several "back up" schools in case your first-choice schools do not work out. Often students will get their hearts set on a college, and if they are not accepted, they feel all is lost. To avoid this disappointment, find several schools that you think best to meet your interests, and that you stand a good chance of gaining admission. In short, "do not put all your eggs in one basket."

Chapter 26
Final Words for Students— The Most Important Principle for a Successful and Happy Life

From time to time, you will not get the grade you would like. You may even get a poor grade. It is not the end of the world. Remember, mistakes are opportunities to learn. Often the best lessons learned are from mistakes. Don't beat yourself up when things don't go your way. If you don't succeed, keep trying. Remember the poem by Rudyard Kipling I quoted in Chapter 6? "HOLD ON"!

Always keep telling yourself how wonderful you are. Accept the guidance and constructive criticism of others. To do so is the mark of a wise learner. Reject destructive criticism from others! When others belittle or tease you, they are not sincere, instead, are being driven by their insecurities and that is their issue, not yours. Your image of yourself is based on how you perceive yourself, not how others see you.

It is not what you get out of life, instead what you give to it. Set your goals, then, "Go for it!"

In closing, I would like to remind readers of a fundamental principle. If all people in the world made the following a core value in their lives, it would make a far better world. Often, how you interact with others is how you feel about yourself. Since we cannot control the negativity of others, we can at least strive to influence them positively. This principle is the cornerstone of success and happiness in life.

Love yourself, Love Others—Unconditionally!

PART TWO

Parents' Guide

Our chief want in life is somebody who
will make us do what we want.
Ralph Waldo Emerson

SECTION H
What Parents and Guardians Can Do

Life loves to be taken by the lapel and told:
"I am with you kid. Let's go."
Maya Angelou

Chapter 27
Helping Children Master Self-Discipline

In the mid-60s, American sociologist James Samuel Coleman, along with several other researchers, published a landmark report, *The Coleman Report*. The release reported that **student background and family environment are more important in determining educational outcomes than the quality of schools and teachers**. In this chapter I will address several behavior modification strategies parents can take to help children during their formative years. Why did I devote a whole chapter to child discipline in a book on school success? Because a critical component to success in life, both in school and beyond, is based on one's ability to manage self-discipline. The young person who learns to control themselves correctly is much more inclined to make wise choices.

I felt it appropriate to address the issue of discipline because no matter what techniques are provided for learning, if a child does not learn how to master self-discipline early in life, then school will be more of a challenge. Effective home discipline strategies will provide a solid foundation for excellent academic skills as well as enhance opportunities for lifelong success. If your student is challenged when it comes to discipline, then this chapter can help. It is the rare parent who has not experienced the struggle of getting a child to do a task that the child does not want to do. The conflict between parent and child often leads to frustration, and the chances of task accomplishment reduced. To help a child gain self-discipline, then it is essential to understand the underlying forces that influence child behavior.

Students who learn excellent organizational skills and use their time wisely will not only do better in school but learn habits that will help them in their personal and work life. One of the critical sub-topics of self-discipline is the issue of organization and using time productively. I provided guidance to your student on these subjects in Chapter 7. In this chapter I have included some "TIPS" that can help you to motivate your child to be efficient with their space and time. A few excellent books for helping instill self-discipline skills in younger children are: *How to Talk So Kids Will Listen and Listen So Kids Will Talk* by Adele Faber and Elaine Mazlish. Another excellent book is *Loving Our Kids on Purpose: Making a Heart-To-Heart Connection* by Danny Silk. Silk provides practical strategies for parents to help children learn to manage themselves and do so in a non-confrontational manner.

The Importance of Boundaries (Limits)

Just as the animal trainer uses some form of structure to contain the animal while undergoing training, so too must the parent establish a "corral" or boundaries for the child. Dr. Michael Popkin in his book *Taming the Spirited Child*, describes an eight-sided "corral" to help define boundaries.

Leadership. Parents are leaders. The effective leader is firm yet fair. He respects his subordinates and gives allowances for growth and is patient when mistakes are made. He knows that others look up to him and will emulate him, so he is careful to act and do things in a manner that he wishes his children to copy.

Prevention. Learn to recognize when the child's temperament is on the rise and find ways to positively redirect his/her attention before the temper becomes anger.

Relationships. Parenting can and should be a fun experience. Building on the friendship aspects of the parent-child relationship is the best way to have an enjoyable, meaningful, and successful experience with your child. To do this, the parent must provide sincere and frequent encouragement. Discourage the child, and you run the risk of harming the relationship.

Power. Understand the principles of "power" and how to avoid power struggles with your child. Misused "power" can de-motivate and discourage. Many believe that they can control others with their anger or violence (verbal or physical). Have you used these strategies? Did they work? If you are honest, the answer would be "no, not really." And if they did, did it last?

Structure. Although humans may resist the constraints imposed by "rules and routines," the fact is we need them. Without rules and routine, we would have chaos. Even though we all must live within limits, it is especially true for the child who has yet to understand and learn that boundaries are essential to safety and well-being.

Discipline. Discipline is an essential element in enforcing limits or structure. To be most effective, however, the discipline must be appropriate, timely, consistent, and not harsh. There is a close relationship between control, empathy, and problem-solving. It is essential to know that before one can discipline another, it is necessary to have discipline oneself. It is a tall task to try to teach something to another if you don't have it yourself. If the adult is disorganized, the probability is that the child will also be disorganized. Parents who react to children angerly may be teaching their children to do the same.

Problems. For the child to learn to solve his/her issues, they must learn to identify decision making options and understand the consequences of those decisions. The child must understand how to control "feelings" and "wants." The key to helping the child use effective communication techniques, and this includes how to argue constructively rather than destructively.

Resources. Often, it is difficult to do it all on your own. There are many resources available to help, including schools, spiritual organizations, recreational leagues, family and friends, mental health organizations, community activities, and youth organizations, etc. Take advantage of them!

TIPS
TO HELP PROMOTE SELF-DISCIPLINE
(AND AVOID CONFLICT)

Keep your cool! There is a power struggle going on between the parent and child. If the parent loses his/her temper, the child wins. The child thinks, "Look how powerful I am, I made you angry."

Set the example. From infancy, children learn to model their parents. They become little mirrors of the authority figures in their lives. If you don't want your child to do it, don't do it yourself! If you use bad language, don't be surprised when your child does. If you throw your clothes on the floor, expect them to do the same. If you holler and scream, they will think, "it is OK for me to do it too?"

Influence rather than control. Force and spanking often lead to more misbehavior and can model aggressive behavior. When pushed, the natural response is to push back. The more one pushes, the less control you have. The goal is to "influence" the child (this works well with adults too), rather than "control" that person. By "influence," the goal is to get the other person to CHOOSE to do the right thing rather than doing it because he/she feels they MUST do it. No one wants to be controlled, even children. However, what they want, and need is guidance.

Listen carefully, speak calmly! The search for self-identity is essential to a child's self-development. This is one reason that young people are so conforming to their peers. They fear being different—at least from their friends. The opinion of their peers is more important than that of adults, and (sorry folks) that often includes parents and teachers. So what can adults do? LISTEN!! Realize and acknowledge that young people do not necessarily see things as adults do. Try hard to see things from the child's perspective. It does not mean that we as adults need to agree, just that we must try to understand. Besides listening to the child, listen to yourself. Continually ask yourself, "How am I coming across? Is my voice tone, choice of words, and body language conveying the desired correction, or do I sound more scolding?" Children may, on occasion, need to be spoken to firmly, but when communication is non-threatening, non-condescending and calm, the chances for achieving the desired outcome will be far greater. **A good rule of thumb is to speak to children as you would like to be spoken to. Remember, the goal is to get the child to perform a task(s) because he/she chooses to, not because you order them to.** This is called "incentivizing," and in the long term, it is far more effective than forcing, scolding or punishing.

Natural consequence. Sometimes it is best to "do nothing." In other words, allow a child to experience the consequences of his/ her actions or inactions. Parents do not want their child to get a bad grade for not doing homework. When their child procrastinates, the natural tendency is to remind, and sometimes to scold them to do the schoolwork. Doing so will get the work done, but what has the child learned? The next day, the cycle starts all over again. What would happen if the parent said nothing or just one reminder with no response from the child? Then when it is time for bed, the parent insists they go to bed — homework undone. The child gets an incomplete or poor mark for not completing the assignment — a "natural consequence." The odds are the student will be more inclined to not make the same mistake again. More importantly, a conflict between parent and child would have been avoided.

Sharing power. Nobody, even children, like to be ordered around. If frequently done, the child comes to expect such disciplinary tactics as nagging, lecturing, threatening, bribing, yelling, hitting, timeouts, etc. The stage for a power struggle has been set, and the child is, by their very nature, a very worthy opponent. Subconsciously they think," I may not get my way, but I can sure show them how powerful I am by not letting them have their way." What can the parent do to erase this thinking by the child? By allowing the child to keep his "power thinking" by sharing the power. The power is shared when strategies are used to encourage the child to want to act rather than forcing them to do something they do not want to do. The goal here is a win-win situation rather than a win-lose struggle. How is this done?

Don't fight, but don't give in. In other words, refuse to fight. You have established rules, guidelines, and consequences. Either they follow the rules, or not. It is their choice. The consequences are theirs, no need for the parent to make a big issue of it.

Give choices, not orders. "When do you want to do your homework now or after dinner?" "Since you have an exam on Monday, do you want to study for it this Friday or on Sunday?" In these examples, the parent is still in control by providing options, yet the child is made to feel they have some say in the issue by getting to make a choice.

"When-then" scenarios. When the child is resisting, you may need to be a bit more assertive. For example, if the child refuses to start homework, the parent might say "When you finish your schoolwork you can have some time on your laptop to play, agreed?" It is also a good idea to set a time limit. For example, "Remember, we agreed that you will shut down your computer by 10 P.M. on school nights?" Incentives work. When the child complies, an incentive may be offered. If the child complies, the reward is given. If the child procrastinates, then later asks for the reward, the parent gently reminds the child, "The agreement was that you would start doing your homework immediately after dinner. You waited 45 minutes before you got to work. I am glad you finished, but the agreement was "right after dinner." Do you want to try again tomorrow?" The parent does not allow herself to be pulled in to a dialogue that could well escalate into an argument. The parent is not seeking the child's approval instead is maintaining control of the situation.

Never insult, complain, criticize, shame, or humiliate. Such tactics attack the person rather than the issue. As humans, when we become fearful, frustrated, and angry, it is natural to resort to such tactics. But they are often fueled by our emotion rather than logic and the results are almost always a prelude to major conflict Focus on the issue, not the person. Instead of "Danny, you are so lazy. Why must I always have to remind you what you need to do? What is wrong with you?" A better approach is, "Danny, you have an examination in history coming up. You want to give yourself enough time so you can avoid a last-minute cram session."

Ask the child to help solve the problem. "I know you want to go to your friend's house now. Earlier you said you wanted to watch some television with the family after dinner. Do you want to go to your friend's house now, then do your homework after dinner instead of TV? Which would you rather do?" The process of including the child in the decision-making process helps confirm the child's feeling and avoid a confrontation.

Encouragement. One of the most powerful tools parents can use to motivate is to lavish praise on the child. Positive self-esteem is best fostered by encouragement. Focus on what the child does right and try not to only focus on the big mistakes and misbehaviors. Choose your battles! If we address every little thing a child does, we will only succeed in frustrating ourselves and discouraging the child. The more you acknowledge the child's strengths, progress, and results, the more we are re-enforcing the desired behavior.

Put it in writing. Often a little note of encouragement can be a potent motivator. "You did a great job of getting to your homework when you came home from school yesterday. It was great having you join us for a television show before bed time." Writing a note (paper, card, e-mail, text message) signifies to the receiver that you cared enough to go out of your way to acknowledge them — a task that takes a bit more effort than verbal praise. Just make sure that the note is specific to the improvement or accomplishment, is sincere, and how his behavior is positively affecting himself or others. Thank him and let him know how proud you are of his success.

Never mix criticism with praise. First, let's distinguish between **"destructive criticism"** from **"constructive criticism."** Destructive criticism is meant to hurt another. It serves no purpose in helping to resolve an issue and often results in making things worse. On the other hand, constructive criticism is meant to provide guidance and help. Although the words, "criticism" and "correction" are often used synonymously, I prefer to use the word "correction" as it better implies the intent of helping to improve. That said, when giving praise, and a correction is needed, give the praise separate from the correction. For example, a father tells his son, "Dave, you did a great job on your school project, but you need to learn to clean up after yourself." How might Dave receive this message? Initially, he will be proud of the fact that his father was acknowledging him for doing a good job, and then comes the "but." Often the "but" wipes out the praise. What does Dave think? "I did a good job on the project but screwed up by making a mess. I guess Dad is disappointed in me." If praise is given, and if a correction is needed, correct later and do it in private. By so doing, the recognition is provided and received as it was intended, a positive acknowledgment without the chance of being negated. Likewise, when the correction is given later, the focus is on the issue at hand, thus helping to avoid the possibility of misunderstanding.

Chapter 28
Helping Children Control Negative Impulses

One of the most valued tools adults can give children is to teach them how to deal with negative emotions. Stress, anxiety, nervousness, sadness, hurt, disappointment, anger, frustration are natural emotions, and for children of all ages, a problematic part of growing up. School is an especially fertile ground for these feelings. Such emotions can be a response when a person's desires are unfulfilled. They are discouraged if they experience an unrealized goal or feeling that they let themselves or another down or have fears.

Children respond to situations or thoughts in different ways, and often much differently than adults. It is important to know that what causes an emotional feeling for an adult often will not produce the same emotional feeling in a child. Usually, their response, if not done appropriately, can result in feelings of inadequacy resulting in loss of self-esteem. It can also result in depression if severe enough, and if left unchecked. The age of a child also affects a child's emotions. Parents should be careful not to dismiss a child's expression of his/ her feelings as irrelevant just because the adult does not feel the same way. For example, a child's attitudes towards the dark are often much different than that of adults. What are some of the behavioral signs of a child who is stressed?

Overly sensitive
Excessive worry
Recurring fears
Passive-aggressive behavior
Bed wetting
Unexplained crying
Persistent headaches and or stomach aches

Irregular sleep patterns
Too critical of self or others
Over or under eating
Withdrawal or isolation
Obsessive-compulsive tendencies

It is difficult for parents to see their children experience negative feelings. Thus they often take steps to shield them from the hurt. By so doing, although well-intentioned, it could result in contributing to the child's inability to cope with the emotion. It is essential for children to learn how to self–regulate their feelings. If parents try to protect the child from their pain, the child will not learn to deal with it. If they do not learn to deal with it, they will not learn useful coping skills and thus less able to deal with emotions as they grow older. These children may have more difficulty with peer relations and schoolwork than children who are better able to address their emotions and effectively resolve problems.

Controlling negative impulses are often difficult for a child to regulate. Although experiencing such emotions is inevitable, the yucky feelings can be minimized by maximizing resilience and confidence. Adults in a child's life can teach strategies to help children learn to cope with such emotions. Although tools for self-regulation can be acquired at any age, they are best learned when young. Some strategies include modeling, reframing, and self-awareness. When adults (parents, grandparents, caregivers, and teachers, etc.) use a team approach and work in harmony, the better the outcomes will be. Let's look at these strategies.

TIPS
To Help Children Cope with Negative Emotions

Modeling. When a child experiences an emotion such as anger, frustration, fear, etc. the adult can share with the child how they responded to the feelings when they experienced them. For example, a teacher I knew told her class that when her dog died, she felt sad and cried. Then she began to feel anger because she would no longer have her dog to love and care for. To help herself feel better, she took several deep breaths and began to tell herself that it was OK to feel sad, but not be angry. Besides, who was she going to be mad with, anyway? The students laughed at this. Then the teacher said she thought about all the good times she had with her dog, and the many memories she had with him. She explained how talking to herself was able to control her anger, thus help alleviate her sadness.

Be aware of how you and other family members handle emotions, both negative and positive. Children will pick up on your feelings and react accordingly. When your child has negative thoughts, try to re-frame them from a negative viewpoint to a positive one.

Another modeling strategy is to show a child how to **respond (not react)** when a situation stimulates an emotional feeling. Children learn by copying. Explain to the child what you did, and what you did to effectively respond to your feelings. Since adults are not superhumans, we will on occasion (hopefully infrequently) react in a less than appropriate manner. This can be a good teaching moment. Rather than ignoring it, confess to your child how you felt and how you might have handled it differently. It is OK to let your child know you make mistakes and react to various situations. But when you do, you learn from the mistake and try to do it better next time. Isn't this precisely what you want your child to do as well? The key to self-regulation is to remain calm when confronted with disappointments, frustrations, rejection, etc. One of the best tools for modeling is the attitude demonstrated by the adults in a child's life. When children observe adults display a positive and enthusiastic manner when confronted with disappointments (and other strong emotions), children will often follow suit.

Reframing. Show children how to see things differently. Professionals call this "reframing." Often, children and adults are a victim to misinterpretation of events that result in an adverse reaction. When one child knocks over another's carefully constructed tower of blocks, the first child will usually immediately accuse the other of having done the dastardly deed intentionally. This child may even strike out at the second child. Having been falsely accused, child number two may strike back, cry, or react in some other negative, albeit perfectly understandable way. In such a situation, the adult can help de-escalate the situation, and teach a more appropriate manner of responding by using reframing. In other words, the adult can show the child how to substitute a more effective way of dealing with the situation. One strategy that is used typically by behaviorists and schools is the "turtle technique" (Havighurst et al. *Building Preschool Children's Emotional Competence: A Parenting Program.* Greenberg et al. *Promoting emotional competence in school-aged children in Emotions in Development Psychopathology.* Early Education and Development). The technique includes the following steps:

- Help the child recognize his/her feelings.
- Have them say to themselves, "stop."
- In their mind pretend they are a turtle. Go into their shell, just as a turtle does.
- Have the child take three deep breaths.
- Think calming thoughts, such as "It was an accident that my brother knocked down my blocks. I can control my anger and think of ways to handle this, so we don't get into trouble, and I do not lose my friend over a few building blocks."
- When the child feels in control, they come out of their shell.

The use of puppets and or dolls can be used effectively in role-play to help younger children learn emotional control strategies. The puppets can share ways to calm down, respond, and problem solve. Children love to play make-believe, and what better way to teach skills than through make-believe games. Just look at all the wonderful children's programs on television that effectively teach life skills. Sesame Street, Peppa Pig, Chuggington, Clifford, Danial Tiger's Neighborhood, to name a few. There are many children's TV shows that are entertaining but provide little or no educational value. My recommendation is to choose the ones that teach and entertain, rather than just entertain.

Self-Awareness. Sharianna Boyle, author of *The Conscious Parents Guide to Childhood Anxiety*, says that one of the best ways to help the child develop skills to be aware of emotions and thoughts without identifying with them. In other words, because a person can experience feelings of sadness, frustration, or fear, does not mean they are good, bad, competent, or worthy. When a child learns to recognize emotions as experiences and not become overwhelmed by them, their ability to cope is increased.

The myth of "perfection." To do well at something does not mean a person needs to be perfect. When a child believes that he/she must be "perfect" and unable to achieve perfection, feelings of negativity such as inadequacy and incompetence can result. Listen for such statements as, "I am stupid," "Why am I not liked," "Why can't I do better." Such negative thinking is painful is stressful and can block success thinking. Parents and adult leaders must teach children that they are not perfect. Rather than worry too much about outcomes is to try hard, learn from mistakes, and focus on the joys and experiences of the present.

Advance preparation. One of the best ways to help children handle negative emotions is to prepare them for it. When children expect one thing and get another, they may feel disappointed, angry, frustrated, sad, etc. An effective strategy is for the parents to provide options. For example, if a multiple children family can only allow one child to go shopping with Mom, tell all the children that only one can go, but another will go next time. Each one will get a chance to go shopping with Mom, but they will have to be patient. Reinforcement may be used as an incentive for those who are left behind, such as having them help put the groceries away upon Mom's return. Prepare your child for life events that can trigger stress by explaining ahead of time what to expect. The more they know about what to expect, the better they will be able to cope. Ask them to gather what they need for school, extra-curricular activities, social events, etc.

False hopes. It is essential not to give false hopes unless you are entirely sure that you can deliver on the promise. Sometimes it may be best not to tell a child of a pending favored activity until it is going to happen. If a child experiences a disappointment, try not to respond with your disappointment, frustration, or anger adding to the child's negative feelings. A better approach is to respond with encouragement to learn from the experience and not allow a temporary setback to discourage them. Convey to your child that you have confidence in their ability to meet life's challenges.

Breaking down tasks into small chunks helps make large tasks simpler to manage and less overwhelming. Review with your child Chapters 5 on being prepared and Chapter 7 on being organized.

The strategies of modeling, reframing, self-awareness, and preparation can help those of any age to respond to emotions healthily and positively. Doing so plays a vital role in intellectual and social development that contributes to school and life success, and with less stress.

School-Related Anxiety and Stress. As I stated in the opening paragraph of this chapter, school is a fertile ground for children to experience negative feelings, particularly anxiety and stress. School related potential stressors include new experiences/transitions, peer relations, teacher/coach/parental expectations, fear of failure, and feeling overwhelmed. Review the signs listed in the second paragraph of this chapter. A few signs/symptoms not listed are skipping school, refusal to do or complete homework assignments, or excessive delay is starting homework. What can you do when such situations arise?

Speak to your child to ascertain what is bothering him/ her.
Speak to teachers, coaches, and counselors, as appropriate.
Help children to learn and use the principles outlined SECTIONS A through F.
Consider limiting after school activities if the child feels overwhelmed.
Promote proper balance of academic, extracurricular, social, and relaxation activities.
Explain that some anxiety is normal, such as before a test or a class presentation.

Encourage children and adolescents to express opinions and feelings about school.

Give praise for schoolwork done well.

Refrain from criticism when they falter.

Deliver guidance and corrections in a non-confrontational manner.

Listen more, talk less!

Promote socially appropriate and positive peer relationships.

Discourage or even prohibit peer relations that will negatively influence your child.

Encourage (but do not force) participation in youth groups

Get involved in your child's extra-curricular activities, if practicable. Attend events!

Use relaxation strategies and self-calming strategies such as meditation, calming music, guided imagery.

Limit the use of social media, especially during the school week.

Seek professional help if symptoms persist.

Chapter 29
The Mind of the Teenager How
to Respond and Support

When I served as a volunteer Emergency Medical Technician, our crews were often called to the scene of accidents in which teens had made poor choices. One that will always stand out in my mind was an incident in which four teens were speeding down a country road trying to out-run other teens who were chasing them after an altercation at a bowling alley. Sadly, the driver of the first car lost control and slammed sideways into a tree, throwing the two who were riding in the rear seat out the side windows. The teen riding in the front passenger seat was also thrown from the car. The three passengers died. The two who were thrown from the back seat were brothers. In the hospital, I still remember the mother's anguish when she had been told her two sons were dead. It is the rare family who has either personally or know of someone who has experienced the heartache of teens who have made poor decisions resulting in tragedy or near tragedy.

"Why," parents ask, "do teens make such poor choices, often ending badly?" "Why does my teenager focus so much on things that matter so little to life success?" "Why are they so self-centered?" "Why do they think that adults know so little, yet (they think) they have so much wisdom—even though they have only been on God's green Earth for only a few years?" "Why do parents feel as if they are speaking to a foreigner sometimes?" "Why can't my child seem to make logical decisions?" "Why do they take reckless risks?" No wonder tensions often run high in homes when teens are expected to yet often challenged when managing emotions, handling risks, responding to relationships, and engaging in complex schoolwork or employment? There are, believe it or not, some perfectly reasonable reasons for such strange behavior.

Although the teenage thought processes have bewildered adults for millenniums, it was not until the late 20th century that science researchers began to understand better the physiologic development of the human brain. Development of brain image technology greatly facilitated research and provided insight into why teens think and act the way they do. A study conducted by the National Institutes of Health (NIH) showed that brains undergo a significant transformation between the ages of 12 to 25 years old longer than had been previously thought. During this time frame, the brain undergoes a re-wiring, like a re-wire of a computer network.

Two doctors who have been exploring the unique structure and chemistry of the adolescent and brain are David K. Urion, and Frances E. Jensen, professors of Neurology Children's Hospital Boston and Harvard Medical School (HMS). Debra B. Ruder, in an article titled *The Teen Brain* published in the Harvard Magazine (Sept/Oct 2008) reported that Jenson and Urion explain that "The teenage brain is not just an adult brain with fewer miles on it," says, Jenson. "It's a paradoxical time of development, these are people with very sharp brains, but they're not quite sure what to do with them." The portion of the brain that acts as the "traffic cop" is called the prefrontal cortex. Located in the front part of the brain, it directs self-regulation, focus, organization, attention span, risk and reward, prioritizing, and self-evaluation. The prefrontal cortex also communicates with other parts of the brain, including those that are particularly associated with emotion and impulses, so that all areas of the brain can be better involved in planning and problem-solving. The main component of the body's nervous system is the neuron, or the "brain cell," as many like to call it. The neuron is a highly specialized cell that transmits information by electrochemical signals throughout the body. The transmission process between neurons is called "synapse." There are as many as 1,000 trillion synaptic connections. To give you an idea as to how huge this is, it is equivalent to a computer with a one trillion bit per second processor. The brains memory capacity ranges from 1 to 1,000 terabytes. Ten terabytes equal about 19 million books. Wow! That is a massive library in our brain!

The research has revealed that young brains have both fast-growing synapses and sections that remain unconnected. The gray matter in the brains of the young adolescent is more significant than it is in adults leaving teens easily influenced by their environment and more prone to impulsive behavior. Add hormones and genetic predispositions, as well as family and socio-economic factors, it is easy to see why teens often do not seem to be Earthlings. Jensen and Urion point out that the brain is only about 80 percent developed in adolescents. Around the onset of adolescence, the frontal cortex is the only brain region that has not reached adult levels. This helps explain why teens behave the way they do.

With repeated stimulation, synapses become more robust, thus contribute to faster learning in children and adolescents than in adults. No wonder young people can learn languages and instruments in less time than adults. So I do not suggest that you compete in learning games with your adolescent, as they will, no doubt, win. If you and your teen decide to learn to play an instrument together, you may find yourself being outperformed by your kid. Younger children can absorb information even more quickly. Just watch how fast an infant develops. There are also gender differences in brain development. The ability to process information will peak for girls between the ages of peak 12 to 14 years old and in boys about two years later.

Jensen and Urion also state that adolescent brains more are susceptible to alcohol-induced toxicity than are adults. They point out that the use of marijuana (cannabinoid) blocks cell signaling in the brain. Jensen says, **"We make the point that what you did on the weekend is still with you during that test on Thursday. You've been trying to study with a self-induced learning disability." (This may be a paragraph you wish to share with your teen.)**

Sleep and exercise are also crucial for learning and memory. "Many teens," state the doctors, "do not get enough sleep or exercise, thus adversely affecting their ability to maximize study time and memorize required material."

Teens are bombarded by information in this electronic age. Jensen highlights a recent study showing how sensory overload can hinder a student's ability to recall words. "It's truly a brave new world. Our brains have never been subjected to the amount of cognitive input that's coming at us," she says. "You can't close down the world. All you can do is educate kids to help them manage this." By raising awareness of this paradoxical period in brain development, the neurologists hope to help young people cope with their challenges, as well as recognize their considerable strengths.

Beatriz Luna, a professor of psychiatry at the University of Pittsburgh, has been studying the teen brain with neuroimaging. She found that compared to adults, teens were less able to use the portions of the brain that monitored performance, planned ahead, and remain focused. Thus, adults can better resist temptations, whereas teens more readily give in to impulsivity. Is it any wonder that teens will text while driving even though it is against the law, and dangerous? She also found that when offered rewards, teens focus would improve.

Urion believes programs aimed at preventing risky adolescent behaviors would be more useful if they offered practical strategies for making in-the-moment decisions, rather than merely lecturing teens about the behaviors themselves—my failing as a parent. I was always under the assumption that my children would understand and respond to my "lectures." I sincerely believed that they "understood," but they did not know how to "respond." When my daughter was about 8, she would ask permission to do something. She then would say, "Daddy, just say yes or no." Translation, "I don't need nor even understand your reasoning; just keep it simple." A classic example of how child and adult thinking sometimes just do not connect.

One area of focus in the study of neuroscience is the plasticity of the brain. Repeated stimulation of a synapse allows the brain to make new neuron connections, thus able to pass on messages more readily. This process is the basis of how we remember. Although this occurs in adults of any age, it is more so in the young adult. The process is what many term "emotional intelligence" or "social intelligence." Some educators argue that these may be better predictors of adult success and happiness than IQ or SAT scores. So the question remains, are social memory, emotional perspective taking, impulse control, empathy, ability to work with others, and self-regulation better indicators of lifetime success rather than the ability to memorize formulas, valance tables of elements and vocabulary words? I will speak more about this in SECTION K, "Our Education System (and Students) at Risk."

The developmental process has a purpose. B.J. Casey and Kristina Caudle Casey wrote in *Current Directions in Psychological Science* that, *"*We are so used to seeing adolescence as a problem. But the more we learn about what makes this period unique, the more adolescence starts to seem like a highly functional, even adaptive period." Put another way, the changes in the adolescent brain and associated thinking and conduct are preparing them for the transition from home to the outside world. Although impulsive behavior can sometimes be risky, it also allows for experimentation, learning, and socialization. For example, the teenagers urge to make friends, turns their focus from home-related interests to interests outside of the home. These experiences are necessary for growth and transition. Granted, they take more risks, but many behavioral scientists argue that teens know the risks they are taking. So why do they take risks? Because taking risks provides gratification to the adolescent brain. It is all part of the "plan." Parts of the information in this chapter were taken from an article which appeared in the October 2011 edition of the *National Geographic* magazine, "Beautiful Brain" by David Dobbs.

TIPS
To Motivate Your Teen

Dr. Daniel Amen, director of the Amen Clinic for Behavioral Medicine in Fairfield, California, in his book, *Change Your Brain, Change Your Life* describes the role that the deep limbic system has on human behavior and survival. It is the storage place for emotional memories (good and bad); it affects motivation and drive, sleep and appetite, smell, bonding, and social connections. Whereas a therapist would focus on such things as dealing with bad memories, building positive interpersonal relations, and other mind-body connections— parents, guardians, teachers, coaches, etc. can use the power of the deep limbic system in dealing with teen behavior. Some of Dr. Amen's suggestions include:

Spend time with your teen. Let them know that you value alone time with them. Do something they would like to do. They may sometimes resist, as they may prefer to do teenage interest things, and that is OK. Don't push it. Just keep offering. Many teens would welcome a "date night" or maybe a dinner and a movie. During this time, refrain from the temptation to interrogate, lecture, or give unsolicited advice. It is an opportunity for relationship building, not resolving the behavior. Do more listening than talking.

Note positive behaviors and thoughts of your teen and give positive feedback. Avoid critical comments, even though tempted to do so. Give hugs!

Here are some more suggestions, taken from *Teenagers 101* by Rebecca Deurlein; as well as experiences of my own, my family and my friends.

Be involved with your teen's activities. If you have the time and inclination, participate as a leader or coach in their extracurricular activities. If unable to do so, as a minimum, attend games, shows, and events. Let them know you are their biggest fan! Caution— don't overdo it! Sometimes teens want a little space from parents. So give it to them.

Establish a routine and set standards. Have family routines, chores, and family activities. Make it clear that your children are expected to participate in these activities. Teenagers are masters at procrastinating, making excuses and blaming. Just don't play their game.

Inspect what you expect. When tasks are not performed to standards, show them what to do, then have them repeat it. Repeat as often as necessary until they master the task. Provide gentle corrections.

Foster organization kills. Help teens set goals and a plan for achieving their goals. Encourage your teen to have a calendar and "to do" lists. Assist them with effective prioritization skills.

Motivators. Use rewards (motivators) sparingly. It is essential that children learn to perform from internal motivation, i.e., because it is the right thing to do, rather than for external motivators, i.e., for what they may get out of it. In other words, homework is done to gain knowledge, not for a gift. When motivators are used, try to make them relevant to their established goals and interests. For example, if your teen achieves a specific milestone in an extracurricular activity, you might reward her with an outing to a similar discipline (theatre, professional athletic event, museum, etc.).

Teamwork. Although family members may have differences regarding interests, abilities, and beliefs, all must be on the same sheet on values and standards and the teaching and enforcement of those values and norms. Not doing so will send mixed signals and hence, confusion. When adults disagree—and they will form time to time, never disagree or argue in front of the child as this will give them ammunition for playing one adult against the other.

Promoting positive self-image for teenagers is just as important as it is for younger youth. Parents ask, "How do I deal with this strange person living in my house?" Challenges to authority, tradition, habits, and attitude can be frustrating for parents. As they transition between childhood and adulthood, they are striving most for self-identity, caused, in part, by physiological changes. Their bodies are changing, they are afforded new freedoms and challenges, different expectations of adults, and opinions of friends and acquaintances. Boundaries (as explained in Chapter 27) are just as important for teens as it is for younger children. **As teens discover themselves, the best support parents can give is positive reinforcement for what they do right, for accomplishments, and effort.**

TIPS
To Influence Your Teen

So how can parents and guardians influence teens to help them make wise choices? In Chapters 27 and 28, I provided some strategies to help parents teach children self-discipline, control anger, and disappointment. Although those chapters were directed more for young children than teenagers, many of the strategies work with teens as well. But teenagers are not small children and require different parenting strategies. Michael Resnick, Ph.D., conducted a study published in *The Journal of the American Medical Association* in 1997. Dr. Resnick reported that teenagers who feel loved and connected with their parents have a significantly lower incidence of teenage pregnancy, drug use, violence, and suicide. He termed this connection, "limbic bonding." The degree of this bonding with parents and teachers is the most crucial determinant of whether a teen will engage in risky behavior.

Because teens need to feel that they are loved and capable, they will often strive to meet these needs with attention-seeking behavior or misbehavior. Examples are failing to do chores or homework, being mischievous, expecting to be waited on, disobedience, rudeness, limited effort, violence, withdrawal, self-inflicted pain, purposefully being annoying, etc. Such conduct elicits in parent's feelings of frustration, anger, and hurt. They may feel threatened, disrespected, and fearful. So how can parents deal with such behavior? **To influence teens to make wise choices it is imperative that parents' guide and respond in a polite, yet firm manner (note again I said "respond" not "react"). Here are TIPS on how to do that.**

Do not allow their actions to suck you in. Ignore, if possible.
Don't do things for them that they can do for themselves.
Refuse to fight, but don't give in.
Allow for natural consequences, as described in Chapter 27.
Refrain from the temptation to attack or hurt back.

Do not accept excuses nor self-defeating attitudes such as "I can't."

Refrain from criticism. Distinguish between sound coaching and lecturing.

Do not be sarcastic.

Give praise when they act or speak appropriately.

Allow them to make their own choices when reasonable and safe.

Express confidence in them.

Treat them fairly and respectfully.

Focus on strengths and talents.

Praise wise choices.

Celebrate accomplishments.

Be frank and honest yet do so tactfully and sensitively.

Never lie to your child. If they catch you telling the untruth, they will lose respect for you.

To help use these responses, it is important that you be in the proper frame of mind. So, to prepare yourself, try the following strategies.

Admit your feelings. If you have reacted in ways that have been ineffective in the past (anger, attacking, playing the pity party, blaming, rationalizing, enabling, avoiding, etc.), honestly recognize such reactions then commit to changing to more effective ways to respond to your teen.

Watch body language and tone of voice. Raised or scolding voice tone, crossed arms, pacing, scowls, and rolled eyes often do more to break down communication than what is said.

Avoid impulsivity. Take a moment to calm down before addressing the teens inappropriate behavior.

Learn relaxing techniques.

Use humor, if it is appropriate and not hurtful.

Ignore excuses. Focus on the issue.

Remind them of their commitments.

Point out natural consequences if they do not follow through when and how expected.

Avoid nagging, frustration, or anger.

Be consistent in enforcing routines and standards.

Let them know you understand their view or how they might feel. It does not mean you have to agree.

Make allowances for the individual differences in each of your children. Work to the unique strengths of each.

Provide positive feedback when things are done well. Children, especially teens, respond much better to encouragement than to criticism.

Guide, don't control.

Prevention and treatment of substance abuse and addictions. Open dialogue is essential. Educate pre-teens and young teens about drugs, alcohol, and smoking. If you see signs that your teen has started to take risks with drugs, alcohol, tobacco, or anything else that places their health and well-being at risk, takes immediate action! Do not give in to any temptation to avoid talking about the issue of concern for fear of creating an altercation. Use the communication strategies described in Chapter 11 and the suggestions on helping children with self-discipline and negative impulses in Chapters 27 and 28. If necessary, get assistance from a counselor or coach. Sometimes teens will respond better to a person other than parents. Dialogue that leads to early intervention can often prevent serious addiction issues.

Since all teens are different, no one strategy or technique will fit all. However, recognizing the basic psychological needs of teens and how to respond best to meet those needs will significantly increase the chance of successfully directing teenage behavior.

Drug Abuse

Regrettably, the teenager's inclination for experimentation and risk-taking makes them susceptible to drug and alcohol abuse. Drug use is a guarantee for struggles in and out of school

and causes extreme stress for the student and his/her family. Drug addiction has become the "worst epidemic in U.S. history," reports the Center for Disease Control and Prevention. Drug abuse is the leading cause of death for Americans under the age of 50, according to a June 2017 article in the *Democracy Now*. The report points out that "opioid deaths have now surpassed the peak in deaths by car crashes in 1972, AIDS deaths in 1995, and gun deaths in 1993. Drug abuse can involve a variety of physician-prescribed medications. Examples are the treatment of depression, anxiety, and sleep disorder, stimulants to treat attention-deficit hyperactivity disorder (ADHD), and opioids used to treat pain. The National Institutes of Health reports that over the last 15 years, there has been a steady increase in emergency room visits and overdose deaths due to misuse of prescription drugs. Common "recreational drugs," also termed "street drugs" include cocaine, ecstasy, methamphetamine, and LSD. Have you ever heard of Molly? I am not referring to the female band "Red Molly," rather an illegal recreational drug often found at concerts and parties. According to *WebMD*, between 5 percent and 7 percent of high school students have tried "Molly," thinking it was the drug MDMA or Ecstasy, which produces feelings of euphoria and lowers inhibitions. But Molly can be anything the producers want to put in the drug, often containing synthetic drugs, many of which are more dangerous than pure ecstasy. Many teens are ignorant of this, resulting in serious side effects, often seizures, anxiety, depression, memory loss, and death. **(This is another paragraph you ought to share with your teen).**

To get a momentary high young people will often resort to solvents such as glue, aerosols, nail polish, and gas lighter fluid. When taken irresponsibly, alcohol and cannabis (marijuana) can result in adverse consequences. Once a child begins to experiment with any mind-altering drug, it could well start a very miserable journey—for themselves and their families. I am not suggesting that everyone who correctly takes prescription medications, or even tries marijuana, alcohol, or a recreational drug will become an addict. But one thing is for sure, 100 percent of addicts started with one or more of the mind-altering substances mentioned. **The lie that young people tell themselves, "I can do it a few times. I am in control. I will not become addicted." Over 700 youth who died this year believed the lie.**

In an August 2017 article of *U.S. News & World Report,* referring to the National Institute on Drug Use, about 4,000 children under the age of 18 begin using illicit drugs every day. This is indeed scary! Thus, parents must start teaching their children about the dangers of drug use while they are still in grade school. Do not rely on schools, the government, and certainly not the entertainment media—they all get poor grades in the drug education department. The parents are the most powerful source when it comes to drug education.

In PART ONE, Chapter 24, "Obstacles to Achievement" I addressed the dangers of drug and alcohol abuse to young readers. I provided a list of warning signs and told them that I also listed them for parents in PART TWO and warned them not to try to pull the wool over your eyes. Here are the signs to watch. Be advised, however, just because your teen may display a few of these signs does not necessarily mean that they are using mind-altering substances. Any of the listed "symptoms" should be investigated as a cause for possible medical concern. If symptoms are seldom experienced, it may not be indicators of the use of dangerous substances. If, however, you notice several signs, especially over a period, then do not hesitate to seek medical help.

Mood swings, easily irritated, quick to anger
Poor hygiene, organization, and eating habits
Unexplained weight loss
An unusual drop in body temperature (they are cold when most others are comfortable)
Indifference or withdrawal from family
Poor academic and extracurricular performance
Change in normal sleep routines
Dishonesty/stealing/excuses
Scratching

Bloodshot or glassy eyes
Drowsiness and drifting off when others are speaking
Poor judgment, irrational
Forgetfulness
Delayed motor skills/reflexes

Sadly, some teens will not heed the warnings and indulge in mind-altering drugs anyway. If you notice your child is beginning to show any of the symptoms listed above, dig deeper! Check rooms, backpacks, clothes pockets, under or even in mattresses, under beds, or any other possible hiding place. If your child knows you are doing a shakedown inspection, they will not like it. But the truth is the "clean child" may complain a bit but will not fuss too much as they know they have nothing to hide. Congratulate them! A child who is using, on the other hand, will likely become angry and do everything they can to try and deter you from searching their room. They react this way because they have something to hide. If you discover drugs or drug paraphernalia, it will be upsetting to you, but try hard not to over-react. An angry parent will do little to encourage a productive dialogue with their child. **Caution!** Your teen may promise not to do it again, but the probability is that they will. With this in mind, seek help! There are many resources online, as well as organizations and professionals that can assist. The sooner drug use can be stopped the better chance your teen has of not developing a full-blown addiction.

TIPS
If Your Teen Is Using Drugs

Using the strategies described in the preceding paragraphs of this chapter, try to get your teen to admit to using drugs. If they do, do not overact or become angry, as hard as this may be. Scolding will prevent the adolescent from opening up to you. During your dialogue, try to determine if the use was a single experiment or has it become frequent and becoming a problem. Regardless of the frequency, teens who are shown love and support are more inclined to respond positively.

If your teen denies using drugs, reassure them that you are concerned. Tell them that you will not sit idly by and allow them to sabotage their future, their health, and even their life. You will be inspecting their rooms, administering unannounced home drug tests, and seeking professional help from therapists. Be aware of what your teen is always doing. Do not allow unsupervised activities! Establish clear rules and consequences for violating the rules. Know your child's friends. Step in if you suspect your child's peers are pressuring them to use drugs. You will get pushback on this but be firm! You are dealing with potential life and death of your child. Also, carefully monitor prescription and even certain over-the-counter drugs in your home.

Caution! There is a difference between enabling and supporting. Enabling is helping a person to do something. To enable an addict is to promote the dangerous behavior by ignoring, covering for, excusing, paying for their irresponsible financial errors, doing their work, and condoning misbehavior and disrespect. Doing so only serves to encourage their continued abuse rather than helping them take responsibility and the consequences for their actions. Support them by getting them involved in extracurricular activities, restrictions (long ones, if necessary), caring for them when sick, transporting them to doctor's appointments, and taking them to AA or NA meetings, etc. The line between enabling and supporting is often a thin one. To help distinguish, ask yourself the question, "If I help, will it encourage him/her to take responsibility for what he/she has done or has failed to do?" Addicts are masters at manipulation. Thus, it is often difficult to ascertain the difference between an actual need and when they are taking advantage of you. No doubt the most challenging thing a parent can be faced with is not helping when their child is screaming for support. You can get help from others who are experiencing similar challenges through ALANON.

If your child (or you) has a condition that requires a physician-prescribed medication, and the physician suggests an opioid, consider the alternatives listed below. Opioids contain codeine, and methadone and include Vicodin, OxyContin, Percocet, Percocet, Opana, Demerol, Darvon, and Duragesic (these are the brand names). U.S. Public Health's Rear Admiral Joyce Johnson suggests these alternatives:

- Ask about other pain-relieving options, such as nonsteroidal anti-inflammatory drugs, acetaminophen (Tylenol), antidepressants, and anticonvulsants, osteopathic treatments, physical therapy, nerve block, steroid injections, or behavioral therapy. To Dr. Johnson's suggestions, I would include homeopathic medicine and mind-body exercises such as Yoga and Tai Chi.
- If your provider insists that an opioid is appropriate, ask that the prescription be for a limited time with safer drugs prescribed for long-term use.
- Discard leftover any medication that could be abused.

Tobacco Use

In Chapter 8 I spoke about the importance of physical health as one of the "five essential columns." In that chapter, I did not speak to the use of tobacco products by young people and the effects on health and productivity. I did, however, address it in PART I, Chapter 24, "Obstacles to Achievement." Sections include: "Tobacco Addiction," the physical and health effects of smoking, "Avoiding the Smoking Habit," and "How to Quit Smoking." You may wish to review these sections, so you know what I said to your kids.

Here are some important facts reported by the U.S. Department of Health and Human Services, National Center for Chronic Disease Prevention and Health Promotion, Office on Smoking and Health, Atlanta."

Adolescents who start smoking are generally characterized by one or more of the following: (*Preventing Tobacco Use Among Youth: A Report of the Surgeon General.* 2012).

The perception that smoking helps to control stress or lose weight.

Lower socioeconomic status, including lower-income or education.

Lack of skills to resist influences on tobacco use.

Lack of support or involvement from parents.

Accessibility, availability, and price of tobacco products.

Low levels of academic achievement.

Low self-image or self-esteem.

According to the CDC report, "The teen years are critical for brain development, which continues into young adulthood. Young people who use nicotine products in any form, including e-cigarettes, are uniquely at risk for long-lasting effects." The report also states, "Because nicotine affects the development of the brain's reward system, continued nicotine products use cannot only lead to nicotine addiction, but it also can make other drugs such as cocaine and methamphetamine more pleasurable to a teen's developing brain." (*The Health Consequences of Smoking—50 Years of Progress: A Report of the Surgeon General.* 2014).

Electronic cigarettes also referred to as e-cigarettes, e-vaporizers, and vapes, resemble tobacco products. They are battery-operated devices that are used to inhale a gas that usually contains nicotine and other chemicals. According to a National Institute of Drug Abuse (NIDA) report, *E-Cigarette Use Among Youth and Young Adults: A Report of the Surgeon General.* 2016 **"E-cigarettes are popular among teens and are now the most commonly used form of tobacco among youth in the United States."** Further, a study of high school students found that one in four teens reported using e-cigarettes for dripping, a practice in which people produce and inhale vapors by placing e-liquid drops directly onto heated atomizer coils."

The NIDA reports that evidence suggests that the use of e-cigarettes by high school students are seven times more likely to use smokable tobacco products than those who have not used e-cigarettes. Thus, it can be reasonably concluded that use of e-cigarettes can be a pre-curser for pre-teens and teens to use tobacco products. In 2016 the Federal Drug Administration established regulations prohibiting the sale of e-cigarettes to persons less than 18 years of age. The FDA did this because e-cigarettes contain nicotine and other harmful chemicals, many of which can cause cancer. Side effects include nausea, stomach pain, high blood pressure, seizures, and death.

TIPS
To Discourage Teen Smoking
or
To Help Them Quit

The best way to combat pre-teen and teenage smoking is to prevent it. The best prevention is education. Once they start, it is more challenging to get them to stop as the addiction quickly sets in. Suggestions on what you can do to help prevent your child from using tobacco products are presented in the "TIPS" section, Chapter 24, "To Help Address Drugs and/or Alcohol Abuse".

If your adolescent is thinking about smoking or is already smoking, an excellent resource for helping is "smokefree.gov." (https://teen.smokefree.gov/become-smokefree/tools-for-quitting). The "smoke-free" resource provides free tools to help teens quit. Included are "Smoke-free Text Messaging," and "teen.smokefree. gov" provide guidance, inspirations, and challenges. Try the National Cancer Institute's LiveHelp online chat. You will be connected with a trained specialist who can answer your questions and give information about quitting smoking. LiveHelp is available Monday through Friday from 9:00 a.m. to 9:00 p.m. Eastern time. LiveHelp also is available in Spanish. Their number is 877-448-7848.

All states provide trained counselors who can assist smokers to quit. Call 800-784-8669 to connect directly with your state counsel.

Chapter 30
Parenting Styles—What
Works, What Doesn't

Parental involvement and encouragement are essential to the academic success of their children. Indeed, there are many parenting styles. What might work for one child may not work for another. I know. I have five children, and they are all very different. Each responded to varying strategies of parenting, coaching, and corrections. Some strategies seemed to work consistently. Based on research and experience, behavior professionals can point to the parenting styles that, often, result in children who are more successful in life and generally happier. So, what kind of involvement is most effective? Let's look at a few different parenting styles.

Child psychologists have studied parenting styles for years. They have generally come to agree on four main parenting styles: Authoritarian, Authoritative, Indulgent, and Neglecting. The four styles are categorized according to levels of control, warmth and support. Each of the four parental methods can be categorized along two fundamental dimensions of "high" or "low." Parents are not necessarily totally one style or the other, instead will lean towards one or more style depending on the situation. In other words, few parents will demonstrate one method exclusively. As you read through the definitions, try to relate to your style. Also, think about your parent's style. What seemed to work best and what didn't?

Authoritarian

Controlling and strict.
Rules are rigid and sometimes have little if anything to do with safety or learning.

Demand compliance with no or little opportunity for parent/child discourse.

Communication usually one way-parent to the child.

Knows about the child's social life (if they have one).

Shows little interest in and do not promote positive children's activities. Accomplishments are taken for granted.

Little or unenthusiastic praise. Admonish for failures.

React with anger.

Show little empathy. Insensitive to feelings.

Punishment, often harsh, may be applied inconsistently, or unfairly may be inappropriate for the infraction.

Disrespectful and insensitive. Sometimes verbally or physically abusive.

The child is not allowed to express needs, wants, and feelings. Parents needs and wants take priority.

Children taught to make decisions based on right or wrong view. Subjective thinking.

Activities and interests are unbalanced in favor of adults.

Quick to anger. "React" to stressful situations.

Teaching and modeling appropriate and successful behavior and decision making are minimal.

Warmth and support are limited.

Results. Children often have low self-esteem and have difficulty making decisions later in life. Often obedient and proficient but insecure, low self-esteem, and prone to resentment and depression. They may excel in academics and the career field. But when they do, it can be due to obedience rather than a desire to pursue their interest and talent, thus are not happy.

Authoritative (supportive)

Controlling, but not overly strict.

Have rules that are relevant to safety and learning. Rules are consistently and applied.

Expect compliance, but the opportunity is provided to dialogue and learn from the experience.

Communication is two ways between parent and child.

Knows about and involved in their children's social life.

Show interest in their children's activities. Praise accomplishments and supportive when there are failures. Ensure opportunities for positive social experiences.

Empathetic to the child's feelings and emotions. Use effective behavior modification strategies (see Chapter 27)

Punishment administered firmly, consistently, and fairly and appropriate for the infraction.

Shows respect and sensitivity.

Child allowed to express needs, wants, and feelings, even when encouraged.

Family needs and wants are balanced.

Children taught to make decisions considering all views.

Objective thinking.

Consensus building. Prioritize family activities are balanced to meet the needs of all family members.

Slow to anger. "Respond," too stressful situations.

Are proactive in teaching and modeling appropriate and successful behavior and decision making.

Results. Children have high self-esteem, good interpersonal relations, and are happy. They perform well in academic and professional settings. They score high in warmth and support.

Indulgent (permissive)

Not strict.

Few if any rules and standards.

Desire compliance but do not enforce it.

Communication is two-way.

Knows about the child's social life but not necessarily knowledgeable of who they are with or what they may be doing.

Show interest in their children's activities. Praise accomplishments and supportive when there are failures. Ensure opportunities for positive social experiences.

Empathetic to the child's feelings and emotions. May or may not use effective behavior modification strategies.

Punishment not administered firmly and consistently.

Shows respect and sensitivity. Child allowed to express needs, wants, and feelings, even encouraged to do so.

Family needs and wants are often unbalanced in favor of the child's demands.

Children taught to make decisions based on considering all views. Slow to anger.

Are ineffective in teaching and modeling appropriate and successful behavior and decision making.

Score high in warmth and support.

Results. Children with indulgent parents are often spoiled, self-centered, and lack self-discipline. They tend not to do well in school and struggle with authority. They often have a poor work ethic, thus will be challenged in the job market.

Uninvolved or Neglecting

Few rules or demands.

Little communication.

May meet the basic needs of children but often neglect the needs, wants, and desires of their children.

Score low in warmth and support.

Results. Children of neglectful parents feel rejected and unloved. They tend to lack self-discipline, have low self-esteem, have poor social skills, and are unhappy and even depressed. They often do not perform well in school or in the job market.

Since the authoritative parenting style will most likely result in the happiest and successful children, why don't all parents utilize an authoritative parenting style? The answers are complicated, but generally involve differences in culture, educational and socioeconomic status, and religion. Also, personality differences and parenting styles of each of both parents may differ, thus creating a mix of styles and confusion to children. Parents who grew up under the influence of poor parenting styles will often pass on their ineffective parenting strategies to their children, going on for generations unless the cycle is broken by those who can change the ineffective parenting they were exposed to as children. Parents who have experienced childhood traumas can result in psychological issues that influence how they react to their families. A child who experienced abuse will sometimes become an abuser. A child who was not made to feel loved may have difficulty in loving. When a child has a disability or a strong temperament, it will add even more significant challenges for parents. Authoritative parents can have children who choose to behave in a defiant or delinquent behavior. Conversely parents with permissive styles can have children who display personality traits that result in positive outcomes in school and socially. There is no single template that applies to every child.

Somewhere between the authoritarian parent and the authoritative parent is the "helicopter" parent. They care deeply for their children and want their children to succeed but do so by controlling every aspect of their lives. They set high goals, then to meet these goals, they strictly enforce rigid schedules and demand adherence to exacting structure and standards. Children must strive to always win in a "win-lose" scenario. Many psychologists theorize that such parents are attempting to fulfill their own unfulfilled personal and professional dreams by having their children accomplish what they were unable to do. Of course, a parent who tries to live their life or some aspect of it through their child may not necessarily manifest all the parenting styles of a real "helicopter parent."

The development of a cohesive parenting approach requires considerable cooperation, communication, and compromise. Parents are not purely one style or another but will vacillate between the different styles. The goal should be to study and focus on the authoritative style. Try to emulate it as much as possible and be willing to adjust as required. Most of you reading this book are proficient in some area. Few, if any of you can honestly admit you learned your parenting skill all by yourself. You learned because of what you were taught from your parents or grandparents. You took a course, you read, you checked things out on some media source. Do not feel you need to perform the most crucial assignment you have been given in life all by yourself—being a parent. There are thousands of resources available to you. Friends and extended family members, books, videos, TV specials, support groups, professional counseling services, case managers, church, and community organizations, to name a few. Seek them out, use them! Doing so will help with parenting and can help relieve much of the stress associated with raising your children.

It has been shown that a child's chances for success in school and life are most influenced by parenting styles that establish clear rules and guidelines that are consistently enforced fairly and equitably, and combined with open communication, support and encouragement.

Chapter 31
How to Maintain Family Harmony

It does not take scientific research to prove that disharmony in a family will have negative consequences on a child's ability to perform efficiently in school or socially. Going through life without conflict is impossible. For many, this conflict turns into arguments, fighting and discord resulting in miscommunication, hurt feelings, sadness, broken relationships, and on occasion, physical violence. The parties strive to get over on the other with an attitude that someone must "win" and someone must "lose." But conflict does not always have to result in discord or have a "win-lose" philosophy. It is possible to create a situation where all win. When discussing a topic that has the potential for conflict, it is essential to share opinions and feelings. If you hold on to your position and don't ever hear or understand the views or feelings of others, the conflict will not be resolved and probably escalate it into something ugly. To keep this from happening, agree to a few rules that will help reduce discord and increase peace. Family harmony is created by the ability of family members to live together in balance, with mutual respect and support. Under the "TIPS section, I provide suggestions for having to avoid family discord and promoting harmony. But first, let's look at what NOT to do.

The key to family harmony—effective communication

Ineffective communication often ends up in disagreements escalating into hurt feelings, anger, loud arguments often including shouting and screaming, breaking things, and even violence. When there is no resolution, the issue(s) causing the conflict to remain, only to be raised again in the future. When you send a message to another, do you want the other person to retaliate in anger or to shut you out in frustration? Or would you rather they hear you out and try to understand your feelings and views.

Here are a few things to avoid when having a sensitive conversation with another.

- **Poor timing.** Frequently, when a person feels highly emotional about something, they feel a need to resolve it right away. But the time to discuss it may not be the best time for the other party. If one or the other is tired, stressed, busy, drinking, or with other people, the chance for a successful outcome is significantly reduced.

- **Blaming.** The presumption of "I am right, and you are wrong" will often result in efforts to blame the other. This can take the form of accusing ("you failed to…"), exaggerating ("you always…"), or assuming evil intentions ("you cheated"). Note how often the word "you" appears in these examples. The use of the word "you" will often be perceived as blaming and judgmental. Using the word "you" is like pointing a finger. People don't like it so don't use it unless, of course, you are looking for pushback.

- **Too many issues.** When angry, it is common to use as much ammunition as possible. Bringing up any topic you can think of to support your position and "defeat" the other is the objective.

- **Anger** is the only emotion expressed. Other underlying feelings, such as fear, sadness, guilt, envy, disappointment are obscured by the anger.

- **Impossible demands.** Unfair fights often include obscure and vague demands, such as "don't be so picky" or "be more considerate." Such orders seldom work because changes in habits or personalities do not change quickly.

- **Threats and ultimatums.** "If you do that again, I'll leave." "If you don't stop that, I'll smack you." "I won't love you anymore."

- **Names or labels** such as selfish, foolish, stupid, liar, lazy, worthless, mean, bully, thief, drunk, are meant to hurt, and they usually do. Because they do hurt, expect the other person to defend themselves. Do not expect the conflict to end constructively.
- **Sarcasm**. Sarcasm is usually couched in humor that covers some negative emotion such as anger or hurt. Unless the listener is exceptionally naïve, they will pick up sarcasm and either retaliate in anger or be pushed away.
- **Dragging up the past.** Often, when frustrated or angry, we tend to bring up issues from the past. Interestingly, they seldom even have any relevance to the current discussion. We do this because when we are in a high-emotional state, our temper rises. Issues that are still unresolved will come up, if for nothing else, to get them off our chest. The result is it confuses the issue at hand and opens old wounds rather than helping resolve the current dilemma.
- **Negative comparisons**. Comparing a person to another to put that person down sends the message that you think he/she is somehow inferior. No one likes to be put down, even if they may be guilty of something.

If someone else came at you with remarks like those above, how do you think you would feel and react?

Here is an example of a mom who is setting up a situation that will create negative feelings. Mom sees her son with a shirt on that she feels inappropriate to wear when getting ready to visit with relatives. Mom says to her son (in a loud voice), "Gary, I see you are wearing that silly shirt again. Go change it right away." What kind of reaction do you think Mom is going to get from her son? Even if Gary obeys, it probably will not be done willingly.

Let's try re-structuring this message so that Gary will be more inclined to respond to Mom's wishes agreeably and not be made to feel controlled. When speaking with another, try using these four types of expressions: what you see or **observe,** what you **think**, what you **feel**, and what you **need or want.** To use this strategy, you must be sincere with yourself and with the other person(s). It does not mean blaming, accusing, or dumping on others. It means to focus on yourself, not the other. It means expressing your feelings and how you came to feel this way. It does not mean it is OK to be rude, aggressive, or insensitive. How is this done? Let's look at an example.

"Gary, I **see** you are wearing your pants that have holes in them." **(Observation)**

"I know they are the fad. However, I don't **think** it is appropriate for the family reunion." **(Thought)**

"**I feel anxious** that your aunts and uncles might think I don't provide you with nice clothes." **(Feeling)**

"I would be more comfortable if you wore pants without holes in them." **Would you mind changing**? **(Want)**

Here are a few examples that do not use the **Observation, Thought, Feeling,** and **Want/ Suggestion/Request)** technique.

Words that create disharmony:

"Gary, you **need** to go change right now!" (People do not like to be told what they "need" to do. Try to avoid that word.)

"If only **you** would learn to dress appropriately for the occasion." (The word "you" is often perceived as accusatory.)

"**I can't believe** you would do that." ("I can't believe" is a put down).

"Wear what **I tell you** to wear, **or we will** leave you home." (A demand, followed by a shallow threat)

"I **know what your problem is** you like to party too much." (An accusatory judgment of the other person… probably incorrect)

"**Stop that** right now **or you cannot go** out Saturday." (A demand followed by a consequence that has no connection to the misdeed, and often will not even be enforced.)

If someone else came at you with remarks like those above, how do you think you would feel and react? Note that these examples have one or more of the following implied messages: demanding or ordering, accusative, blaming, judgmental, and threatening (sometimes shallow, as in the last example). It should be noted that these types of messages are often delivered in a tone of voice that helps to elicit even more defensiveness than the words alone. In other words, the tone of voice (yelling, scolding, nagging, belittling, whining, etc.) adds fuel to the fire. Body language can also send messages that result in defensiveness. Crossed arms, shaking fingers, waving of hands are but a few examples negative body languages.

Here are more examples of parents using the **Observation, Thought, Feeling, Want/Suggestion/Request strategy.**

"Kevin, you are making quite a bit of noise." **(Observation)** "Do you think this may be interfering with your big sister's ability to concentrate on her homework?" **(Thought)** "How do you feel about that?" **(Feeling)** "I am sure she would appreciate it if you were quieter." **(Suggestion)**

"Susan, I noticed that your school papers were left on the dining room table." **(Observation)** "When we clear the table in preparation for dinner, the papers may get misplaced." **(Thought)** "We don't want that to happen." **(Feeling)** "How about if you put your papers in your folder, so you will know where they are later?" **(Suggestion)**

"George, I had to close the front door after you left for school this morning." **(Observation)** "This sure does not help our electric bill, does it?" **(Thought)** "Dad gets upset when we don't help conserve electricity." **(Feeling)** "Dad would appreciate it if you would remember to shut the door when leaving the house." **(Want/Request)**

"Ann, you got home late last night and did not call to tell us you were going to be delayed." **(Observation)** "We expected you back at midnight." **(Expectation)** "When you did not get home on time or call us, we worry." **(Feeling)** "Can we count on you in the future to adhere to the house rule?" **(Request)**

Family meetings: A key to family harmony is the ability to communicate with one another effectively. An excellent way to maintain family harmony is to establish procedures that prevent discord in the first place. When issues do arise, have a system in place to address and resolve them in a logical, non-confrontational manner. An excellent method to help promote family communication, promote harmony and balance, and avoid conflict is to have periodic family meetings. But for family meetings to work, the family must use it. It cannot work if not used in a conscientious, routine manner. Get the family together and present the idea. If all agree to use it, then agree to an established time to meet. NO excuses! Turn off the television, turn off cell phones. Just do it!

TIPS
FOR RESOLVING FAMILY ISSUES (AND AVOIDING DISCORD)

All families have issues that must be addressed from time to time. When not addressed early, they can (and often do) escalate into dispute. An effective way to avoid dis-harmony is to have family meetings. A family meeting can involve two or more family members, depending on the situation. Here is how to do it.

Rules: First, establish ground rules. All family members old enough to understand must agree to the rules. For example:

- Be honest.
- Take responsibility for your actions and feelings.
- No blaming or finger-pointing.
- Give others the right to their own opinions. In other words, "agree to disagree."
- No complaining.
- Control emotions. If one feels themselves getting emotional or angry, leave the room until composure is regained.
- Encourage participation by all, but do not force.
- Take turns speaking and listening. When one is talking, give that person your undivided attention. Do that for them and the more likely they will do the same for you.

When you are the speaker:

- Explain your point of view. But keep it brief and use the "Rules for Effective Messaging" presented below.

- Use the "Observation," "Think," "Feel," "Want/Suggestion/ Request" technique.
- Avoid blaming, name calling, and game playing.

When you are the listener:

- Give your full attention to the other person. Strive to understand their feelings, opinions, and needs.
- Do not disagree, argue, or correct anything the other has to say.
- Use the listening strategies described in Chapter 11.
- Once the speaker has finished his/her thought, the listener concludes by paraphrasing or summarizing what he/she heard the speaker said to help ensure a complete understanding as possible. Now the roles are reversed, and the "speaker" becomes the "listener."

 Family meetings: Set aside a time for family meetings. Emphasize that there are one or more issues the family must address, and it is best done when all are involved. Preferably the meeting should be on the same day and time every week. Sunday evening is a good time, as weekly schedules and plans can be discussed and coordinated as well as any issues of concern. Any family member can call special meetings should they feel the need. If one person attempts to avoid the discussion, state something like, "This is important to me and it will not go away. I want to resolve it. Can we talk it out? How about tonight at 7?

- Have an agenda. Make a list of items to discuss. All family members can contribute even the youngest ones. Cover old unresolved issues first, then go to new topics of concern.
- Take turns facilitating the group. The leader starts the meeting and makes sure the rules are followed and ends the session at the agreed-upon time. Meeting should not go beyond 60 minutes. The shorter the better.

 Constructive discussion strategies: Whether in a family

meeting or a one-on-one discussion, there are effective ways to communicate that can maximize effective communication and minimize the chance of disharmony. Here are some strategies.

- **State the problem**. Clearly say what the issue is. If you can put it in the **Observation, Thought, Feeling** and **Want/Suggestion/Request technique, do it!**

- **Stick to the issue**. Discuss only one issue at a time. More than one can obscure the current issue or tempt one or the other to bring up past issues.

- **Use "I" messages and express "feelings" as much as possible.** For example, rather than saying, "*You* made me so angry this afternoon," say, "*I* felt so angry this afternoon."

- **Propose change.** State what is needed or desired and be as specific as possible.

- **Describe consequences.** Describe any emotional, practical, financial, or health benefits.

- **Prevent escalation.** If the conversation begins to get emotional, try these preventive measures. (1) Watch non-verbal behavior—rising voice, pacing, finger or arm-waving, clenched fists, head shaking, etc. (2) Stop talking and breathe deeply. Take a few minutes to calm down. (3) If necessary, take a "time out." To do this agree, in advance to signal, such as a T sign as is used during a sports time out. No "last words." As soon as a time out is called, stop talking immediately. Leave one another for a short break and return at the agreed-upon time.

- **Avoid using the word "you"** when you have a concern about what another does, doesn't do, or is not doing. "You" statements, often are perceived by the other as an attempt to place blame on the other person, resulting in their becoming defensive. In so doing they counter-attack and potential for an argument is the result.

- **Focus on your feelings and thoughts.** When you focus on the other, you are telling them that you have more authority about their thoughts and feelings, and you are going to tell them how it is can often elicit defensiveness from the other person. Continual focus on the other is also a way for some to avoid accepting responsibility for one's thoughts, feelings, and actions. It may take practice. Many of us have become so accustomed to focusing on others that we forget to focus on ourselves. Ironically, it is when we begin to focus on ourselves that opens the door to the resolution of problems.

- **Express feelings.** A better strategy than focusing on another ("you") is to focus on yourself by using words that express your feelings, such as I am hurt, worried, sorry, confused, or angry. Define your concerns by stating, "I feel...," or "It makes me feel..."

- **Ask everyone's opinion.** Consider the pros and cons of all the options.

- **Timing**: When you have an issue that you feel needs discussion, set a time and place with the other person. Avoid pushing an issue that one or the other has energy on or that has the potential to become emotional. Addressing such a point at the wrong time will usually result in a disappointing outcome. Examples of poor timing are when one or the other is preoccupied, stressed out, or emotionally strained. When the discussion does take place, turn off all distractions such as television and music. If children are in the household, have the conversation when they are not present. Emotional discussions are best done face to face. Telephone or e-mail should only be used if necessary.

- **Use the "and" stance**. Using the word "and" helps to underscore the fact that there is more than one view on issues. "I believe in you, and I am sure you can do it, *and* I am fearful of a few things that may be challenging." Do not use the word "but." "But" tends to negate. "I believe in you, and am sure you can do it, *but* I am afraid some challenges will be too tough." Note that the first example sends the message that you have more than one feeling on an issue, whereas the second example negates the vote of confidence of the words "I believe in you."

- **Explore the facts.** Often, something that happens is the result of one or more things that each has done or failed to do. Take the time to be a detective and thoroughly and honestly find out what is giving rise to the issue. For example, a Mom is upset at her teenage daughter for leaving dirty glasses and dishes around the house after use. What Mom may not realize is that she has helped to contribute to her daughter's bad habit of not picking up after herself by previously picking up after her daughter. In other words, she has enabled the practice even though it bothers her. For years she has continued to do it rather than addressing the issue promptly. Once you have a good idea of what may have caused the concern, rather than emotionally reacting, explore ways of possible resolution or compromise and how the problem can be avoided in the future.
- **Get the other's viewpoint.** To argue about who is right and who is wrong will do little to resolve a conflict. It is essential to realize that you don't know the other person's thoughts, feeling, and opinions. If we do not understand the other person's viewpoint or story, we tend to try to persuade the other to our way of thinking. People do not like to be forced, told, or persuaded. When done, it often will end up in an argument and arguments push others away rather than pull them together. More compelling is influencing the other to consider options and make a choice on their own. When self-choices are made, the likelihood of following through is significantly increased. Sometimes understanding the other person's story will not solve the problem, but it will promote discussion and avoid an argument. To help find the other's viewpoint, try these strategies.
- **Ask questions** to increase understanding.
- **Appreciate differences** in values, habits, thoughts, feelings. We are all different. Trying to get others to our way of

thinking may merely be an exercise in futility with resulting in disharmony. Avoid value judgments.

- **Do not assume you know the other person's "intent."** Just because we perceive something as so, does not mean another sees or thinks the same way. Many arguments can be avoided by merely trying to understand the other person's viewpoint, feelings, and priorities. This does not mean that we must agree, by the way. What should be sought is "understanding," not necessarily "agreement."

- **Disagreements are inevitable:** People will always have different opinions, values, and feelings, tastes, preferences, fears, and needs. Thus, it is unavoidable that family members will not always agree on everything. There is no avoiding it. Disagreements are OK— discord is not OK

Two final suggestions:

Forgive! Often it is difficult to forgive another when you are angry at them. I recently saw a billboard that said, "Forgive! Now!" What is behind the two-word powerful message? Because when you do not forgive, you get to keep your negative feelings. Holding on to negative emotions also contributes to dis-harmony with family and friends. It can be stated that unwillingness to forgive has created more interpersonal discord than any other factor. Distinguish between "forgiving" and "forgetting." When you forgive you free yourself of a burden. "Forgetting" would be ideal, but if the hurt is so great, you will remember. But learn from the issue and move on.

In Chapter 9, I addressed the importance of forgiveness. Although the guidance provided herein can apply to anyone, often it is one or more family members with whom we have emotional issues. These are the person(s) we are most likely to have hurt or have been hurt by. I recently heard a sermon by a local pastor who has been speaking on Jesus' parables (stories). At this sermon, he spoke on forgiveness. Pastor Josh explained that when we feel that an injustice has been inflicted on us, we feel hurt. To try to make the hurt go away, we are tempted to inflict hurt on the other. When we do so, what happens? Discord! Does it make the pain go away? No! It often makes things worse. What can we do then? Forgive! "What, forgive the person who has hurt us?" "Yes," says Pastor Josh. Doing so may not make the pain go away (at least right away), but it will not make it worse. Retaliation, on the other hand, will make it worse. "Do not try to make the other forgive you," warns Josh, "rather forgive yourself and forgive the other. If you cannot forgive, at least have pity." Try hard not to re-play the issue(s) in your mind over and over. When you find yourself doing this (and you will), re-focus on more pleasant memories. Think of what you have rather than what you do not have. I have a close friend whose mother abandoned her as an infant. Years later, after meeting, even though the daughter had become successful, rather than asking for forgiveness, the mother unjustifiable criticized her daughter. The daughter, rather than retaliating with resentment and anger, forgave her mother. By so doing, she was able to rid herself of the pain she had been carrying. By the way, my friend's inner strength—the ability to forgive, came from her sincere spirituality.

Finally, remember to laugh. Humor is one of the Lord's greatest gifts. Laugh at yourself and WITH others, but not AT them.

Chapter 32
Helping with Organization, Time Management and Homework

In SECTION B of the "Students' Guide," I provide suggestions for students on strategies for goal setting, preparation, dealing with obstacles, and organization. SECTION D is devoted to studying strategies. In this chapter, I will offer suggestions on what parents can do to support children with the organization, managing time, and homework.

Unfortunately, few children enjoy doing things that involve work and that includes homework. It is natural to do preferred activities over non-preferred activities. Thus, children will find ways to do the preferred activity (do you blame them?). Being with friends (either in person or on their computer or cell phone), watching television, listening to music, playing games, sleeping, will often win out over starting the drudgery of doing the most important things first.

Like it or not, homework is essential for school success. The challenge is how to get children to do homework without causing conflict. Parents also ask, "How do my support strategies differ as my child progresses through school." Here are a few suggestions. Keep in mind that they are only general guidelines. Procedures will vary from child to child depending on their individual needs, personalities, strengths, and weaknesses. For detailed guidance refer to books such as *How to Help Your Child with Homework* by Marguite C. Radenich and Jeanne Shay, or *Homework Without Tears* by Lee Canter and Lee Hausner.

It is important to realize that your role as a parent is to supplement the teacher by encouraging, guiding, and supporting your child. **The parent can best help by re-enforcing what the teacher is teaching at the time.** For older students, if you are comfortable with the subject matter, parental tutoring can help. But don't be tempted to do the child's homework for them (and this is a big temptation, I know). The goal of the parent is to make homework a positive experience.

Helping your child to establish effective organizational and time-management habits will have a direct bearing on their ability to deal with homework.

TIPS
To Help Students with Organization and Use Time Efficiently

Organization. It is no secret that good organization and time management skills will go a long way to helping students do well in school, home, and on the job. For many people using strategies that help with organization can be a challenge. When was the last time you misplaced your car keys, cell phone, or remote control? It can be a struggle for parents as well. Look at these "TIPS" to see if there might be a few ideas that may help.

Start with a Time Log. Before your students can get started on how to improve their time management, they need to know how they are currently spending their time. Have them record (out of school) on paper everything they do for one week. Review the log with your child at the end of the week. Ask them how they think they can better use their time to help meet their goals and priorities more effectively. You may wish to review Chapters 4 and 7 that guide the student on goal setting, organization, and time management. The log, when done faithfully and honestly, will quickly identify time zappers. Look for things such as spending time on the cell phone or social media, watching television, surfing on the internet, looking for items that have been misplaced, or oversleeping. Point out that when they can identify just 30 minutes of non-productive time per day, they will add over 3 hours per week or over 12 hours per month towards achieving their high-priority goals. If they can find 1 hour per day, it equals 7 hours per week or 28 hours per month. That is a lot of saved time!

Review the goals they set for themselves. What did they do or fail to do that would help them achieve the goals they set for themselves? What can they do to help improve their productivity? How can they work on "habits" that are robbing them of using their time wisely? See Chapter 32.

Review with your student the technique for prioritizing, as described in Chapter 7.

Encourage them to have a "plan" and a method to routinely evaluate that plan. An efficient way is to include in their plan: 1) What they plan to do, 2) When they plan on starting and finishing, 3) After completed, have them record the actual time they started and finished. Without comments on your part, ask them to critique themselves by telling you what went right and what can be improved. They will figure it out themselves, which is the best learning experience.

When your child procrastinates. Don't nag or scold! Doing so will cause resentment and do nothing to motivate. Suggest that they take a few moments to relax and then proceed with the task. Encourage them to use the strategies described in Chapter 16, which explain how taking breaks and studying when most productive can help with recall. These strategies can help to deal with procrastination. Remember, we usually put off doing things we would prefer not to do. When we use strategies to help take the pressure off, such as knowing that we do not have to work when we are not mentally and physically at our best, or that we will not be subjected to countless hours of tedious work, one is more motivated to get started. Have them post a sign in their room that says, "Am I making wise use of my time?"

Allow your child to experience the consequences of not managing their time. One or two times of staying up until the wee hours, getting a poor grade, or missing a favored activity because they failed to complete an important project can serve as a powerful motivator.

Use calendars! Have your child mark due dates, test dates, birthdays, school holidays, special events, extracurricular activities, etc.

Encourage them to prepare for the next school day before they go to bed.

Help them organize their rooms and study area. When children have developed habits that foster good organization, it will have positive effects on their ability to perform homework. Desks should be appropriately stocked with necessary items such as pencils, pens, pencil sharpeners, paper, erasers, reference materials, and anything else your student needs. They should not have to waste valuable time looking for items they need to do their homework efficiently.

Help organize backpacks and binders. Use pocket folders for handouts and assignments to avoid loose papers. Use resealable plastic bags for small items such as pencils, pens, paper clips, erasers, etc. Binders should be organized by subject. I prefer three-ring binders to spiral binders. The reason is papers are more secure. Students will fold papers and place them in the spiral binder and guess what… they fall out.

TIPS

To Help with Homework Elementary School

Provide a homework area that has adequate workspace, lighting, and no distractions.

Establish a written schedule that includes extracurricular activities, relaxing/down time, family time, and study time. Also, consider the needs of the child. Some children may prefer to study right after they get him from school—others later in the evening. There is no uniform "best time" to do homework. But once the time is established, it is important to lock study time into the schedule and stick to it. Help your child keep to the schedule! Children will try to wiggle out of it. And there may be exceptions from time to time. But the more routine the schedule becomes, the more comfortable your child will grow with it, and the less resistance you will get.

Clearly express your expectations and standards. Communicate in a firm yet unemotional manner. Avoid anger, arguing, or begging. Doing so will de-motivate.

Insist that homework be done according to the teacher's expectations and deadlines. Listen to excuses, but do not give in to them. Do not show disappointment when a child does not do well or perform to your expectations. Just keep encouraging positively. Provide incentives when children comply with the schedule and adequately complete homework assignments.

Apply natural consequences (Chapter 27) if your child does not comply with repeated requests.

Avoid last-minute cram sessions or written work that is hastily done. Communicate with your child's teacher. Doing so will not only ensure that you know what is expected, but it will also keep your kid from the temptation to manipulate.

Teach your children the study skills outlined in SECTIONS D and E.

Have fun. Make learning enjoyable with games and "hands-on" examples to demonstrate concepts.

Link new ideas and concepts to what the child already knows. In other words, use "mental pictures."

Read. Reading is essential for learning vocabulary, grammar, and spelling. Insist that your child turn off the TV, put down his/her mobile device, and read at least an hour every day. Set an example by reading yourself.

Review tests and written assignments with your child. Make corrections and emphasize that learning from mistakes is part of the learning process. I stress again, do not scold, instead encourage.

Adjust your support according to age and grade.

Middle School

The middle schooler should now be able to start his/her homework on their own. Gentle reminders may be necessary. If they do not respond, then keep reminding without showing anger. Apply "natural consequences as described in Chapter 24 if necessary.

Encourage and praise but don't overdo it, and when you do, do it with sincerity.

Communicate with your child's teacher. Middle schoolers are becoming much more independent and better at manipulating. Thus, regular communication with teachers is even more important than when your child was in elementary school.

High School

High school students are expected to begin and complete homework independently.

Re-enforce. You may have to re-enforce organizational habits and their use of weekly planners.

Acknowledge and praise. Teenagers do not expect nor wish continual praise as was done when they were younger. But this does not mean that they should not be acknowledged for effort and jobs well done.

Attend parent-teacher conferences. Do not hesitate to speak with teachers in person or by email if you have questions or concerns about your child's school performance.

Suggest. Teachers welcome suggestions as to how you can be supportive of them or your child. Encourage the use of strategies presented in SECTION E.

SECTION I
Different Paths

Invest in the human soul.
Who knows, it might be a diamond in the rough.
Mary McLeod Bethune

Chapter 33
Learning Differences

In this chapter, I review many types of learning differences to help you identify your child's learning style or learning challenges, if applicable. Many students underachieve in school because they have trouble completing assignments, difficulty with comprehension, or behavioral problems. There are many reasons for academic challenges. I will not attempt to address all of them. Although psychological, sociological, motivational, and economic factors come in to play, often the culprit may be a learning preference that affects academic success. Everyone does not learn in the same way. There are generally three types of learners.

1. Sensual learners: auditory, verbal, visual, and kinesthetic (feeling)
2. Reasoning learners: deductive, inductive, logical
3. Environmental learners: intrapersonal, interpersonal

Classroom instruction favors auditory and visual learners. A kinesthetic learner or a child whose strength is other than the auditory or verbal can be at a disadvantage in the traditional school. Modern-day education systems are much more knowledgeable about learning styles than in years past. Many teachers are taught to recognize and respond to such differences. By identifying learning preferences, study methods can be altered to favor the student's strengths rather than his/her weaknesses. When a student has a teacher, who does not seem to recognize a learning difference or how to teach to varied learning differences, a student may not be able to do much about it. Nevertheless, the student can better respond and adjust if he/she is aware of what works best for them. The following is a little more about these learning styles to help students identify their preferred style.

Auditory are effective listeners. They prefer to follow verbal stimuli rather than written or visual stimuli. These students would prefer the lecture over reading assignments. Listening to educational broadcasts on the computer, podcasts, CDs, etc. are effective for the person with an auditory preference.

Verbal learners think while speaking thus may tend to be verbose. Verbals are good speakers. They may become bored with subjects such as math but may like to read. For verbal learners, reciting out loud and repeating lessons to other, is effective.

Visual learners, (sometimes referred to as "spatial" learners), prefer to see things to understand better. In general, visual learners like anything that is in pictures such as charts, photos, films, outlines, diagrams, and things are written on the black/green board. They like art and would prefer reading a textbook over lecture. Mind Maps, as described in Chapter 16, is useful for a visual learner.

Kinesthetic (tactile learning) learners prefer physical activity such as hands-on assignments, writing, and individual assignments. Kinesthetic learners may find sitting in a classroom and listening to a lecture too confining. They want to be actively doing something, such as making a model or poster. Role play, demonstrating, and teaching others works well for the student with kinesthetic bias.

Deductive reasoners like to look at the big picture and then focus on the details. They want to be clear on the instructions before embarking on an assignment.

Inductive reasoners like to see examples when first introduced to a new subject, before developing an overview. They prefer to learn as they go along.

Logical learners tend to be organized and are planners. They can easily see patterns. They do well in math and science. They generally do well in the traditional classroom but may be challenged with tasks requiring creative tasks.

Intrapersonal learners are more introverted and independent. They prefer to work alone or with only one other person rather than a group. They work well in quiet places.

Interpersonal learners are social and prefer interacting with others. They like group projects, debates, and open discussions. On the downside, the interpersonal student will often get admonished for talking in class.

Although people prefer one or two of the described learning styles, most will use several. In other words, we may be able to identify a primary preference, but we should be able to also see your child in several.

The term **"Learning Disability" or "LD"** was coined in 1963 by parents and educators determined to better understand and assist children who were smart but were challenged in the classroom. The group came up with the term "Learning Disability" to help define different learning styles. They begin working with school systems on how best to adapt teaching methodologies to children who require different teaching approaches to maximize learning in school. The group called itself the "Learning Disability Association (LDA)." There may be a local chapter in your area. Although the LDA and some educators and behavior specialists use the term "Learning Disability," many parents and professionals prefer to use the term "Learning Difference." I prefer the latter. Just because one person is challenged with math and another with reading, for example, does not mean that either has a "disability." It is quite possible, if not probable that the student who has trouble with math is a strong reader, and the weak reader is strong at math.

Even though I have used the term "Learning Differences," the federal definition of a "Learning Disability" includes "such conditions as perceptual disabilities, brain injury, minimal brain dysfunction, dyslexia, and developmental aphasia. LD does not include visual and hearing impairment, motor disabilities, mental retardation, emotional disorders, environmental, cultural, or economic disadvantage. LD is also not the same as autism. For these reasons and because of the complex nature of LD's, diagnosing and treatment can be challenging. (Turkington, Carol, and Harris, Joseph R. *The A to Z of Learning Disabilities*)

A "learning disability" is a general set or group of disorders that can affect a person's ability to understand, speak, listen, read, write, spell, calculate, or reason. An LD can affect school, work, daily routines, family life, and interpersonal relationships. Because learning disabilities cannot be seen, such as is the case with a physical disability, they can often go unidentified.

More examples of LDs: Dyslexia is a common condition that results in students having problems primarily with reading, but can also affect writing, spelling, and speaking. Students who have Dyscalculia have difficulty with numbers and how to manipulate numbers, thus resulting in challenges with arithmetic. Auditory Processing Disorder (APD) is a condition manifested by problems in the auditory modality that affect day-to-day communication and learning abilities. APD has been called the auditory equivalent of dyslexia. Parents, if you suspect your child has a learning difference or a condition that interferes with their ability to perform well in school, speak to your child's school counselor or your primary care physician. **Such conditions can cause children to not only fail in school, but can adversely affect family, social, and career. Thus, it is imperative to identify and begin treatment as soon as possible.**

Here are other kinds of disabilities: "Academic Learning Disability" (trouble learning reading, writing, or math); "Language Learning Disability" (difficulty expressing thoughts and ideas, or understanding others words); "Motor Disability" (difficulty with motor skills such as holding a pencil, games, or sports); "Social Skills Deficit" (difficulty understanding how others feel, or reading others' non-verbal signals, such as body language. (Fisher and Cummings. *The Survival Guide for Kids with LD)*

A prevalent condition that adversely affects learning, yet many professionals may not classify it as a Learning Disability, is Attention Deficit Hyperactivity Disorder (ADHD). ADHD can often co-exist with an LD. Symptoms of ADHD are inattention, impulsiveness, and hyperactivity. Such traits often adversely affect a student's ability to succeed in school. Fortunately, most ADHD challenges can be treated with medication and behavior therapy. If your child is being treated with medication, ask the practitioner if a behavior therapy program combined with medication may be more effective than just medication alone.

Other disorders that are not technically defined as LD and can affect success in school and can even co-exist with an LD include Manic Depression, Anxiety Disorder, and Information Processing Disorders.

What are some signs that may indicate a learning difference (disability)?

Problems getting along with peers.
Difficulty with reading, writing, or math.
Visual or hearing problems.
Disinterest in age-appropriate activities.
Difficulty communicating.
Extreme emotional swings.
Slow to respond to change, or resistant to change.
Anxiety with test taking.

In their book *Bright Kids Who Can't Keep Up.* Ellen Braaten, Ph.D., and Brian Willoughby, Ph.D., define a condition they term "processing speed." It is a complex neurological condition that is more common than many parents realize. The condition can "cut across disorders such as learning disabilities, developmental disabilities and attention problems, and can be quite frustrating for children and their parents." Generally, the processing speed can be defined as the amount of time it takes to perceive information and to respond effectively. In other words, state Braaten and Willoughby, it is "how long it takes to get something done." After evaluating and treating hundreds of children, both psychologists noted that many diagnosed with processing speed issues are quite intelligent, although actions and thought processes were slower than the average student.

Braaten and Willoughby provide a checklist for parents to help identify processing speed issues. They divide them into five categories: Verbal/Listening Processing; Visual Processing; Motoric

Processing; Academic Processing; and General Processing with Processing Speed.

1. **Verbal/Listening Processing**

    Appears not to listen to others

    Doesn't seem to understand directions.

    Can't seem to follow instructions.

    Becomes overwhelmed with too much verbal information.

    Needs more time to answer questions.

    Answers questions with short responses.

    Does not participate in class discussions.

    Has trouble retrieving information from memory.

    Can't keep up with the pace of lectures.

    Makes a lot of grammatical errors in writing.

    Had problems sustaining focused attention during social activities.

    Needs additional time to respond to conversations.

2. **Visual Processing**

    Don't pay close attention to details.

    Has difficulty proofreading work.

    Makes careless errors.

    Don't grasp the subtle visual cues of social relationships.

    Neglects to look at important visual information.

    Omits phrases or words in writing.

3. **Motoric Processing**

    Seems tired, even after a good night's sleep.

    Seems lazy or unmotivated.

    Moves slowly on fine motor skills (e.g., writing); or gross motor skill (e.g., catching a ball).

    Reluctant to start tasks.

    Can do assignments, but not in the time allotted.

    Slow to physical aspects of writing.

4. **Academic Processing**

   Frequently seems absent-minded.

   Has difficulty taking notes in class.

   Has trouble formulating and expressing ideas in writing.

   Exhibits inconsistent academic performance.

   Lacks fluency when reading aloud.

   Becomes distracted during academic tasks.

   Makes punctuation and capitalization errors.

   Makes spelling errors in writing spite or otherwise being a good speller.

5. **General Problems with Processing Speed**

   Often looks confused.

   Frequently seems absentminded.

   Lacks persistence in completing any task.

   Avoids tasks that require sustained attention or focus.

   Generally, seems slow much of the time.

   Needs extra time to complete tasks.

   Forgets information that he/she just learned the day before.

   Frequently responds, "What?"

   Starts strong but then wanders off task or "time out."

   Impulsively rushes through tasks.

   Is hesitant to participate in social situations or conversations.

TIPS
FOR ASSISTING CHILDREN WITH LEARNING DIFFERENCES

As you match the characteristics as they relate to your child, realize that most children will manifest only some descriptions. Recognize the frequency and the intensity that your child exhibits the various symptoms. If your child displays many symptoms, then it indicates the justification for consultation with professionals such as a psychologist or certified social worker trained in testing and assessment of children. Not all professionals are trained to test and assess for developmental, disability, and processing speed problems. So if you (or your child's teacher) suspect that your child may have a Learning Disability or other condition that may be blocking their ability for success in school, here are the steps that should be taken.

Schools are required to have a screening process that identifies students who may need special assistance. This screening includes a review of academic and attendance records, observations of behaviors, and a vision and hearing assessment. If the school does not conduct vision and screening evaluation, do it with your practitioner. As a result of the screening, the school may recommend a formal review. However, parents may request an assessment at any time. Although many schools may accept a verbal request, I suggest that you do it in writing. The letter can be to the principal or the school psychologist. It is also possible that the school may recommend an evaluation. In either case, you will probably be asked to sign a "permission to evaluate/consent" form. When the review is completed, it will include information about learning strengths and weaknesses, social-emotional issues, behavior modification, and educational needs.

School officials and parents/guardians will conduct a meeting to develop an **Individualized Education Plan or IEP.** School officials may include the psychologist or school counselor, teacher, and school district Special Education Supervisor. The IEP will recommend educational goals and plans that are best suited to the students learning needs. An IEP meeting is scheduled for review every year. Students will be re-tested every two to three years to determine changes to the IEP or if further enrollment in a Special Education program is indicated.

Parents be aware that it can sometimes be a challenge wading through the school bureaucracy to get your child properly diagnosed and placed in the Special Education Program. Seek assistance from medical providers or counselors knowledgeable of the Special Education requirements for your state and school district. Even if you cannot get your child admitted into a special education program, at least you will have learned more about his/her strengths and weaknesses. You will be better able to respond to your child's learning style and provide the appropriate support. Be advised, however, that special education programs and learning support, as are all school programs, are supported by budgets. When money is tight, school programs get cut. Consequently, administrators are forced to allocate scarce dollars according to assessed priority. And "assessed priority" is not always dictated by actual need but also by how hard parents/ guardians are willing to advocate for their children. The squeaky wheel gets the grease!

There are many accommodations available for special needs students. Included are visual aids, adjusted class schedules, extra time for tests, computer-aided instruction, modified homework assignments, and one-on-one instruction, to name a few. Once a student has been enrolled in a Special Education Program, it can often be utilized through high school and even college.

Support outside of school is available. There are a variety of programs and professionals who can help in providing support for your child. You may also consider the aid of tutors trained in teaching to your child's special needs.

For more information, go to www. disabilityinfo.gov. Note that the Disabilities Act of 1975 (Public Law 94-142), along with revisions enacted in 1990 (Public Law 101-476) and 2004 (Public Law 101-476), commits the U.S. government to the right of people with disabilities to get the maximum benefit from our school system. Along with these laws, the "Individuals with Disabilities Education Improvement Act" or IDEIA states that the opportunity for quality education should not be denied on the basis of physical, mental or cognitive disability. Help is available, take advantage of it!

SECTION J
Looking Ahead

Destiny is not a matter of chance;
it is a matter of choice.

Chapter 34
Facilitating Your Child's Choices

Career Fields. It is never too early to expose children to various career fields. When children are younger, do this by pointing out, discussing, and even having them meet and speak with people in various career fields. When watching TV together or reading books, point out what people do for a living and some things that make their jobs enjoyable. Another option is to have an adult family and friends speak to your children about their careers. Invite children to go to work with you and others. Do not rely on school career days! Often, such events do not provide enough information for students to make informed career choices.

Exposing children to various career options will help them match interest with opportunities. Some will grasp a possible career that interests them as early as when in elementary or middle school. Although such early interest usually does not last, it enhances curiosity. As children get older, try to focus on the details of various careers. Many, if not most, students have little idea of what they want to do career-wise even well into their college careers. This is not necessarily a bad thing, as exposure to various college courses, professors, clubs, and other students is all part of the process. A college major usually does not have to be chosen until the second year. Caution, however! The National Center for Education Statistics reports that only 39 percent of college students graduate in four years. Students change majors, transfer schools, or take courses that do not count towards the degree they are aspiring to. Such changes result in extra costs and possible increased debt. When a high school student has a good idea of what they would like to do for a career, it can make choosing a college much more straightforward. High school students can help themselves and help their college selection process if they have a good idea of the career field they would like to pursue.

Alternatives to a College Degree. In Chapter 25, I discuss career fields that do not require a college degree. Technical training may be needed that can be achieved with on-the-job training, vocational training, or junior college. Not every child aspires to a career requiring a college degree. Many students spend four or more years pursuing an undergraduate and even graduate degree only to find that their degrees are not very marketable. Sometimes they end up in a career field that is not related to their degree. Many parents expect their child to go to college because they feel it is the proper thing to do, such as provide status and increased opportunities. Whatever the reason, it is vitally important not to try to live your life through your children. By this, I mean sometimes we adults have unfulfilled dreams that we may attempt to live out through our children's lives. Although tempting to do so, this is not only unfair to your child; it often creates resentment and possible parent-child conflict. Also, the child may end up in a career he/she is not content.

A good handle on your child's talents, interests, and desires will go a long way to helping make the correct post-high school education choice.

If Your Child Chooses to Go to College, proper preparation is essential to making good choices. It is a rare student and parent who do not worry about all the things needed for college admission. Daunting perquisites, lengthy applications, choosing a college or university, outrageous costs, etc. can assuredly seem overwhelming, especially for those families traveling down this path for the first time. When broken down into parts, combined with a plan, the process can be made to be much less worrisome. I am not a college admissions officer and will not attempt to provide detailed counsel on a subject for which I am not qualified. However, I have spoken to several high school counselors and college admissions staff and did a bit of research to help my readers better maneuver the college search and admissions process. Once the decision has been made to go to college, it is wise to set a plan in place. The process is not the same for all families. Chapter 25 D can help provide students (and parents) with vital information to consider when planning for college and the process of college admissions. **I urge you to review Chapter 25 with your students.** Do so early in your student's high school career and review periodically throughout the high school years. Included are guidelines on choosing a possible career field, college options, and preparation TIPS for admission. Suggestions for helping to pay for college are provided below.

In Chapter 25 C, I discussed the Pros and Cons of a "Gap Year." A Gap Year is a year a student may choose to take off between high school graduation and the start of his/her freshman year in college. It is not a "vacation year," rather a time to explore and learn about one's personal and professional self-awareness. A common question many parents have, "Is my son/daughter ready for the temptations and challenges of independently living away from home in a college environment?" Of course, every child is unique and responds to life situations differently. If you have any concerns, you may want to consider a Gap Year for your son or daughter. Consider this, researchers (Birch and Miller 2007; Crawford and Cribb 2012)" discovered that in Australia and the United Kingdom taking a Gap Year had a significant positive impact on student's academic performance in college. The study also found that students in the United Kingdom and the United States who had taken a Gap Year were more likely to graduate from college with higher grade point averages than individuals who went straight to college from high school. This effect was seen even for Gap Year students with lower academic achievement in high school. Data also indicates that students who have completed a Gap Year report that they are more likely to be "happy" or "extremely satisfied" with their careers. For more details go to americangap.org

Chapter 35
Paying for College

Paying for college. If a college education is the goal of your son or daughter, unless you are very wealthy, costs ought to be an essential criterion in helping to select a college. Although I could have included this Chapter in PART ONE, since most parents are more knowledgeable about finances, it seemed more logical to place the chapter of paying for college in the parent's part, regardless of who will be paying the bills.

Many students (or parents) are burdened with substantial financial costs for years after college. According to the National Center for Education Statistics rapidly. College costs include tuition, room, board, lab fees, books, transportation, and other miscellaneous expenses. Tuition and books alone can range from $3,000 per year for community colleges in which the student commutes, to over $40,000 per year for private colleges that include tuition, room, and board. More than 70 percent of graduates leave college with debts averaging $28,000 according to Student Loan Report. There are several reasons for these staggering costs. Included are university over-spending and rising costs, Congressional acts that tossed money-making opportunities to the private sector, stagnation of income for the middle class, and states retreating from support to higher education. According to the U.S. Bureau of Economic Analysis, nationally, state contributions to higher education decreased from 58 percent in 1975 to 37 percent in 2016. Of course, as state funding decreased, college expenses increased.

Several options can be considered in helping to pay for college, without incurring a huge debt.

Financial Aid

Financial aid programs. The Pell grant assists low-income students. The amount awarded depends on the Expected Family Contributions (EFC), the cost of the college expenses, and if the student is part or full time. Money awarded from grants does not have to be paid back. Federal loans, such as Direct Loans (formally Stafford), and Perkins Loans must be re-paid, plus interest.

The EFC is calculated by the school to determine eligibility amount for federal student aid. It is not the amount you will have to pay rather the amount you are eligible to receive. For more information request a free copy of *Funding Your Education: The Guide to Federal Student Aid*. Go to https://studentaid.ed.gov/resources#information-on-getting.

QuestBridge. QuestBridge connects promising high school students from low-income backgrounds with leading colleges and universities. The program assists in applying for and securing scholarships. High school juniors regardless of citizenship currently attending high school in the U.S. are eligible for the College Prep Scholars Program. Go to www. questbridge. org for details.

The FAFSA. The U.S. Dept. of Education's *Student Financial Aid Handbook* advises applying for Federal student aid; you must complete and submit the Free Application for Federal Student Aid (FAFSA). It is not so difficult once you get into it, and it is free. The application will tell you if you qualify for one or more federal aid packages such as Pell Grants, Direct/Stafford Loan, and work-study programs. The application also can be used for institutional loans and state aid. Questions include name, address, and Social Security Account Number, educational plans, dependency status, parent's financial status, student income, and assets. The formula used to determine financial need is simple: Cost of attendance less Expected Financial Contribution=Need. If there are scholarships, they are calculated in. Although scholarship money is calculated in the formula, they do not have to be re-paid as loans do.

Some colleges may require a Financial Aid Profile. This

information is used by colleges to determine financial aid from sources outside the federal government. The higher the family's worth, the more they are expected to finance college expenses. There is a small fee for filing the Profile-about $25 as of this writing. Deadlines may vary for different colleges, so check with each college or their requirements. Go to collegboard.org/css-financial-aid-profiles for detailed information.

The FAFSA must be filed on time. The earliest one can file is October 1 for the following academic year. The deadline is June 30.

Double-check all information entered on the FAFSA form. Is data entered in the correct spaces? Are social security and birth dates correct? Is financial information accurate?

Much of the information asked for on the FAFSA is the same as can be found on your tax return. So, it helps to do your taxes first. But if not feasible, that is OK, gather taxable income (wages, interest earned, capital gains, other income, pensions, etc.). Also, have non-taxable income information available. Do not miss deadlines because you do not have the final data. If you don't know the exact amounts, estimate, then go back and correct as the updated information becomes available.

Financial aid packages can vary quite a bit from one college to another, so consider them carefully when comparing colleges. It may seem elementary, but you would be surprised at how many students will place a higher value on other factors, and then later regret their decision when payback time comes. Check out financial aid information on each college website that you are considering. If one of the colleges you are considering is close to your home, visit the office of financial assistance. They will be glad to answer your questions and help. If considering a private college, ask about discounts. Many will offer discounts for qualifying prospective students.

Refinancing and consolidating student debt. It is not uncommon to end up with several loans that must be repaid when college is completed. Besides having to juggle repayments to several agencies, not to mention the fact that interest on several loans can be more expensive, consolidation of loans could be a solution, reports "Kiplinger's Personal Finance" in the July 2016 edition. *Kiplinger's* suggests that you carefully examine each outstanding loan for interest rates, repayment plans, and duration. Would accelerating or consolidation be a wise option? Conditions for private and federal loans differ, and you do not want to lose valuable benefits of federal loans that private loans do not provide. The Department of Education's Consolidated Student Loan program allows for the combining of several loans into a single loan with only one bill and one interest rate. It will not give you a lower interest rate, rather a repayment plan that can be easier to manage. There is no cost for this consolidation. If unemployed or other financial challenges occur, payments can be postponed or even reduced. Go to the loan consolidation at www.findaid.org/ calculators to check interest rates according to the federal loans you have. Repayment plans can be located at www.studentloans.gov. and www.loanconsolidation.ed.gov.

Private loans can also be consolidated, but you cannot mix federal and private loans. Good credit history and stable income are generally required. Since public service loan forgiveness is complicated, some private companies offer to assist for a fee. Not necessary! You can do it yourself. A free checklist is provided at Saving For College.com/article/checklist-for-public-servive-loan-forgiveness.

Beware of scams! If you receive a phone call, e-mail, or see an ad that offers opportunities to reduce student loans, do not enroll! These scammers have you make loans directly to them rather than to the lender. By doing so, they claim they will pay down the loans at a reduced rate. Rather than paying the lender, they keep the money. Some scammers strive to obtain the Federal Student Aid ID, user names and passwords. Doing so provides an opportunity for them to alter confidential information on the original loan. Never respond to such ads. There are a few legitimate loan-forgiveness programs, but they charge you for assisting. Why pay them when you can do it for free?

Grants and Scholarships

Non- Federal grants and scholarships are awarded for many reasons to include financial need, affiliation with civic or fraternal organizations, religious groups, employers, schools, non-profit organizations, and veteran organizations, to name a few. To find sources check with the financial aid office at college, the U.S. Department of Labor scholarship search tool, your state grant agency, or your high school counselor. Ask parents, grandparents, relatives, and friends if organizations with whom they are affiliated offer tuition assistance or scholarships. Many on-line sources provide information on how to apply for grants and scholarships. Cappex. com is a free database of scholarship sources. Another is Unigo. com. Both sites offer information on scholarships, awards, and grants available from public and private sources. Two other good on-line sources are SallieMae.com and the U.S. Department of Education's *Federal Student Aid Program*. The sites provide guidance on how to apply for scholarships. Some sites ask you to register. Registering will permit them to send you notifications of scholarship opportunities.

Many private for-profit companies attempt to sell loans. Private loans can have higher interest rates than government, and non-profits- and can be quite unforgiving in terms of repayments.

Types of scholarships. Many associate scholarships with athletics and high honor students (merit-based). Although this is true, there are many scholarships awarded for other than sports and merit. For example, "need-based" scholarships are awarded based on a family's financial status. Many states and colleges allocate funds for low-income students who also meet basic academic criteria. Merit-based scholarships are based on grades, accomplishments, potential, interests, and even background. Believe it or not, scholarships are available for such things as choosing a specific major, community service, children of alumnae, and church and civic affiliation. My granddaughter received a $1,000 scholarship from a law firm and a summer internship because she planned on majoring in pre-law in college. A suggestion provided by Kristina Ellis in her book *How to*

Graduate Debt Free is to do an internet search by typing in keywords such as "science scholarships," "leadership scholarships," "returning students scholarships." Kristina recommends a book written by Gen and Kelly Tanabe titled *The Ultimate Scholarship Book*. The high school counselor's office will have potential sources. Ask the college admissions office if the school offers need and merit-based scholarships.

529 College Savings Plans. A great way of helping to pay for college is to open a college savings account when the child is young. These are 529, "Qualified Tuition Plans." There are two types of 529 plans - individual and custodial. Individual plans remain in the account owner's portfolio. In a custodial plan, the account owner serves as the custodian until the beneficiary (child) reaches the age of majority. The beneficiary then becomes the account owner. Plans are administered differently by each state.

There are two types of investment plan options. Prepaid and College Savings Plans.

Prepaid Tuition Plans. With this plan, you purchase college credits for future enrollment in participating colleges and universities at today's prices. Thus, you are **locking in a tuition rate** helping to avoid increasing future costs. Payments are based on the child's current age and the number of years purchased. Many states will guarantee prepaid plans. These plans allow investors to save for qualified college expenses while avoiding income tax and capital gains taxes on investment gains. Unlike College Savings Plans (explained below) there are no sales fees.

One of the limitations of this kind of plan is that they usually restrict you to colleges in the state where you set up the plan (which needn't be your state of residence, however). You can always get the money out later, but in that case, you've eliminated the one advantage of all prepaid plans, the locked-in tuition rate. Funds can only be used in the state prepaid plan for in-state public colleges. Private College 529 plans can only be used for member colleges. Room and board are not covered.

Savings Plans

529 College Savings Plans. Contributions are invested in bond mutual funds, stock mutual funds or money market funds and will fluctuate with the market. State or federal governments do not guarantee these plans. However, unlike prepaid tuition plans, savings plans cover room and board and other fees such as books and computers. Enrollment in College Savings Plans, both prepaid and investment plans, are done through investment management companies. Management fees vary, so it is wise to shop around. Go to your search engine and type in your "(state) 529."

Restrictions. Since 529 plans are intended to pay for college. If funds are withdrawn for other purposes, a penalty will be assessed. Since the funds are considered assets, it can affect financial aid. However, funds can be transferred to another eligible family member according to Mark Kantrowitz, a financial aid expert on college savings and publisher of SavingForCollege.com. If you own one or more 529 plans, you can withdraw up to $10,000 to repay qualified education loans. Federal and many private loans qualify. Owners of a 529 account can change the beneficiary (family members, to include grandchildren, nieces, and nephews) who have outstanding education loans. For example, if the plan owner has $10,000 leftover, he could apply it to a Stafford loan. The owner could then change to the beneficiary to another and pay down that loan.

Research! Since every family's needs and wants are different, it is wise to compare plans and options. A good source is The College Savings Plan website. The site has a plan comparison tool for all states. https://plans.collegesavings.org/planComparisonState.aspx.

Although 529 accounts are an excellent way to save for college expenses, there are a few things that investors must be aware of. 529 Plans differ from state to state, so investors are advised to do their homework. Some states do not offer income tax breaks. As of the date of this writing, these states include California, Delaware, Hawaii, Kentucky, New Jersey, and North Carolina. Some states offer a tax break even if you choose that states plan or a different states plan.

These states include Kansas, Arizona, Kansas, Missouri, Montana, and Pennsylvania. Some states do not have a state income tax, so there would be no advantage to a state tax break. States that do not have a state tax include Alaska, Florida, Nevada, New Hampshire, South Dakota, Tennessee, Texas, Washington, and Wyoming. Early withdrawals from 529 plans that are not used for qualified education expenses can incur income tax and a 10 percent tax penalty on a portion of the withdrawal. Money from 529 plans can be used for tuition, room and board, books, computers, and computer-related internet access. Travel expenses are not permitted expenses under 529 plans. Investments from 529 plans can also be used for off-campus housing and food if it is equivalent to the on-campus costs.

A few other factors that should be considered are the timing of withdrawals, effect on financial aid, and who initiates withdrawals. Consult a financial advisor to discuss your situation, needs, and desires. Gain more insight into 529 Plans and compare plans at www. savingforcollege.com.

Coverdale Education Savings Accounts. Coverdale accounts are like 529 plans and can be used for qualifying private elementary and school tuition.

More Ways to Finance College Expenses

Military. Active duty military members of all services can have up to 100 percent of tuition expenses paid. Each service has different criteria and application procedures. Reserve and National Guard service members can also receive college tuition assistance. For example, National Guard members can receive $250 per semester hour. Amounts and conditions vary by state and service, so check with service representatives. Go to "Military.com" for more information.

Post high school programs include college, job training, certificate programs, and apprenticeships. A maximum of 36 months of tuition is provided. If the service member does not use the entire 36 months benefit, he/she may pass the remainder of the benefit period on to dependents. Benefits can be divided among dependents. Even if the service member used all 36 months, an additional 12 months tuition could be earned under the "Forever GI. Bill." This Bill was signed into law in 2017 and expands education benefits for veterans, service members, and their family members. Included is in-state tuition for public universities and a portion of private university tuition. However, the selection for benefits under the Forever GI Bill must be made while still on active duty. The service member must have complied six years of service plus an additional four more years after the request for transfer has been made and approved.

The Yellow Ribbon Program provides additional funding for college out-of-state private or graduate programs that the post 9/11 GI Bill does not cover. Benefits from the Yellow Ribbon Program do not affect GI Bill benefits. Not all schools participate in the program, so check. Go to your search engine and type in "Yellow Ribbon Program."

Survivor's and Dependent's Educational Assistance (DEA) program. Dependents of deceased and disabled veterans are eligible can get educational assistance.

Veteran service organizations (VSOs) offer scholarship and tuition assistance. There are many VSO's… too many for me to review here. Search the internet, ask for assistance from VSO educational assistance officers, or the Veterans Administration website.

Reserve Officer Training and Service Academies: If so inclined, college students who enroll in Senior Reserve Officer Training (ROTC) may be eligible for scholarships, if they qualify. During the advanced course (junior and senior years), cadets receive a stipend that can help with costs. Service Academies are free. There is a service obligation following graduation.

More Options

Individual Retirement Accounts (IRA). Although primarily used for retirement, IRAs can also be used for college expenses. Up to $10,000 can be withdrawn for college expenses for the account holder, a spouse, child, or grandchild. Interest is deferred, so is compounded during the life of the fund. Distributions are taxed. Unlike a traditional IRA, Roth IRA taxes are paid upfront so taxes will not be taken out when funds are withdrawn. If an IRA is opened for saving for higher education, there is nothing wrong with this. However, if the IRA is opened for saving for retirement, then taking early withdrawals can deplete funds meant for the golden years.

Public service loans and forgiveness. Persons who work for the government or a non-profit 501c (3) may qualify for loan forgiveness or a re-structure of outstanding federal student loans. Private loans are not eligible but do not disqualify you if you have a federal student loan balance. Benefit calculations are based on ages of federal loans, adjusted gross income, family size, etc. More information can be found at www.forgivemyfederalloan.com.

Online Classes. Many colleges are now offering flexible scheduling and online courses. An entire degree can now be done online. Although online programs can vary considerably in cost, savings can be realized because there is no, or little driving involved and no room and board expenses. More and more colleges now offer both traditional classroom and online classes.

Junior college and vo-tech. A good option many high school graduates are taking is the less costly route of a junior college, technical school, or a local community college instead of a four-year college. If you decide to go on for a bachelor's degree, you can certainly do so. Besides, it is often easier to gain admission to more selective colleges when transferring to the sophomore or junior class, as opposed to the more competitive freshman class. Many junior colleges have affiliation agreements with four-year universities whereby the credits earned for the two-year associate degree are accepted towards a bachelor's degree at the university. One of my sons, for example, earned an associate degree in Criminal Justice from Delaware Technical and Community College. He then matriculated to the University of Delaware's Criminal Justice program. By so doing, he saved a lot of money.

Using the "magic of compound interest." Compounding is earning interest on initial savings, then more interest on the accumulated interest of the previous savings and interest. Why is it often called "magic?" Because the savings grows "like magic." Here is an example. If a person starts with $200 and invests $100 per month for 10 years at 4 percent interest, the interest earned would be $5,583. Total savings would be $29,883. Interest is essentially "free money." The amount earned will depend on several factors: how early the savings is started, how many years the savings is maintained, the interest rate, and the type of investment (savings plan, CD, stocks). The critical thing to remember is to get started saving for college early, then faithfully make monthly contributions as much as your budget allows. With all the temptations today to buy things "wanted" rather than "needed," many do not save. An excellent way to ensure you take advantage of the "magic of compound interest" is to "pay yourself first." By that I mean allocate your monthly savings before you pay for anything else. Automatic deductions help to avoid the temptation of spending the money for other than what it ought to be intended—college savings. Check with your financial advisor for these and other options.

Have a budget. It is essential that all households have a written budget. Those who do not have a budget are at financial risk. When at financial risk, dreams and goals are at risk. A budget spreadsheet can be set up on Excel, pencil and paper, or with an online budget tool. Here are a few to check out. BudgetSimple.com, YouNeedABudget. com, Everydollar.com/Simple/Budget, and Kiplinger's Household Budget Worksheet.

SECTION K
Our Education System (and Students) at Risk

Chapter 36
Why Many Asian Students
Do Well Academically

The Program for International Student Assessment (PISA) measures students in reading, mathematics, and science literacy. The National Center for Educational Statistics (NCES) Commissioner Jack Buckley stated, "conventional wisdom is that top U.S. students do well compared to their peers across the globe. According to this line of reasoning, the U.S. doesn't make it on the list of the top 25 countries in math (or top 15 in reading) because America has higher poverty and racial diversity than other countries do, which drags down the national average—wrong!" says Buckley. Top U.S. students are falling behind even average students in Asia, and they also have poverty and diverse populations. Asian countries dominate the top 11 in all subjects: math, reading, and science. This feature appeared in the Hechinger Report, titled *Top U.S. Students Fare Poorly in International PISA Test Scores,* posted by Jill Barshay on December 3, 2013.

Over the past several years my wife and I have been host parents to five Chinese high school students. I have also come to know a score of others through fellow host families and working with the agency that sponsors them. I am impressed by the devotion of these children's parents to allow their child to travel halfway around the world to gain an education in the United States—at great emotional and monetary expense. Many Asian students also find their way to the United Kingdom, Canada, and Australia for schooling. For the students, it certainly is no small challenge to face a new and strange education system and culture. Although most started learning English when in grade school in China, many are challenged by new words, slang, and colloquialisms. Depending on their fluency in English, in schoolwork, they may have to translate from English to Chinese then back to English. Having to face unfamiliar customs, values, lifestyles, and language can create profound stress and anxiety. This is frequently referred to as "culture shock." Yet despite their challenges, most of the children are committed to doing well. In China a very high emphasis is placed on study and grades. Chinese parents take their children's education seriously. Many feel that their family prestige is dependent on their child's academic success. Thus, parents place high expectations on their student to excel. Just because their child is sent to another country to go to school does not lessen the expectations for their child to achieve top grades. A typical school day in China is from 8 a.m. to 8 p.m. six days a week. Although the government is now striving to limit the number of school day hours, many schools are still holding to the extended school day.

How did this high emphasis on education come about? After the death of Mao Zedong the Chinese Communist Party leadership led by Deng Xiaoping placed top priority on education, especially in science and technology. Although the humanities were considered important, vocational and technical skills were paramount for meeting China's modernization goals. The policy encouraged learning and borrowing in the scientific fields from abroad. Asian students consistently outperform other countries on the PISA. However, controversy has surrounded the high scores achieved by Asian students due to the spread of the numerical data and sampling bias. Regardless of the question of the validity of the testing, many Asian students do perform very well academically, especially in science and math, despite the language and cultural challenges for those studying abroad.

The British newspaper, *The Guardian*, printed an article by Warwick Mansell in February 2011 entitled *Hidden Tigers: Why do Chinese children do so well at school?* The article pointed out that students of Chinese heritage do better in national average testing than those of other ethnicities regardless of socio-economic class. Although formal research on the subject is limited, one study conducted by King's College London interviewed 80 Chinese pupils and 30 Chinese parents and 30 teachers. One of the researchers, Becky Francis, of the UCL Institute of Education, and Director of

Education at the Royal Society of Arts said, "Our main argument is that families of Chinese heritage see taking education seriously as a fundamental pillar of their Chinese identity, and a way of differentiating themselves not just within their own group, but from ethnic groups as well." The *Guardian* article stated that in 2010, Ramesh Kapadia, a visiting professor at London University's Institute of Education presented a paper and said, "I think within Chinese society, there is an emphasis on practice. Children are told, "If you want to learn something, practice, practice, practice, and practice again, and you will get better. It may be that this helps to motivate pupils when the rewards can seem a long way away."

Thus, it can reasonably be concluded that an emphasis on education by government and parents is essential for encouraging students to do well in school. High expectations and social pressure on students to excel provides little wiggle room for students to avoid not studying hard.

Chapter 37
What Some Asian Students Are Missing
(What We Can Learn from It)

Chinese students (Singapore, Taipei, Beijing, Shanghai, Jiangsu, Guangdong) score well on the PISA and academically, especially in math and science. It is all about grades and high-test scores. According to persons I have interviewed who work with Chinese students, many of the young people do not have a definite life purpose or are not innovative in their thinking. Generally, they participate in few, if any, extra-curricular activities in China. Thus, they have limited opportunity to develop self-management and leadership skills. Many of the Chinese students with whom I have been acquainted, must be encouraged and often pushed, to participate in extracurricular activities.

Yong Zhao, born and raised in China and now a professor with a presidential chair at the University of Oregon, author of *Who's Afraid of the Big Bad Dragon? Why China Has the Best (and Worst) Education System in the World*, points out that although Chinese students score very high on tests, they lack creativity, divergent thinking, originality, and individualism. The reason for this can be traced, in part, back to the 1,300-year-old tradition of *keju* that conferred societal rank based on examinations. Although outlawed during the Qing dynasty in 1905, the *keju* philosophy (adopted by other East Asian countries such as Japan, Korea, Taiwan, and Viet Nam) has endured through modern-day China. The focus on examinations in China, argues Zhao, "rewards obedience, compliance, and homogeneous thinking. This authoritarian social control may have fostered good test-taking abilities but, unfortunately, diverted scholars away from exploration, innovation, questioning and challenging." There has been no Enlightenment Industrial Revolution in Mainland China. Zhao contends that China's remarkable economic growth over the last three decades is due to China's opening its markets to foreign capital and enterprise, not to an educational system that still emphasizes memorization and testing. Despite China's emphasis on education, they recognize that they are lagging in western technology. In fact, according to Zheng Yefu, a professor at Peking University and author of *The Pathology of Chinese Education*, of the one billion people who have been educated in Mainland China from 1949 to 2016, China has produced few Nobel Peace prize winners. According to Wikipedia, only seven Noble peace prize winners were from China compared to 363 from the United States and 123 from the United Kingdom.

Most "Made in China" articles are conceptualized and developed in other countries, just assembled in China due to cheap labor. In May 2017, *Forbes* magazine listed the top 100 most innovative companies. The United States had 50 (including 9 of the top 10), whereas China registered 6 (1 in the top 10). Zhao argues that China needs technological innovation, which it will not develop until it reforms its test-based education system. In response to China's need for technical and creative innovation, China is sending students to Western private high schools and universities in droves. According to the Institute of International Education, as of 2016, there were over 300,000 Chinese students in the United States. In fact, 2 out of 5 international students in the U.S. are from China. The numbers have nearly quintupled from just over 62,000 to over 300,000 in 10 years. This trend shows no sign of slowing down; a recent *Huran Report* stated that an annual survey of China's elite, 80 percent of the country's wealthy families plan to send their children abroad for an education. It can be concluded, in part, that a centralized, authoritarian education system that emphasizes grades over diversity in subject matter measured by standardized testing, results in students who make good grades, but is often devoid of the skills for innovation, exploration, questioning, and challenging. Yet, China recognizes that it has lagged in its ability to be innovative and is taking steps to address the challenge. For example, in 2018 China spent $400 billion in technological research and development (R&D). Although the United States spent over $500 billion in R&D, China is catching up. A report by CNBC (July

18, 2017), stated that American companies and universities have an inclination not to share research due to competition concerns, thus tends to stifle innovation progress.

An article that appeared in the January 2015 Journalist's Resource, Harvard Kennedy School citing authors Xie Yu Zhang and Chunni Lai Qing, *China's Rise as a Major Contributor to Science and Technology, Proceedings of the National Academy of Sciences, July 2015, Vol 111, No 26.* "China launched its 'indigenous innovation' campaign in 2006 to turn the country into a science powerhouse by 2020." China wants to lure back Chinese students studying in other countries. "The number of Chinese graduate students attending the science and engineering programs in the United States nearly tripled between 1987 and 2010, growing from 15,000 to 43,000." More science and technology doctoral degrees are awarded to Chinese nationals from American universities than any other foreign country. This raises the question, "Will the U.S. fall behind in the field of innovation in the coming years?"

Because competition is so fierce for college spots in China, parents with financial means will go to extremes to help ensure their child is afforded the opportunity to get a college education. So passionate about their child's success, some parents hire an agency in China that "selects" the student's colleges then apply on their behalf. I asked one high school senior what colleges she had applied to. She did not know. Surprised, I asked why not. She explained that an agency in China was applying on her behalf. I then asked how an agency could know what she wanted regarding a major, career choice, or even college campus environment. She replied that although the agency representatives interviewed her and her parents, she ultimately had little voice in the matter as the parents and agency had made the choices. Thus, the child's wishes and often personal talents to pursue a career field to which they are best suited takes a back seat to the parent's zeal to get their child into an elite college in an English-speaking country. One student whom I was close to was thinking about teaching or social work, career fields that would have well suited her given her aptitude and interests as supported by her results on the Myers Briggs Personality Type Indicator. Yet, her mother insisted she major in business or economics in college. The mother's reasons were so she could later work for her uncle back in China. The daughter obediently complied despite her personal wishes and aptitude. Of course, not all parents are so controlling.

Zhao says that there is a billion-dollar industry in China that sells scientific papers to students and professionals who lack the skills to write their own essays. In China, the system for getting into elite high schools and colleges is based on two examinations: the *zhongkao* that determines what high school students can attend and the *gaokao* that determines what college a student can attend. Consequently, Zhao explains, many courses are designed to pass exams rather than learning how to learn. By contrast, in the U.S. and UK, colleges and universities use several criteria to determine college admission, i.e., high school grades, class rank, one or two standardized tests, extracurricular activities, recommendations, and sometimes essays and interviews.

A Chinese high school junior with whom I am acquainted attended boarding school from the second grade through 9th grade in China. Her parents and the rigid academic environment instilled in her lessons of conformity, obedience, and loyalty. "At school," she told me, "the emphasis was on memorization and passing examinations. Independent thought was not promoted." In classes, students are called on by teachers to answer questions. Class participation is not emphasized as it is in American schools. Although a good student, she said that before transferring to the United States she dreaded the idea of more years studying for the *gaokao* exam, which would be the sole criterion for entrance into a Chinese university. Once the decision is made not to follow the *gaokao* track, it is irreversible. At this point, the student is compelled to *"tuochan,"* meaning "relieved of productive duty." At this point, all efforts are focused on gaining acceptance into international educational systems.

Dexter Roberts in the May 2015 edition of *Bloomberg* wrote in an article titled *China Exam System Drives Students Suicides* that Beijing-based 21st Century Education Research Institute reported just under 93 percent of student suicides happened after arguments with teachers or were attributed to the intense pressure to study put on young people. It is understandable that many Chinese students and their parents are choosing to avoid the dreaded *zhongkao and gaokao* examination by studying abroad. Fortunately, China's education system is now taking steps to lessen the intense pressure it places on students by shortening the school week and broaden the criteria by which students are selected for universities. Thus, they are moving away from China's traditional reliance on a single test. Yet, reform is slow, and the pressure on students and families continue. Wagner and Dintersmith in *Most Likely to Succeed* state that Chinese leaders are concerned about the lack of creativity and innovation in their graduates. In fact, many Chinese educators are seeking answers to the question of why China is primarily a manufacturer of other countries innovations and have come to the United States to help answer the question.

Chinese society and employers place a high value on degrees from elite colleges and universities. Thus, many parents push their child to seek admission to Ivy League schools. Because the competition to gain acceptance into an elite American university is tremendous, in 2105 of the nearly 40,000 Chinese students who applied for admission to U.S. universities only about 200 were accepted into Ivy League schools. In addition to grades and college entrance exams, United States colleges place a high value on extracurricular and life experiences; areas not emphasized in the Chinese educational system where it is almost exclusively about academic grades. The natural parents of most of my students did not encourage participation in extracurricular activities. Consequently, Chinese students in American high schools tend to shy away from extracurricular activities, especially those that are competitive. Even though many had excellent grades, they were declined offers of admission to elite colleges because they were not "well rounded"—an important criterion that elite American colleges expect.

The good news for Chinese students seeking an American college education is that the United States has thousands of colleges and universities and anyone seeking a higher-level education can gain acceptance, even if they are weak in one or more areas most often valued by admissions officers. Once admitted, the value of their education is based more on effort. Many highly successful people did not attend an elite school. Many were rejected by an Ivy League school, including Warren Buffett, Ted Turner, Tom Brokaw, Art Garfunkel, and John Kerry, to name a few of the many hundreds of thousands who gained life success without an Ivy League degree.

Zhao encourages the American education system not to model the Chinese centralized authoritarian education system that focuses on testing and a primary concentration in math, science, and reading. In contrast, western education has always placed importance on reading, writing, and arithmetic (the three R's), but also provides exposure to a wide variety of subjects and extracurricular beyond the three R's. Western countries historically have used individualized testing to evaluate students. Regrettable, standardized testing has gradually crept into the education system throughout the western world. England emulated the Chinese model of standardized testing in the 19th century. Reliance on such testing spread throughout the English Commonwealth, then Europe and finally to America.

Why have I provided a lengthy (sorry about that), elaboration about the Chinese education system? A little background. Faced with new challenges in the 21st century, legislatures and educators agreed that our education system needed to respond to new economic and technological changes. Many legislatures became concerned about the poor scores of American students, as compared to other nations on international standardized tests. They decided that we needed to push our education system harder by calling for curriculum homogeneity, more standardized testing, and teacher accountability measured by student scores on standardized tests. Wagner and Dintersmith hit the nail on the head when they stated, "The United States picked the wrong goal and failed at it. We opted to chase China, South Korea, and Singapore on standardized test performance (a race we never had a chance of winning against children who spend every waking hour cramming for the tests) instead of educating our youth for a world of innovation and opportunity, a race that plays to our strengths."

The question must be asked, are we suppressing the creative spirit in children by continuing to subject them to years of memorizing details of curriculum-based subjects, much of which has little to do with what is needed to compete in the new era?

Chapter 38
Standardized Testing, The
Good and The Bad

When you take the free will out of
education, that turns it into schooling.
John Taylor Gatto

In 2002, Republican President George W. Bush and Democrat Senator Ted Kennedy teamed up to implement standardized tests under the "No Child Left Behind" mandate. Also concerned about the state of our education system, Barack Obama in 2009 created "Race to the Top (RTTT)." The Gates Foundation provided $35 million to develop and implement a new education system in the United States. They called this the "Common Core State Standards Initiative (CCSSI)." It was published in December 2008. The program set national academic standards.

The $4.35 billion program provided grants to states that chose to participate. Implemented under the American Recovery and Reinvestment Act, RTTT had four key goals.

1) Accept rigorous standards and assessments; 2) Recruit, evaluate, and retain highly effective teachers and principals; 3) Build data systems to assess progress; 4) Turn around low-performing schools. A positive result of RTTT is that it served as a motivating force to get state legislatures to deliberate on the challenges of improving education in their states.

Proponents of standardized testing believe that setting high standards and establishing measurable goals can improve individual outcomes in education. They also argue that standardized testing is more valid and reliable than individual testing because they are administered uniformly and evaluated empirically. A 2015 article by William G. Howell in Education Next points out that the RTTT program provided funds to under-funded states resulting in increased public awareness of educational deficiencies, thus stimulating reform. Standardized tests provide more useful information for screening by colleges, employers, and the government. Standardized tests are also valuable tools for helping identify developmental delays for young children. Examples of tests are screening, language, diagnostic, and achievement tests.

Opponents of standardized testing include many educators and parents. They fear the trend in the United States towards centralized government control. A concern that many had about the program was the question whether RTTT would impede rather than encourage teacher autonomy and individual student development. In fact, under pressure to "teach to the test" an Economic Policy Institute report (*Small Successes, Multiple Challenges*), dated September 12, 2013 stated that RTTT resulted in increased distrust between teachers and school administrators. Many are also concerned that centralization and uniformity may stifle student's creativity, innovative thinking, and confidence to explore the values that have, in the past, been the western world's leader in globalization, technology, and the arts.

An article by Elaine Strauss of the Washington Post dated September 12, 2013 referred to an Economic Policy Report stated that the Race to the Top program "... can't deliver much educational improvement in America's public schools because there is a huge mismatch in its mandates and what is actually possible to accomplish with the provided funding and requirements." On May 13, 2019, a Wikipedia report said "although the majority of states have competed to win the grants, Race to the Top has also been criticized by many politicians, policy analysts, thought leaders, and educators. Teachers unions argued that state tests are an inaccurate way to measure teacher effectiveness..."

Over the past 10 years, I have asked many persons involved in education the question, "Do you believe that reforms by the government such as No Child Left Behind, Race to the Top, and Common Core are good or bad for public education?" Most of the respondents felt that the initiatives were well-intended and had some benefits to local school districts, especially in terms of providing funds to educational programs. However, all with whom I spoke thought that the federal government's inclination to attach exacting standards to the awarded dollars was counterproductive. Typical comments included: "The federal government should not be involved in local education," "Children learn best when they are incentivized with hands-on discovery and analysis rather than memorizing to take a test." "Government reforms are noble ideas being drawn up by people with no experience in the field of education." "I agree that teachers should be held accountable, but testing does not consider the many variables a teacher must contend." An argument I often heard was testing makes it difficult, if not impossible, to account for cultural and ethnic differences, teaching styles, and socio-economic variances.

A February 8, 2010 report in Liberal OC titled *Teacher Performance Should Not Be Measured by a Series of Multiple-choice Questions,"* argued that tying teacher's pay to a student's ability to pass a test is inappropriate for many reasons. It directs teachers to focus on subjects being tested and little else. A student who is not strong at math and reading (tested subjects) may excel in the arts (not tested). The article states, "By teaching to a test we end up teaching as though we are programming a computer for limited and simple functions rather than teaching students the full spectrum of knowledge necessary to be productive and involved members of society."

An article that appeared in the Western Journal, October 19, 2018 edition, written by Jack Davis titled *Years After States Adopt Common Core, 2018 ACT Scores See Worst Scores in Over a Decade* stated, "The ACT administers standardized exams used for college entrance, said that students who took the 2018 exam had the lowest readiness for college math since 2004."

Davis reported that Ohio State Rep. Andrew Thompson said Common Core does not deserve all the blame for the falling scores but called it "a significant factor." "I think testimony we took during our attempts to eradicate Common Core showed the dumbing down of curriculum, the social justice indoctrination, the emphasis on social-emotional learning, reduced quantity and quality of reading, emphasizing screen time rather than classroom instruction," Thompson said, according to PJ Media "Destruction of proper math has also been a contributing factor." Common Core proponents, he said, "place a higher priority on indoctrination than education."

So have government-mandated programs such as "No Child Left Behind", "Race to the Top", and "Common Core" as well as state testing programs been effective? The National Assessment of Education Progress (NAEP), a congressionally mandated program administered by the Department of Education, conducts assessments of schools across the country and provides "Report Cards." The assessments look back on student performance across more than four decades. Results showed that average reading and mathematics scores for 17-year-olds were not significantly different in 2012 since the early 1970s. Results have been mixed showing progress in some areas and little or none in others. The National Center for Education Statistics (NCES) compares each state's standard for proficient performance in reading and mathematics by placing the state standards onto a common scale of National Assessment of Educational Progress (NAEP). Results from the 2015 NAEP Reading and Mathematics Assessments, showed "average scores for reading in 2015 declined at Grade 8. There was no significant change in the reading score 4th grade students. Over the long term, however, scores were higher in 2015 in both subject and grades compared to the initial assessments in the early 1990s." In 2017 compared to 2015, there was a one-point increase in the average reading score at Grade 8, but no significant change in the average score for reading at grade 4, or for mathematics at either grade. A 2010 report showed that over eight-year period students in America's largest cities making gains in math. Reading scores in the same cities have shown no progress. But the real question is, given the monetary cost, loss of quality learning on non-tested subjects, teacher frustration, and stress among students, has the mandated programs been a good "return on investment"? The statistics say the answer is "no."

A survey by the Council of Chief State School Officers and the Council of the Great City Schools, showed students taking an average of 113 standardized tests between pre-K and grade 12, with the 11th grade the most tested. (*Student Testing in America's Great City Schools* dated October 2015). "The average student in these districts will typically take about eight standardized tests per year, e.g., two NCLB tests (reading and math), and three formative exams in two subjects per year." Another study entitled *Testing Overload in America's Schools* by the Center for American Progress as reported by Melissa Lazarin on October 16, 2015, looked at 14 school districts. It found that students in grades 3-8 take an average of 10 standardized assessments per year. The emphasis on testing in specified subjects was at the expense of subjects not on the test such as the arts, creative writing, debating, current events, leadership, and other topics that foster social and moral development, initiative, imagination, creativity, conceptual thinking, ethics, and other success principles. What standardized tests do measure is a student's ability to recall facts and knowledge.

Teachers become teachers because they want to teach one or more subjects to the best of their abilities, and they want to enjoy doing it. They want to be committed and enthusiastic. They know that when they are excited, most often, the student is incentivized to learn. Robert L. Fried, the author of *The Passionate Teacher,* says, **"In the debate about national standards and performance outcomes and the legislation to change educational systems, the teacher's role is shunted to a subsidiary role."** Fried argues that teachers face many obstacles, one of which is standardized testing, "that determines who succeeds and who fails, without regard for individual differences or learning styles." Fried uses the term "Game of Schools" to describe an education system in which the... "idea of learning is treated like a mindless duty..." **When required testing and limited classroom time gives way to preparing for standardized tests, it will eventually take a toll on a teacher's joy of teaching and motivation.**

Fried's prediction has come true. In an April 7, 2015 posting in "The Conversation" *Crisis in American education as teacher morale hits an all-time low* the article reported that "...-teachers are leaving the field, and many of those who were considering being a teacher, after hearing the frustration of experienced teachers, choose other career fields." Although there are many reasons for the exodus, one major reason is the decline in teacher morale resulting from standardized testing and centralized government control of education.

A study on youth risk behavior by the Centers for Disease Control and Prevention reported that teen suicide is a growing problem. Nearly 1 in 6 high school students have seriously considered suicide, and 1 in 12 has attempted it. For college students, suicide is the second leading cause of death. Unlike Chinese students who commit suicide because of academic pressures and standardized testing, the reason that American students decide to end their lives appears more related to bullying and depression. However, the question remains, will the emphasis on testing in the United States contribute to increased anxiety and depression in our children? It is unlikely that the western world will get to the point that China has regarding pressure on their students; however, we certainly do not want to go in that direction, which it seems we are doing.

A March 2015 report by Valerie Strauss in the Washington Post titled, *Five reasons standardized testing isn't likely to let up* well summarizes the issue. "For well over a dozen years high-stakes standardized testing has become a hallmark of modern school reform, so much so that an anti-testing rebellion has erupted around the country among parents, students, and educators. Even some of the testing's strongest proponents now say it is time to scale back on the number of assessments students must take. Education Secretary Arne Duncan said that as the 2014-15 school year was beginning, he "shared" teachers concern about too much standardized testing and test prep and that he believed "testing issues today are sucking the oxygen out of the room in a lot of schools."

Strauss quotes Anya Kamenetz, a lead education blogger at NPR, and a former staff writer for *Fast Company* magazine. Kamenetz asks if students, parent, teachers, and even proponents do not like standardized testing, then why do we continue to do it? "Follow the money," she says. Here are her five reasons why our students and education system will continue to be subjected to the hated exams. I will list them, but only briefly state the reasons. For more detail consult Ms. Strauss' article at www.washingtonpost.com/news/answer-sheet/wp/2015/03/11/five-reasons-standardized-testing-isnt-likely-to-let-up/

1. **Companies that publish the tests make tons of money.**

   "In 2012, a report by the Brookings Institution found $669 million in direct annual spending on assessments in 45 states, or $27 per student. When you add administrative costs involved in tests, the total spent on testing rises to $1100 per student."

2. **The test prep industry is lucrative.**

   "Schools spent $13.1 billion dollars in 2015 (including test preparation, tutoring, and counseling). The private tutoring market was estimated at over $78.2 billion."

3. **The people who determine how we reform education are the people who fund education reform.**

   "Among the top donors to public schools are what Diane Ravitch calls 'The Billionaire Boys Club' help drive public school reform." Included are the Bill and Melinda Gates Foundation (Microsoft fortune), the Walton Family Foundation (Wal-Mart), and the Eli and Edythe Broad Foundation (home-building and finance). The Gates, Walton and Broad foundations saw their grants as investments, designed to produce measurable results.

4. **Common Core helps make Ed Tech lucrative.**

   "Before the Common Core, 50 states had 50 standards, creating a fragmented marketplace for texts, materials, and assessments. In a 2013 keynote presentation at SXSWedu, Gates pointed out that standards make it easier for education startups to grow very big very fast." Gates said that test developers would no longer have to cater to many standards but one—the Core. The Gates Foundation spent over 230 million dollars to implement Common Core.

5. **School reform in the United States attracts businesspeople—not educators.**

"Rupert Murdoch, the CEO of News Corp, cast an acquisitive eye on every public dollar spent on education when he announced the beginning of his education technology brand Amplify. At this point, Amplify produces software for the K-12 market, but Murdoch expects to expand his holdings." "When it comes to K-12 education, we see a $500 billion sector in the U.S. alone that is waiting desperately to be transformed by big breakthroughs that extend the reach of great teaching."

The articles written by Strauss and Kamenetz were published in 2015.

Two years later, Joy Pullman wrote in *The Federalist* that Bill Gates admitted Common Core was a failure. Gates wrote in his blog, "Based on everything we have learned in the past 17 years, we are evolving our education strategy," He followed this by detailing how U.S. education has "… essentially made little improvement in the years since he and his foundation — working so closely with the Obama administration, that federal officials regularly consulted foundation employees and waived ethics laws to hire several — began redirecting trillions of public dollars towards programs he now admits haven't accomplished much." Will those and others who have vested and gained so much in standardized testing be willing to turn the tide in the best interest of our education system? Unlikely, but there is hope.

Every April Pennsylvania schools busy themselves with preparing for the state-mandated state achievement exams called the Pennsylvania System of School Assessment tests or PSSA's. The Pennsylvania School Boards Association in 2016 studied standardized testing and concluded, "tests are too long, too frequent, and not developmentally appropriate." Furthermore, the study stated that tests should be used in a way that does not cause teacher anxiety. Nor should they be used to measure teacher effectiveness.

Some national and state legislatures are acting to reverse the trend of more and more standardized testing. For example, Pennsylvania State Senator Andrew Dinniman, Chair of the Senate Education Committee, recently introduced a bill to stop the Keystone Exams as a requirement for high school graduation. This graduation test requirement is tied to the Federal Common Core curriculum. Research by his staff revealed a vast disparity between educational resources (services, teachers, facilities, materials) of more impoverished inner-city schools and the more affluent suburban schools. "The Keystone Exams stated Dinniman, "are neither educationally sound nor fiscally responsible." "The exams would amount to an estimated $300 million unfunded mandate on schools and takes up valuable classroom teaching time." Dinniman has pointed out that in eight years, the state of Pennsylvania and school districts within the state awarded contracts totaling over $1.3 billion for standardized testing. Yet, says the Senator "We had a $15 million shortfall. No wonder property taxes are so high." **Some school districts do not have enough resources to educate students in the subjects upon which they are being tested. Senator Dinniman argues that the millions of dollars spent on testing could be put to better use in educating students instead of evaluating them.**

In June 2017 at a meeting at West Chester University speakers included school administrators, teachers, parents, students, test administrators, and elected officials. Not one presenter spoke favorably about the Keystone Exams. Senator Dinniman said that out of 46 fellow senators all but three supported abolishments of the exams.

Charlotte Iserbyt, who served as Senior Policy Advisor in the Office of Educational Research and Improvement (OERI), U.S. Department of Education, is a primary opponent of Common Core. She argues that the emphasis on performance-based education is stifling innovative thinking. Iserbyt also warns that centralized government control of local school systems will lead to less influence parents have on the education of their children. Currently, parents have several educational choices to which they can send their children, such as public schools, private schools, charter schools, and home-based learning. Many fear that the trend towards centralized government control will threaten private schools in favor of publicly funded schools, thus narrowing the choices parents have.

Many colleges and universities are placing less emphasis on college admissions tests (SAT and ACT). Domenico Grasso, Provost of the University of Delaware in 2017, reported, "After much study and consideration by the Office of Admissions and the Faculty Senate, UD concluded that requiring the SAT/ACT sometimes leads to unintended and or misleading outcomes for students. We will fine-tune our admissions strategy using holistic reviews to encourage all Delawareans capable of success at UD to apply and be subsequently admitted. This will have positive consequences for Delaware students who in turn will enrich the entire University." The University of Delaware is not the first to begin to challenge standardized admission testing. The National Center for Fair and Open Testing reports that as of 2019, over 1,000 colleges and universities that are now de-emphasizing these tests. Many do not require college entrance exams. Others use the tests as optional or flexible. So, there is a trend to deemphasize reliance on standardized testing. Let's hope the trend continues.

I am not suggesting no testing, instead to minimize it. Standards and a means for checking on a student's academic progress are important, but not to the degree that it causes stress on students and teachers, strains educational budgets, and increases costs to taxpayers. Our government is committed to providing the best education possible for our youth. However, politicians and bureaucrats, although well-meaning, may not always make the best choices and must learn from the success and failures of history and other cultures. **It is appropriate to emulate Asian countries that place high importance on education for their children. However, to place emphasis on testing, as the Chinese and other Asian countries do, and as we have been doing since introduction of No Child**

Left Behind, Race to the Top, and Common Core in the United States, undermines the higher value of educating students to be independent and innovative thinkers, and to build character, which are the true cornerstones of a quality education system.

Diane Ravitch, a long-time opponent of government over control of education in her book *The Death and Life of the Great American School System: How Testing and Choice are Undermining Education* argues that fundamentally standardized testing is "... flawed because they are built on a market metaphor. Schools don't work like businesses. Public education should be preserved because it is so intimately connected to our concepts of citizenship and democracy and to the promise of American life." She offers a series of prescriptions:

- Leave decisions about schools to educators, not politicians or people in business.
- Pay teachers a fair wage for their work, not "merit pay" based on deeply flawed and unreliable test scores.
- Encourage family involvement in education from an early age.

If the federal and state governments want to help local school districts, then rather than defining outcomes with test scores, governments can best help by minimizing authoritarian centralized management. Also, educators must be empowered to manage education and encourage parental involvement. If the government and school districts feel compelled to administer standardized tests to monitor progress and evaluate programs, then so be it, but such testing must be minimized. Reducing reliance on standardized testing will allow teachers to focus on the joy of teaching instead of focusing on teaching to the test. Funding must be based on need, and not the results of states and school districts inclination to administer tests. It has been repeatedly proven that when students experience the joy of learning, they will learn best. American education would be wise to follow the Finnish education system which I address in the next chapter.

Chapter 39
Challenges and New Opportunities
for Our Education System

Parents are worried. Technology changes at warp speed, global economic dynamics are getting more competitive, job market skills are challenged to keep up with industry needs, and third world extremists threaten civilized countries through inhumane and despicable acts of terror. Thus, many parents believe a college education, especially from an elite university, is no longer a privilege rather indispensable. This attitude has helped to contribute to the increased competition to gain admissions into elite colleges, says former Yale professor William Deresiewicz, author of *Excellent Sheep—The Miseducation of American Elite*. The seeds of extreme competition in elite colleges were planted back in the 1930s under the administration headed by James B. Conant of Harvard and in the early 1960s under the presidency of Kingman Brewster of Yale. These men recognized that to maintain the elite status of their institutions they needed to change the traditional selection process that focused on male, white, affluent legacies, to a broader base of applicants that did not discriminate, instead based admissions on grades and test scores. It was good in that admissions were now open to all qualified students regardless of race, gender, or creed. But, explains Deresiewicz, the more stringent standards have added requirements for college applicants to include in their dossier's documentation of not only participation in a plethora of extracurricular activities, but leadership in those activities. Over the last 50 years, the expectations of college admissions have become more stringent, and admissions rates have declined.

Consequently, stress on families and students has increased. Many parents are under the expectation that to be successful in a competitive world, their child must attend a top tier university. To gain admission parents pressure their children to make all

"A's", take as many honors courses as possible, participate in as many extracurricular activities as possible, and make high scores on SAT's, ACT's, AP tests, LSAT's, GRE's, etc. Many parents and academicians preach to high school students that to be happy, they must be successful, and to be successful, they must have a college education and preferably from the best colleges in the country. Of course, we know that this philosophy is nice but not entirely accurate.

The introduction of increased selection procedures has spread to colleges and universities across the nation. Indeed, all colleges and universities are not so competitive. It is estimated that hundreds of thousands of high school students are caught up in the game of "race to the top." Deresiewicz argues (with much support from educators across the spectrum) that although many of today's college students are highly educated and competitive, they are more concerned about credentials and prestige than being progressive and innovative. Based on his personal experience at Yale, and after interviewing hundreds of college professors and students, Deresiewicz points out that many students lack an inner purpose and passion, ultimately resulting in frustration with their careers.

The experience and perceptions of many teenagers today was well expressed by Riley Griffin, who wrote a piece when she was a high school senior in 2013, which appeared in the May 19, 2015 edition of the Huffington Post. "The 21st century teenager is unique. More so than ever, there is an implicit obligation to grow up early and have accomplished something significant before leaving for college. The pressure doesn't derive from our motivation for success; rather, it comes from a fear of failure. The academic competition is intense, and in order to keep up the demands of the admissions office, we fill our plate to the brim with extracurriculars, SAT prep, and community service. You know the deal. They want it; we do it. It's a never-ending circle of nervous breakdowns and ceaseless comparisons. A self-fulfilling prophecy (sic). A desperate scramble for achievement, and yes—glory. Nobody is to blame, we all partake in this messed up system—students, teachers, counselors, college rankings—and of course, our parents." To Riley's claim, I would add "politicians."

Riley goes on to say, *"We show you an alternate reality because we believe the 'system' has no room for imperfections. Even our quirks must be scoured and glossed. We are flawless. We are superhuman. We are not associated with words like "average" or 'normal.' To you, we are hardly teenagers. When you look into our eyes, you don't see a kid; you see a future. Nobel laureate, secretary of state, Academy Award winner—take your pick. Essentially, there is a gap between who we are and who we claim to be. This gap fosters insecurities and doubts (ironically) because we believe that every other student actually is what they say on their resume."*

John Holt, the author of *"Why Children Fail,"* claimed that children do poorly in school because they are afraid, bored, and confused." "Afraid" because children do not want to disappoint their parents whose "limitless hopes and expectations for them hang over their heads like a cloud." Bored because "the things they are given and told to do in school are so trivial, so dull, and make such limited and narrow demands on a wide spectrum of their intelligence, capabilities, and talents. Also, students are confused because what they are told in school hardly has any relation to what they really know, to the rough model of reality that they carry around in their minds." A few years later, Holt published *"How Children Learn."* In this work, he quoted Professor Seymore Papert, who wrote in *Mindstorms*, that "... teachers have less say than they used to about what they teach and how they teach and test it." Holt states that, "Schools cling more and more stubbornly to their mistaken idea that education and teaching are industrial processes to be designed and planned from above in the minutest detail and then imposed on passive teachers and even more passive students." Holt further stated that "Our schools have, with few exceptions, moved steadily in the wrong direction. Schools are on the whole bigger than they used to be, more depersonalized, more threatening, more dangerous, and what they teach more fragmented." Surprise! John Holt's books were written over 50 years ago! It seems as if little has changed, and if anything, is worse. I am sure Holt would have embraced the research and publications of social scientists today such as Peter

Gray, who wrote *Free to Learn,* and Dr. Stuart Brown, who wrote *Play.* John Holt's work is being continued by Holt Associates, 2269 Massachusetts Avenue, Cambridge, MA 02140.

Gray and Brown use evidence from psychology, and history to explain the importance of play to the natural development of creativity, problem-solving, social skills, and adaptability. Gray, Brown, and other "free play" advocates disagree with the belief that children learn best in a structured environment controlled by adults both in and out of school. In short, the argument is that if free play is removed from a child's life, the less opportunity they have to take responsibility and to develop their own natural instincts to explore and learn. Despite such research, many school districts in the United States have reduced or eliminated recess to devote more time to academics. Dr. Bessel Van Der Kolk, a professor of psychiatry at Boston University and founder and medical director of the Trauma Center in Brookline, Massachusetts, wrote in his book, *The Body Keeps the Score,* "Sadly, our education system, despite the well-documented effects of anger, fear, and anxiety on the ability to reason, tends to bypass the emotional engagement system and focus on the cognitive capacities of the mind." "Many programs", says Dr. Van Der Kolk, "continue to ignore the need to engage the safety system of the brain before trying to promote new ways of thinking. **The last things that should be cut from school schedules are chorus, physical education, recess, and anything else involving movement, play, and joyful engagement."**

Unlike traditional schools, Montessori schools emphasize self-direction, collaboration, risk-taking, and communication. In contrast to the typical traditional classroom in which a student sits in a seat and listens to countless hours of lecture, Montessori schools promote self-direction. Children are encouraged to find their passions and taught how to set goals. Montessori schools encourage students to explore, to discover, to inquire, to take chances, and to learn from failures. Guess what! Progress is based on feedback from the teacher and fellow students—not tests and grades. According to the American Montessori Society, "Given the freedom and support to question, to probe deeply, and to make connections, Montessori students become confident, enthusiastic, self-directed learners. They can think critically, work collaboratively, and act boldly a skill set for the 21st century."

In his book, *Carrier to Classroom* (Lulu Publishing, 2017), Charles "Chuck" Baldwin provides extraordinary advice to educators and parents on how to manage, or should I say "lead," effective school programs. After performing duties as a public-school principal, Baldwin set his sights on a different course. Frustrated with the micromanagement of school administrators and teachers by school boards, and lack of adequate leadership, Baldwin turned to the charter school model.

For his work in furthering educational programs in Delaware, Baldwin has been formally recognized by the Delaware Adjutant General, the U.S. Senate, the Christina School District as Teacher of the Year, and many other organizations for his success in developing and furthering educational programs. Included among his accomplishments are the co-founder of the Delaware Military Academy, member of the founding committee for the First State Military Academy, and president of the Charter School of Wilmington. All Navy Junior ROTC units in the State of Delaware were initiated by Baldwin. He credits much of his success as an educator from the leadership skills he learned from a career in the U.S. Navy. In his book, he describes the strategies and philosophies he used to create highly successful programs at public and charter schools.

In the first year of eligibility, the Delaware Military Academy (DMA) was honored as the "Distinguished Unit with Academic Honors" by the Navy. Because of DMA's low dropout rate, high retention rate, high achievement scores, high college scholarship rate (92 percent), and satisfaction scores by students and parents, the Academy is considered one of the best high school level military schools in the United States. So, how did he do it? As Baldwin states, "by establishing a strong, positive school culture." This may seem basic, but as Baldwin states, "Most schools invest little or nothing in leadership development among staff." I am not certain how he came to this conclusion, but I can state from my experience as a child behaviorist in several schools at the elementary, middle school and high school levels, Baldwin's observations are accurate. The school administration and teacher's leadership skills are a critical influence on a school's culture. Baldwin uses a model he took from his leadership training and experiences. The model is called "Deck plate Leadership," and entails ten principles. I presented them to students in Part I, Chapter 10, "How to be a Great Leader."

Some educational programs are beginning to "think out of the box." Although many high schools, colleges, and universities continue to teach using traditional methods, some are using technology to complement, and in some cases, replace traditional classroom instruction. Colleges are teaming up with companies such as Udacity and Coursera to provide students affordable, flexible, innovative educational opportunities. Udacity pioneered with AT&T to develop online, affordable courses designed to prepare and compliment software disciplines for employees of companies such as Google, Salesforce, Cloudera, and AUTODESK. As of this writing, Coursera has partnered with over 24 countries and 118 colleges, universities, and non-academic institutions to provide a wide range of online courses that anyone can take at no cost. Although the courses offered by Coursera are non-credit, they can complement classes offered at higher education institutions. Such "blended learning" strategies have shown to increase student engagement and outcomes. Another example of 21st Century learning is the Mathnasium Method that focuses on teaching children mathematics in non-traditional methods. Larry Martinek, the creator of the learning system, is quoted as saying, "Children don't hate math. They do hate being confused and intimidated by math. With understanding comes passion, and with passion comes growth and a treasure is unlocked."

School systems are being inundated with students whose primary language is not English. According to a U.S. Census Bureau, *Language Use in the United States: 2011*, the number of people in the United States whose native language is not English has nearly tripled over the past thirty years. Most are Spanish speaking (37.6 million, up from 11 million in 1980) and the next most widely spoken language is Chinese at around 2.9 million. Census reports reveal that many metropolitan area population growths are due more to immigration from other countries than domestic growth. To ensure that foreign-born children have the best chance to be productive citizens, they must be afforded the opportunity for a good education. In landmark Supreme Court cases of Brown v. Board of Education (1954), and Lau v. Nichols (1974), school districts receiving federal funding are to establish multi-lingual programs to help address the language barriers of non-native English speakers. In a 2005 a Pew Hispanic Center study revealed that teens with language education difficulties have a higher dropout rate than native English-speaking students. When a student has difficulty understanding, they become frustrated, and many just give up. A diverse student body, however, need not be an obstacle to providing a productive learning environment for all children. Finland's school system has met the challenge.

Why Are Finland's Schools Successful, an article by LynNell Hancock published in September 2011 in the Smithsonian Magazine, reported that Finland's schools produce students who are scoring among the highest in the world. In 2009 Finland scored second in science, third in reading, and sixth in math out of 57 countries (half a million students) on the Program for International Student Assessment (PISA). In 2015 Finland scored 5th in science literacy. Ninety-three percent of Finland's students graduate from high school or vocational school (17.5 percent higher than in the United States). The success is the result of a program that emphasizes teacher education, small schools and classes, teacher collaboration and special help for struggling students, flexibility in teaching methodologies, and a de-emphasis on student and school rankings. There are no mandated tests, except an exam at the end of the last year in high school. "We prepare children how to learn, not how to take a test," said Pasi Sahlberg, from Finland's Ministry of Education and Culture. Sahlberg also said, "I think international benchmarking in the U.S. in general focuses too much on measured test scores and country rankings and thereby undermines other features of education systems, such as equality, well-being, and creativity. Sahlberg describes in his book *Finnish Lessons 2.0* the history of the Finnish education system and how the Finnish process of educational reform differed from the American trend that implements competition, and test-based accountability.

Timo Heikinen, a principal in Helsinki, said, "If you only measure statistics, you miss the human aspect." Kari Louhivuori, principal of the Kirkkujarri Comprehensive School in Espoo, said, "Americans like all these bars and graphs and colored charts. It's nonsense; we know much more about the children than any test can teach us." Unlike in the United States, which emphasizes marketplace competition that challenges states to compete for federal dollars, using standardized tests and other measuring strategies, the Finnish system promotes equal distribution of resources across the spectrum. This is significant given the huge diversity of the country with immigrants from Somalia, Iraq, Russia, Bangladesh, Estonia, Ethiopia, and others. Equality among all socio-economic groups is emphasized and supported by both conservatives and liberals alike.

Andress Scliecher, head of the 36-country member for Organization of Economic Co-operation and Development (OECD) points out that the "highest performing education systems always prioritize the quality of teachers. Finland places high importance on teacher training, remuneration, and time to collaborate with administrators, fellow teachers, and parents. OECD data shows that teachers in the United States spend 38 percent more time in the classroom than their international peers. This takes away from time that could be spent in collaboration, and self-improvement and class preparation. The extra time provided to Finland's teachers provides more time for them to prepare classroom curriculums and assessing students.

Scliecher points out that when a choice must be made between smaller class size and a better teacher, the Finnish education system goes for the latter. Rather than putting money into small classes, they invest in competitive teacher salaries, ongoing professional development, and a balance in working time. Students spend more time at play than do American students. Homework is minimal, and compulsory education is not started until age 7. "Children learn better when they are ready, "why stress them out?" says Louhivuori. **School meals, daycare, three years of maternity leave, preschool for 5-year old's, medical care, counseling, and transportation are all state-funded, and at a cost less per student than in the United States.**

One educator who has extensively studied education systems around the globe for 30 years, and published the benefits of non-traditional learning is John Abbott, president of the 21st Century Learning Initiative. In his paper, *Battling for the Soul of Education*, Mr. Abbott asks, "How can we, as a society, leverage this new information to overhaul our education delivery system?" Abbott goes on to state, "Given what we now know from research into human learning, it would seem that what we need is not further school reform, but a radical transformation of the education system based on the complementary roles of home, community, and school-teachers and legislative reform alone will not get us there. Secondly, are we raising our youth to repeat what they see, or are we raising them to think outside of the box for the betterment of their community? Our society must instill and encourage from a very young age curiosity and risk-taking as platforms for discovery and true learning." In his book *Overschooled but Undereducated*, Abbott states that educational systems misunderstand the teenager's instinctive need to do things for themselves, thus goes against the natural grain of the adolescent brain. Hence, "Formal education ends up unintentionally trivializing the very young people it claims to be supporting." Abbot says that by using the physical and social sciences, educational systems can better understand adolescent human learning. His book is based on extensive research. It considers education systems in Scotland, Wales, Ireland, Canada, the U.S., Australia, and New Zealand. It intends to shake education out of its two-centuries-old inertia. **If education in the 21st Century fails, it is because it will continue to hold on to antiquated teaching philosophies and methodologies and not equip students with the tools needed to meet the challenges they**

face today and in the future. Abbott, who is from England, has observed many of the shortcomings of the British education system. Abbot states that "IQ testing and the tripartite system of secondary education has been strangely confused by the ongoing tension between central and local government." Abbot's arguments sound like the debates being made in the United States, China, and elsewhere in the world. Abbott, and the 21st Century Learning Initiative supported by British and American businessmen. Presentations and seminars have been provided in over 40 countries. The 21st Century Initiative utilizes research-based data as a base for its programs.

Abbot poses the critical question, "What kind of world do we want our future generations to live in"? *The answer, he continues, "...* **relies on the collective work of families, communities, and schools."**

An article published in 2017 in the *Business Insider* reported that the U.S. lags behind other countries when it comes to investing in early childhood programs. The U.S. ranked 46th for primary education. The United Kingdom studied the effects of early childhood education and concluded that it results in marked academic benefits. Thus in 2015, 15 hours a week of free child-care or preschool would be provided for 38 weeks a year. In the UK, enrollment rates for 4 to 6-year-olds far exceed OECD averages.

In response to a plethora of research providing educational and parenting strategies that can improve child development, in 2007 three experts in the field from Stanford University, Madeline Levine, Ph.D., Jim Lobdell, MA, and Denise Pope, Ph.D., founded "Challenge Success." The web site states, "At Challenge Success, we believe that our society has become too focused on grades, test scores, and performance, leaving little time for kids to develop the necessary skills to become resilient, ethical, and motivated learners. We partner with schools, families, and communities to embrace a broad definition of success and to implement research-based strategies that promote student well-being and engagement with learning. After all, success is measured throughout a lifetime, not at the end of a semester. The program educates families, communities, and schools with strategies that will help kids be engaged in learning strategies that promote a love of learning and do it in a physically and emotionally healthy manner. Challenge Success provides consultative and training programs to schools, parents, and communities utilizing workshops, presentations, conferences, and educational videos. Participants report a significant reduction in student stress while maintaining and frequently improving student engagement and academic performance. It is important to note that Challenge Success does not seek to change curricula, eliminate homework and exams, rather diagnose areas that are inefficient and ineffective, and frequently contribute to student stress." **Like John Abbot, the founders and staff of Challenge Success agree that the challenge to reduce student stress while improving performance must be collaboratively addressed by all players—schools and school districts, colleges and universities, parents, students, government officials.**

One of the criticisms of traditional education is that it neglects young people's social and emotional skills. Should school help to nurture these soft skills, and if so, how? Some argue that this is not the role of schools, rather better taught by families. Granted, the family plays a major role in teaching soft skills. But that is not to suggest that school officials and legislatures also do not have a responsibility for creating an environment and opportunities for teachers also to be able to teach these "soft skills." A single book, nor many books, nor advocates for education reform such as John Abbot, Deresiewicz, Pinker, Iserbyt, Zhao, and others can bring about change in isolation. It takes many voices to influence change. **Those who have the power of the vote (you and I) must contact our legislatures and school board members and help them understand that what we want is an education system that minimizes government control and let teachers do what they do best, teach course content of how to be successful in the 21st Century, and not how to take a test.**

The formula for academic systems that wish to improve is **basic:**

1. **Study the data and do what has been shown to work best.**
2. **Be willing to change based on the facts, not unproven theories, political or personal self-interest.**

3. **Be open to revising curricula that maximizes curiosity, innovative thinking, encourages the love of learning, reduces student stress, promotes teacher's joy of teaching, and develops essential life success principles.**

4. **Re-direct monies spent on standardized testing to more critical school programs.**

If the United States wants to improve the education system, it needs to seriously consider the suggestions of Abbott, Challenge Success, Finland, and others. Follow lessons learned and be willing to let go of failed strategies.

Epilogue

Following is the text which appears in PART ONE, *Students Guide*

From time to time, students will not get the grade they like. They may even get a poor grade. It is not the end of the world. Everyone does not succeed at everything they try. The important thing to remember is not that mistakes are made; instead, learn from those mistakes. Often, the best lessons learned are from errors. So don't beat yourself up when things do not go your way. If you do not achieve your goals, keep trying. Remember the poem by Rudyard Kipling I quoted in Chapter 6? "HOLD ON"! Always keep telling yourself how wonderful you are. Accept the guidance and constructive criticism of others. To do so is the mark of a wise learner. Reject destructive criticism of others! When others belittle or tease you, they are not sincere, rather are being driven by their insecurities. That is their issue, not yours. Your image of yourself is based on how you perceive yourself, not how others perceive you. Work on your "Life Purpose," as described in Chapter 9 and set achievable goals, as explained in Chapter 4, then "Go for it!"

A final note to parents and guardians.

My goal in *"Student Success with Less Stress"* was to provide many principles for students to achieve the success that, if followed, will guarantee success not only in school but throughout life. PART TWO for parents and guardians provides guidance and TIPS on how parents and guardians can support their children in their quest to maneuver the challenges of the education system, the social pressures children must face, and how to maximize the opportunity for success and happiness in life. I conclude by providing facts that point to risks in our current education system. To help improve the system, parents must be informed and involved. You are now informed. Involvement is up to you.

The principles provided in both Parts was gathered not only from my own experiences and lessons learned over my lifetime, but more so from the minds of many more educated than I. All I have done is to bring these principles together in one guide to make it easier for the student and those who educate and mentor students, to help children be the best that they can be, and do so in an enjoyable manner and with minimal stress. It is no secret that the key ingredient for a child's success in school, and ultimately success in life, is the involvement of parents, guardians, grandparents, and other family members have during a child's developmental. **Although teachers are essential to teaching children, it is what is happening in the home that most influences the child.** Challenges will be placed in the paths of children and parents alike, but if you and your children can "HOLD ON" challenges will be much easier to deal with. Parents who can instill in their children the principles, values, and strategies described in this book, will give your children, and your children's children a gift far more valuable than anything material you could provide. I concluded PART ONE to students with the powerful principle—the cornerstone of success and happiness in life….

Love yourself, Love Others—Unconditionally! And to this I add… Be involved, stay connected, be the best role model you can be.

Appendix A
Chart Your Course, A Self-Assessment Tool

This chart lists the habits and character traits that are typical of students who are honor students and those who are not. This is not to suggest that all honor students possess every trait listed on the "Success" side of the chart or that average or below-average students reflect every trait listed on the "Self-sabotage" side. No one can have all the traits listed on one or the other side of the chart. However, if you want to be an honor student, successful and happy in life, strive to assimilate and reflect as many of the Personal Attitudes, Interpersonal Skills, and Work Habits listed on the "Success" side of the chart. Know too that these qualities not only will make you a great student but also provide the elements for a successful and happy life.

This chart is modeled after a profile comparison entitled "The Sabotage Verses Success Profile" designed by Dr. Daniel Amen and was published in his book "Don't Shoot Yourself in The Foot" (Werner Books, Inc. New York, 1992)

PERSONAL ATTITUDES AND ATTRIBUTES

Self-sabotage	Success
Negative	Positive
Quick to anger	Even-tempered
Reacts	Responds
Subjective	Objective
Lacks integrity	Honest
Non-compliant	Compliant

Blames	Takes responsibility
Externally motivated	Internally motivated
Lacks vision	Visionary
Close-minded/Stubborn	Open-minded/Receptive
Expects to fail	Expects to succeed
Unmotivated	Motivated
Lacks focus	Focused
Lethargic	Energized
Lack of confidence	Confident
Inflexible	Flexible
Gives up easily	Persistent
Disrespectful	Respectful
Dis-loyal	Loyal

INTERPERSONAL

Self-cantered	Sensitive to needs/ wants of others
Does not provide service to others	Provides service to others.
Avoids interaction with others	Proactively interacts with others
Does not learn from others	Learns from others
Poor communicator	Effective communicator
Passive listener	Active listener
Non-team player	Team player
Dependent on others	Independent

Appendix B
Drive Your Car (and Life) to Success

With your car	With your life
Love your car. Be passionate about your car. Love it, nurture it, care for it.	**Love yourself.** Have a passion for life. Count your blessings.
Know your car Idiosyncrasies. Characteristics Use preventive maintenance procedures. Have a good mechanic.	**Know yourself** **(self-analysis)** Strengths and weaknesses (be honest). Live healthy— body and brain. Seek out other's views. Embrace your spirituality.
Know and comply with **motor vehicle laws.** Know where you are going. Follow them, avoid accidents and penalties.	**Follow life's winning** **principles.** Have a purpose and goals. Increase opportunities for success.
The car as a "rolling library." It is OK to listen to music as you travel, but do you sometimes use the time to "learn" by listening to educational programs?	**Do you spend some of your** **leisure time on expanding** **your knowledge?** Listen to news, talk radio, and books on tape. For students, consider recording lessons and listen when traveling.
When stuck. Call for help!	**When feeling stuck.** Ask for help!

Appendix C
Affirmations

Get into a comfortable position. Take two or three large breaths. Breath slowly and deeply.

While slowly and deeply inhaling and exhaling, close your eyes and silently say to yourself one or more of the following affirmations, as you so choose. Repeat the affirmation several times. Although you do not have to, it often helps to play soothing music, as explained in Chapter 20.

I know I can excel in school.

I will not allow anything to interfere with achieving my goals.

I will not allow negative talk to interfere with my success.

When negative thoughts enter my mind, I will replace them with positive thoughts

I am becoming deeply relaxed so that I can completely concentrate.

I will shut out all distractions.

The stress in my life is fading away moment by moment.

I will have a complete understanding of all the material I am about to study.

I will recall all that I have studied and heard in class.

I will be able to transfer all material learned to my conscious mind when I need it.

I am disciplined and enthusiastic.

I let go of worry and free myself of stressful thoughts.

When I catch myself dwelling on the past, I will choose to refocus on the present and the possibilities of the future.

When feeling stressed, I choose to not complain rather see the positive in the situation.

I am open-minded, and others perceive me as a problem solver.

I try to be humble and sincere. I have no need to complain or boast.

I continually remind myself of what I have rather than what I do not have.

I choose to be positive and to help others be positive.

I choose to listen attentively when others are speaking.

I am sensitive to the views, needs, and wants of others.

I will get rid of self-sabotaging traits and strive to manifest successful traits.

When I am tempted to procrastinate, I will tap into my higher self to give me the discipline to begin the task before me.

I have every right to ask for help when I need it.

When I feel overwhelmed, I will break things down into small tasks, and rejoice in every small accomplishment.

I choose to be positive and am enthusiastic about my life and the opportunities in front of me.

I realize that helping others will give me great joy.

I am excited about my self-development and looking forward to new adventures.

Every moment is a gift and a new opportunity that I will not waste.

I will not allow past failures to get me down, rather look to the future with hope and optimism.

I see every adversity as a new opportunity.

I go with the flow and do not try to force things I have little or no control of.

I am lovable and worthy of good things, just the way I am.

I will not dwell in the past or worry about the future.

There is nothing more precious than love. I will love myself and others unconditionally.

Appendix D
Life Lessons from Benjamin Franklin

A friend recently sent this to me. I thought Benjamin Franklin's "Life Lessons" so well synopsized many of the success principles described in this book that it would be well worth including for my readers. Franklin was one of the most admired persons in American history. His ability to manage his time in a productive manner is equaled by few. Yet, those who strive to emulate the success principles espoused by Benjamin Franklin will, without doubt, greatly increase their efficiency and effectiveness.

Benjamin Franklin was one of the Founding Fathers of the United States of America. Franklin was an author and printer, political theorist, politician, postmaster, scientist, inventor, satirist, civic activist, statesman, and diplomat.

As a scientist, he was a major figure in the American Enlightenment and the history of physics for his discoveries and theories regarding electricity. He invented the lightning rod, bifocals, the Franklin stove, a carriage odometer, and the glass 'harmonica.' He formed both the first public lending library in America and the first fire department in Pennsylvania.

His colorful life and legacy of scientific and political achievement, and status as one of America's most influential Founding Fathers, have seen Franklin honored on coinage and money, on warships, in many towns, counties, educational institutions, and companies.

Waste Not

"Do not squander time for that is the stuff life is made of."

Your time is your life. If you waste your time, you are wasting your life. I've never met a successful person who didn't value their time, and I've never met an unsuccessful person who did.

Don't let other people waste your time either, why is it when someone wants to "kill an hour," they want to kill your hour as well? Protect your time; it can never be replaced; it can never be replenished; your time is your life.

Learn

"Being ignorant is not so much a shame, as being unwilling to learn."

Benjamin Franklin said, "He that won't be counseled can't be helped." Always be open to learning. You can learn from anyone, and from any situation. You can learn from the fool as well as the genius.

Make Mistakes

"Do not fear mistakes. You will know failure. Continue to reach out."

Success comes from doing things "right," and doing things right is usually the result of first doing things wrong. You are certain to make mistakes; the path to success is lined with mistakes and failures, just keep moving. Successful people make a lot of mistakes, but they don't quit, they keep moving until they arrive at their goal.

Energy and Persistence

"Energy and persistence conquer all things."

To have energy and persistence, you must have passion; there must be an inner vision that drives you to achieve your goal.

If you don't have a clear picture of where you're going, then you don't have the energy or persistence to make any noteworthy progress. You must be driven by a picture that is bigger than your current reality.

Prepare

"By failing to prepare, you are preparing to fail."

It's better to not have an opportunity and be prepared, then to have an opportunity and not be prepared. Success loves the preparation, are you prepared?

If the perfect opportunity presented itself, would you be ready for it? Spend your days preparing for success, so when your opportunity comes, you will be ready.

Be Diligent

"Diligence is the mother of good luck."

Solomon wrote the diligent shall be made rich. If you want to be lucky, be diligent, the more diligent you are, the luckier you will be. Everyone can increase their luck seven-fold by becoming more diligent.

References and Resources

Abajo, Ramon. *What Every Teacher Should Know About Handwriting.* Downhill Publishing, 2010.

Abbot, John. *Overschooled but Undereducated: How the crisis in education is jeopardizing our adolescents.* Continuum International Publishing Group, 2010.

-----*Battling for the Soul of Education,* 2010. Accessed March 2018, www.21learn.org/archive/battling-for-the-soul-of-education./

ADDitude Mag. *ADHD & Iron: Can Nutritional Supplements Improve Symptoms?* Archives of Pediatrics and Adolescent Medicine, 2004

Adler, Ronald; Rosenfeld Lawrence and Proctor, Russell F II. *Interplay-Process of Interpersonal Communication.12th ed.* Oxford University Press, 2000.

Alcoholics Anonymous, Alcoholics Anonymous World Services, Inc., 1976.

Alston, J, and Taylor, J., *Handwriting Theory Research and Practice.* Nichols Publishing Company. 1987.

Akman, Terri, and McAnuff, Courtney. *What Colleges Want,* Nov 2015. www.metrokids.com/MetroKids/What-Colleges-Want.

Amen, Daniel. *Don't' Shoot Yourself in the Foot.* Werner Books, Inc., 1992.

-----*Change Your Brain, Change Your Life.* Three Rivers Press, 1998.

-----*The Secrets of Successful Students.* MindWorks Press, 2005.

American Demographics. *Cost-of-awful-handwriting-set-at-200-million-a-year.* St Louis Post-Dispatch (MO)*:* Knight-Ridder Newspapers: 1994. Accessed May 2016. www.questia.com/newspaper/1P2-32906154/cost-of-awful-handwriting-set-at-200-million-a-year.

American Gap Association. Posted by Heritage Valley Credit Union. *Could a gap year after High School make financial sense?* August 2017. Accessed September 2019. blog.heritagevalleyfcu.org/2017/08/could-a-gap-year-after-high-school-make-financial-sense/.

American Montessori Society. Accessed March 2018. amshq.org/Montessori-Education/Introduction-to-Montessori/Benefits-of Montessori.

American Psychological Association. *Teen Stress Rivals That of Adults. Stress in America.* Washington D.C.: 2014. Accessed June 2016. www.apa.org/pubs/contact.aspx.

Assagioli, Roberto. *The Act of Will.* Penguin Books, 1993 (first published 1973).

Atkinson, William. *Eliminate Stress from Your Life Forever.* AMACOM, 2004.

Baden-Powell. *Scouting for Boys.* London, Windsor House. First published 1908.

Baker, Jed. *No More Meltdowns.* Future Horizons, 2008.

Baldwin, Charles. *From Carrier to Classroom.* Lulu Press, 2017.

Barnes, Robert G. Jr., *Who's in charge? Overcoming Power Struggles with Your Kids.* Word Publishing, 1990.

Barshay, Jill., *Top U.S. Students Fare Poorly in International PISA Test Scores,* The Hechinger Report. December 2013. Accessed July 2017. http://educationbythenumbers.org/content/top-us-students-fare-poorly-internation.

Bathia, Dhaval. *Verdi Mathematics.* JAICO Publishing, 2005

Bellis, Teri J. *When the Brain Can't Hear. Unraveling the Mystery of Auditory Processing Disorder.* Pocket Books, 2002.

Benjamin, Arthur, and Sheoner, Michael. *Secrets of Mental Math.* Crown Publishing Group, 2006.

Bennis, Warren and Nanas, Burt. *People don't want to be managed.* Published in the Wall Street Journal by United Technologies Corporation. Harper and Row, 1985.

Benson, Lee. *Brain Bullet.* Self Development.net, a Kaleidoscope Global Brand.2018.

Berenbeg, Ben R. *The Churkendoose.* Wonder Books, 1946.

Berninger, V., Graham, S. *Language by hand: A synthesis of a decade of research on handwriting.* Handwriting Review, *12*, 11-25. 1998. Accessed July 2017.

http://ldonline.org/spearswerling/The_Importance_of_Teaching_Handwriting.

Best Colleges. U.S. News & World Report. usnews@rifgts media, 2016.

Birch, Elisa-Rose, and Miller, Paul W., *The Characteristics of 'Gap-Year' Students and Their Tertiary Academic Outcomes.* Economic Record, Vol. 83, No. 262, pp. 329-344, September 2007. Accessed

May 2018. https://ssrn.com/abstract=1014707 or http://dx.doi. org/10.1111/j.1475-4932.2007.00418.x

Bledsoe, Mac. *Parenting with Dignity.* Alpha Books, 2003.

Bowers Ellen, and Lynam, Edward. *The Everything Parent's Guide to Teenage Addiction.* Adams Media, 2014.

Boyle, Sherianna. *The Conscious Parents Guide to Childhood Anxiety.* Adams Media, 2016.

-----*The Four Gifts of Anxiety.* Adams Media, 2015.

Braaten, Ellen, and Willoughby, Brian. *Bright Kids Who Can't Keep Up.* The Guilford Press, July 2014.

Brown, Stuart. Play. *Play.* Avery Press-Penguin Group, 2009.

Buckley, Jack. *The Nation's Report Card: Mega-States* National Center for Educational Statistics (NCES). February 2013.

Bureau of Labor Statistics (BLS) report *Education Pays* February 2019. Accessed September 2019. www.bls.gov/careeroutlook/2019/ data-on-display/education_pays.htm.

Burns, Ken. T.V. special, *The West*, Season I, Episode 9, 1996.

Business Insider. *US Schools Lag Behind Other Countries.* Accessed Feb. 2017. www.businessinsider.com/ america-low-preschool-enrollment-oecd-2017-90.

Buzan, Tony. *Make the Most of Your Mind.* Fireside Book, February 1984 (First published, 1977).

-----*Mind Map Mastery: The Complete Guide to Learning and Using the Most Powerful Thinking Tool in the Universe.* Watkins Media, March 2018.

Camera, Lauren. *Teen Overdose Death Rate Rises.* U.S. News & World Report. August 2017. See also www.usnews.com/topics/subjects/drug abuse.

Canter, Lee, and Hausner, Lee. *Homework Without Tears.* Harper Perennial,1987.

Can Texting Help With Spelling. Scholastic Teacher. Accessed June 2017. http://scholastic.com/teachers/articles/content-can texting help.

Carlson, Richard. *The Don't Sweat Affirmations.* Hyperion, 2001.

Casey, B.J., Caudle, Kristina. *The Teenage Brain: Self Control.* Current Directions in Psychological Science, 2014.

Carter, Les. and Mirth, Frank. *The Anger Workbook. Thomas Nelson,* 2012.

-----. *The Freedom from Depression Workbook.* Thomas Nelson, 1996.

Center for Disease Control and Prevention (CDC), Division of Adolescent and School Health Resources and Services. *Improving the Health of Adolescents and Young Children,* 2004. www.cdc.gov/.

-----National Center for Injury Prevention Suicide: Fact Sheet. *Teen suicide is a growing problem.* Accessed November 2017. www.ct.gov/dmhas/lib/dmhas/prevention/cyspi/suicidefactsheet.pdf.

-----Office on Smoking and Health. *Preventing Tobacco Use Among Youth.*

Centers for Disease Control and Prevention, Office on Smoking and Health. *Smoking and tobacco use: Tobacco industry marketing.* Accessed February 2016. cdc.gov/tobacco/data_statistics/fact_ sheets/tobacco_industry/marketing/index.htm.

Challenge Success. Accessed June 2018.

Coleman, Samuel. et. al. *The Coleman Report. Equality of Educational Opportunity*, for the U.S. Department of Health, Education, and Welfare. Washington, D.C. 1966.

College and Career Preparation: How Will I Afford College. Quizlet. Accessed August 2018. quizlet.com/86973092/college-and-career-preparation-how-will-i-afford-college.

College Savings - Understanding 529 Plans. Accessed August 2018. http://cheapscholar.org/2012/10/24/college-savings-understanding- 529-plans-fees/

Colligan, Louise. *Help! I Have to Study.* Riverview Books, 1987.

Council of Chief State School Officers and the Council of the Great City Schools, *Student Testing in America's Great City Schools.* October 2015. Accessed April 2018. www.cgcs.org/cms/lib/ DC00001581/Centricity/Domain/87/Testing%20Report.pdf.

Crawford, Claire, and Cribb, Jonathan. *Gap year takers: uptake, trends, and long term outcomes.* Institute for Fiscal Studies through the Centre for Analysis of Youth Transitions (CAYT). Department for Education. United Kingdom, Nov 2012.

Crook, Thomas H. and Adderly, Brenda. *The Memory Cure.* Pocket Books, 1998.

Daniels, Peter J. *How to Reach Your Life Goals.*The House of Tabor, 1985.

Davidson, Jeff. *The Complete Idiots Guide to Reaching Your Goals.* Alpha Press, 1998.

Davidson, Paul. *Why China is beating the U.S. at innovation.* U.S.A. Today. April 2017.

Davis, Jack. *Years After States Adopt Common Core 2018 ACT Sees Worst ACT Scores in Over a Decade.* The Western Journal. October 2018. Accessed May 2019. www.westernjournal.com/ years-states-adopt-common-core-2018-sees-worst-act-scores-decade/

DeAngelis., Barbara. *Living with integrity.* Simple Reminders. com. January 2015. Accessed May 2017. gomcgill.com/ living-with-integrity-by-barbara-de-angelis.

DeFoore, William. *Anger: Deal With It, Heal With It, Stop It From Killing You.* Health Communications, Inc., 2004.

Democracy Now. *Worst Epidemic in U.S. History? Opioid Crisis Now Leading Cause of Death for Americans Under 50* June 2017. Accessed December 2017. www.democracynow.org/2017/6/7/ worst_epidemic_in_us_history_opioid.

Department of Health and Human Services. A Report of the Surgeon General. *Preventing Tobacco Use Among Youth and Young Adult,.* 2012

Deresiewicz, William. *Excellent Sheep, The Miseducation of the American Elite.* Free Press, 2014.

Deurlein, Rebecca. *Teenagers 101 What a Top Teacher Wishes You Knew About Helping Your Kid Succeed.* AMACOM Books, October 2014.

Dew, et al. *Religion/Spirituality and Adolescent Psychiatric Symptoms: a review.* Child Psychiatry. Human Development. Volume 9. December 2000. Accessed June 2018. www.ncbi.nlm. nih.gov/pubmed/.

Diagnostic and Statistical Manual of Mental Disorders (DSM-5). American Psychiatric Association, October 2018.

Dinehart, Laura et al. *Handwriting in early childhood education: Current research and future implications.* Journal of Childhood Literacy. Published online March 2014. Sage Publications. Accessed June 2014. www. journals.sagepub.com/doi/abs/.

Dinniman, Andy. *Pennsylvania is failing students by forcing PSSA's.* Editorial in Avon Grove Sun, West Grove, PA: Southern Chester County News, April 2017.

Dobbs, David. *Beautiful Brain.* National Geographic, October 2011.

Drew, Naomi. *Peaceful Parents, Practical Ways to Create a Calm and Happy Home.* Kensington Books, 2000.

Drouin, Michelle A. *College student's text messaging, use of texting, and literacy skills.* Journal of Computer Assisted Learning, Volume 27. online library/wiley.com/doi/abs/Jan 2011.

Drouin, Michelle; Davis, Claire. Journal of Literacy Research, vol 41 2009. Accessed 12 February 2013. *R U Txting? Is the Use of Text Speak Hurting Your Literacy?*

Economic Policy Institute report by Weiss, Elaine. *Race to the Top, Small Successes, Multiple Challenges, and Lessons Learned,* 12 September 2013.

Ellis, Kristina. *How to Graduate Debt Free.* Worthy Publishing, 2016.

Esquith, Rafe. *Lighting Their Fires-How Parents and Teachers Can Raise Extraordinary Kids.* Penguin Books, 2010.

Eyre, Richard and Linda. *Teaching Children Joy.* Shadow Mountain, 1984.

-----*Teaching Children Responsibility.* Shadow Mountain. 2nd ed. 1984.

Faber, Adele and Mazlish, Elaine. *How to Talk So Kids Will Listen and Listen So Kids Will Talk Loving.* Scribner, 2nd ed., 1996

Facts for Families. All Family Resource. San Rafael, CA. Accessed May 2016. http://familymanagement.com/facts/english/index.html.

Forbes Magazine. *The World's Most Innovative Countries.* May 2017. Accessed January 2018. www.forbes.com/innovative-companies/list/.

Fried, Robert L. *The Passionate Teacher,* Boston, MA. Beacon Press. 2nd ed. 2001.

Fisher, Gary, and Cummings, Rhoda. *The Survival Guide for Kids with LD*: *(Learning Differences).* Free Print Publishing. 1990, reprinted 2002.

Forbes Magazine. *100 Most Innovative Countries,* May 2017.

Foreman, George. *Guide to Life*. Simon and Schuster, 2002.

Frank, Steven. *The Everything Study Book*. Adams Media Corp, 1996.

Francis, Becky. *The glaring gap in the English education system is social class*. The Guardian, October 2015.

Fritz, Robert. *The Path of Least Resistance*. Stillpoint Publishing, 1984.

Fry, Ronald W. *How to Study Program*, 4th ed. Career Press, 1996.

-----*Ace Any Test*. 3rd ed. Career Press, 1996.

-----*Take Notes*. Audio Cassette. High Bridge Company, 1994. 2nd ed 1996.

Geisen, Michael. *How to become a Super Star Student*. The Great Courses, 2011.

Generalized Anxiety Disorder. WebMD. http://webmd.com/anxiety-panic/guide/generalized-anxiety-disorder#1. Accessed June 2016.

Goldenthal, Peter. *Beyond Sibling Rivalry*. Henry Holt and Co., 1999

Goleman, Daniel. *Social Intelligence: The New Science of Human Relationships*, Bantom Books, 2006.

Gottesman, Greg. *College Survival*. 3rd Ed. MacMillan, 1994.

Graham, S., Harris, K. R., Fink, B. *Is handwriting causally related to learning to write? Treatment of handwriting problems in beginning writers*. Journal of Educational Psychology, 92, 620-633. 2000, and 93, 488-497, 2001.

Granic, Isabela, et al. *The Benefits of Playing Video Games,* University Nijmegen 2013.

Grasso, Domenico. *Welcome back, Blue Hens!* February 16, 2106. Accessed February 2016. https://provost.udel.edu/resources/letters-from-the-provost/2016-letters-from-the-provost/welcome-back-blue-hens/.

Graves, Donald, and Kittle, Penny. *My Quick Writes: For Inside Writing.* Heinemann Educational Books, Sept 2005.

Gray, Peter. *Free to Learn.* Philadelphia, PA, Basic Books, 2013.

Greenberg, Mark, et al. *Promoting emotional competence in school-aged children in Emotions in Development Psychopathology* Volume 7, Issue 1. Cambridge University Press. 1995. Published online March 2009. Accessed June 2018. www.cambridge.org/core/journals/development-and-psychopathology/article/promoting-emotional-competence-in-school-aged-children-the-effects-of-the-paths-curriculum.

Griffin, Riley. Huffington Post, May 19, 2015.

Grosshans, Beth A. and Burton, Janet H. *Beyond Time Out.* Smithsonian Magazine. Sterling Publishing, 2008.

Guillen, Michael. *Amazing Truths: How Science and the Bible Agree.* Zondervan, 2015.

Haidt, Jonathan. *The Happiness Hypostases.* New York. Basic Books, 2006.

Hancock, LynNell. *"Why Are Finland's Schools Successful."* September 2011. Accessed June 2018. www.smithsonianmag.com/innovation/why-are-finlands-schools-successful

Hansen, Mark V., and Canfield, Jack. *Dare to Win*. New York, NY. Berkley Book, 1994.

Sophie, S; Harley, Ann; Prior, Margot. *Building Preschool Children's Emotional Competence: A Parenting Program*. Early Education and Development. Journal Article. ERIC. Lawrence Erlbaum Associates, Inc. 2004. www.LEAonline.com.

Hay, Louise L. *The Power is Within You*. Hay House, Inc., 1991.

-----*You Can Heal Your Life*. Hay House, Inc., 1985, 2004.

Healing Power of Nature. Time Magazine. June 2017. See also www.h.chiba-u.jp/prof/graduate/ryokuchi/ymiyazakie.html.

Hill, Napoleon. *Think and Grow Rich*. Flip Publishing, 2017 (First published, 1937).

Holt, John. *How Children Fail*. Pitman Publishing, 1964, revised edition Delacorte 1982 3rd ed, Perseus, 1995.

-----*How Children Learn*. Pitman Publishing. 1967; Revised Merloyd Lawrence, 1983.

How A Gap Year Can Prepare You for University. Up with People. January 2018, Accessed March 2018. https://upwithpeople.org/uwp-blog/gap-year-can-prepare-university/.

How to Save Money for College—Accessed June 2017www.savingforcollege.com.

How Will I Afford College? College and Career: ElfGutz. 2015. Accessed June 2017. https://quizlet.com/86973092/college-and-career-preparation-how-will-i-afford-college.

Howell, William G. Education Next. Fall. *Results of Presidents Obama's Race to the Top.* 2015. Accessed April 2019. www.educationnext. org/results-president-obama-race-to-the-top-reform.

Hudson, Michael. *Public Speaking Secrets...52 Proven Ways to Increase Your Impact Every Time You Speak.* CreateSpace Independent Publishing Platform, July 2016.

Huran Report. *Immigration and the Chinese.* July 2015.

Iyer, Ravi. *What are the basic foundations of morality?* Your Morals Blog. WordPress: Accessed May 2016. November 2009. www.yourmorals.org/blog/2009/11/what-are-the-basic-foundations-of-morality/.

Jackson, Abby. *Global Competitiveness Report, 2016-2017.* World Economic Forum (WEF). Business Insider. 6 October 2016. Accessed June 2018 www.businessinsider.com.au/world-economic-forum-report-on-us-competitiveness-2016-10.

James, William. *The Principles of Psychology,* 1890.

Jensen, Eric. *You Can Succeed; The Ultimate Study Guide for Students.* Barron's Educational Series, 1979.

Johnson, Sharon. *Facts for Families.* Harris Interactive for the American Psychological Association on Stress. Published in U.S.A. Today, February 2014.

Journal of Computer Assisted Learning (Volume 27, Issue 1). *Mobile technology and literacy: effects across cultures, abilities, and the lifespan,* February 2011.

Kamenetz, Anya. *Testing: How Much Is Too Much?* NPR Ed. Nov.17, 2014. Accessed March 2019. www.npr.org/sections/ed/2014/11/17/362339421/testing-how-much-is-too-much.

Kantrowitz, Mark. *529 Education Savings Plans*. Bottom Line Personal. Volume 40, Number 14, August 15, 2019.

Kelly, Gerard. *"Short-Cut Math."* Courier Corporation, 1969.

King, Daniel, and Delfabbro, Paul. *Internet Gaming Disorder Treatment: A Review of Definitions of Diagnosis and Treatment Outcome.* Journal of Clinical Psychology. Volume70, Issue10. October 2014. Accessed January 2018. https://doi.org/10.1002/jclp.22097.

Kipling, Rudyard. Poem, "If." First published in *Rewards and Faries* circa 1895.

Kiplinger's Personal Finance. July 2016 edition. Accessed June 2017. www.zinio.com/kiplinger-s-personal-finance/july-2016-

Lazarin, Melissa. *Testing Overload in America's Schools.* Center for American Progress. October 16, 2015. Accessed May 2018. www.bing.com/search?q=testing+overload+in+america%E2%80%99s+schoolsby+mela+laza

LD On-Line. *The Importance of Teaching Handwriting.* Accessed May 2015, www.ldonline.org/spearswerling/.

Leider, Richard J. *The Power of Purpose.* Berrett-Koehler Publishers, 1997.

Leman, Kevin. *Have a New Kid by Friday.* Baker Publishing, 2008.

Lester, James D., and Lester James D. Jr. *The Essential Guide for Writing Across the Disciplines, 2 ed.* Addison Wesley Educational Publishers, 2002.

Liberal OC. *Teacher performance should not be measured by a series of multiple-choice questions,* February 2010.

List of Nobel laureates by country. Accessed May 2018.Wikipedia. wikipedia.org/wihi/list of NobelLaureatesbycountry.

Logan, Arthur. *Remembering Made Easy.* Areo Publishing, 1981.

London, R. A., Westrich, L., Stokes-Guinan, K., and McLaughlin, M., 2015. *Playing Fair: The Contribution of High-Functioning Recess to Overall School Climate in Low-Income Elementary Schools.* Journal of School Health, 85: 53–60. doi: 10.1111/ josh.12216.

Lowe, Tamara. *Get Motivated.* Doubleday, 2009.

Lozanov, Georgi. and Gateva, Evalina. *The Foreign Language Teacher's Suggestopedic.* Routledge,1988.

Lumina Foundation. *Americas Call for Higher Education.* Foundation of American Public Opinion on Higher Education, 2013.

Luna, Beatrice. Professor of Psychiatry and Pediatrics and Director of the Laboratory for Neurocognitive Development. Accessed Dec 2016. https://psychology.pitt.edu/people/beatriz-luna-phd.

Lynum, Edward, and Bowers, Ellen. *The Everything Parents Guide to Teenage Addiction.* Adams media, 2014.

MacArthur Study Bible. Scripture taken from the *New King James Version (NKJV)*, Thomas Nelson, Inc. 1979, 1980, 1982. Used by permission.

Madeline Levine, Jim Lobdell, and Denise Pope. *Challenge Success. Strategies for Student Well Being and Engagement with Learning.* Accessed May 2018. www.challengesuccess.org/..

Mansell, Warwick. *Hidden Tigers: why do Chinese children do so well at school?* The Guardian, February 2011.

Marshall, David. *The Truth Behind the New Atheism.* Harvest Hous,. 2007.

Mathnasium, The Math Learning Center. 21st Century Learning. Accessed March 2017, www.mathnasium.com/carmelvalley/

Matrix Blog. Accessed February 2019. https://www.matrix.edu. au/coping-with-stress-how-maintain-your-mental-health-during-hsc/

Mayo Clinic Newsletter. *Stress Relief.* April 23, 2016. Accessed August 2016, www.mayoclinic.org/healthy-lifestyle/stress-management/ in-depth/stress-relief/art.

McKay, Mathew. Davis, Martha. Fanning, Patrick. *Thoughts and Feelings: Taking Control of Your Moods and Your Life.* New Harbinger Publications. 3rd Ed., 2007.

-----*Messages, The Communications Skills Book.* New Harbinger Publications, 1995.

Mehrabian, Albert. *Silent Messages,* Wadsworth. 1981.

Miech, R.A., Bachman, J. G., and Schulenberg, J. E. *Monitoring the Future: National Survey Results on Drug Use,* 1975-2016: The National Institute on Drug Abuse at The National Institutes of Health, Institute for Social Research, The University of Michigan, 2017. Accessed December 21, 2017. www.monitoringthefuture. org/pubs/monographs/mtf-overview2016.pdf.

Mindell JA and Owens JA. *A Clinical Guide to Pediatric Sleep: Diagnosis and Management of Sleep Problems.* Lippincott Williams and Wilkins, 2015.

Minirth, Frank, and Meier, Paul. *Happiness is a Choice.* Baker Books. *1978, 1994, 2007, 2013.*

Miracles of Faith. Time /Life Special Edition. January 2019.

Mitchell, Michael. Leachman, Michael. Masterson, Kathleen. Center on Budget and Policy Priorities. *A Lost Decade in Higher Education Funding: State Cuts Have Driven Up Tuition and Reduced Quality*, August 2017.

Miyazaki, Yoshifumi, et al. *Psychological benefits of walking through forest areas.* International Journal of Environmental Research and Public Health, 15(12), 2804.2018. Accessed Dec 2018. *www. mdpi.com/.*

Mokdad, A. H., Marks, J. S., Stroup, D. F., and Gerberding, J. L. *Actual causes of death in the United States.* Journal of the American Medical Association, 2004.

Moore, Linda. *The Everything Parent's Guide to Children with Special Needs.* Adams Media, 2009.

National Assessment of Educational Progress. *Mapping State Proficiency Standards.* May 2018, Accessed June 2018. https:// nces.ed.gov/nationsreportcard/studies/statemapping/

National Association of Colleges and Employers NACE). www. naceweb.org/ Accessed May 2015.

National Center for Chronic Disease Prevention and Health Promotion. Office on Smoking and Health *Smoking and tobacco use: Tobacco industry marketing.* 2015. Accessed February 12, 2016,// www.cdc.gov/tobacco/data_statistics/fact_sheets/tobacco _industry/marketing/

National Center for Education Statistics. *Graduation Rates for Selected Cohorts, 2009-14; Outcome Measures for Cohort Year 2009-10; Student Financial Aid, Academic Year 2016-17; and*

Admissions in Postsecondary Institutions, Fall 2017 (Provisional Data). U.S. Government Printing Office, 2018.

National Center for Fair and Open Testing-Fair Test. fairtest.org. Accessed June 2018.

National Institute of Drug Abuse (NIDA) *E-Cigarette Use Among Youth and Young Adults: A Report of the Surgeon General,* 2016.

National Institute of Health. *Become Smoke-Free.* "smokefree. gov." Accessed August 2018. https://teen.smokefree.gov/ become-smokefree/tools-for-quitting.

National Survey of Student Engagement (NSSE). Accessed May 2018. http://nsse.indiana.edu/.

Nightingale, Earl. *Lead the Field.* Simon Schuster Audio/Nightingale-Conant, a CBS Company: 2002. (first published January1976).

-----*Acres of Diamonds.* Amazon Digital Services LLC. Audio. 2012. (first published October 11th, 2010).

-----*The Strangest Secret.* Simon Schuster Audio/Nightingale-Conant, a CBS Company. 1986. (first published January 1976).

Opioid Deaths: Worst Epidemic in U.S. History. Democracy Now. June 2017. Accessed September 2017. www.democracynow. org/2017/6/7/

Olney, Claude W. *Where There's a Will, There's an A.* American Educational Publishers, Inc. 1988.

Peal, Norman Vincent. *The Power of Positive Thinking.* Fireside Books: 2007. First published by Simon and Schuster, 1952.

Pelzer, Dave. *Help Yourself. Finding Hope, Courage and Happiness.* PLUME, 2000.

Pennsylvania Department of Education, Bureau of Special Education. *Parent Guide to Special Education.*

Peters, Ruth. *Laying Down the Law, the 23 Laws of Parenting.* New York, NY, Rodale, 2002.

Poley, Michelle F. *A Winning Attitude.* SkillPath Publications, 1992.

Popkin, Michael. *"Taming the Spirited Child."* Fireside, 2007.

Preventing YouthTobacco Use. A Report of the Surgeon General. 2012. Accessed July 12, 2016. www.surgeongeneral.gov/library/ reports/preventing-youth-tobacco-use/.

Prochaska, James. Norcross, John. Diclemente, Carol. *Changing for Good,* Harper Collins,1994.

Pullman, Joy. The Federalist. *Bill Gates Tacitly Admits His Common Core Experiment was a Failure.* October 2017. https:// thefederalist.com/2017/10/25/bill-gates-tacitly-admits-common- core-experiment-failure/ *Accessed May 2019.*

Purdue University Online Writing Lab. *Is It Plagiarism Yet?* February 2008, library.csusm.edu/plagiarism/howtoavoid/how avoid common.htm

Radencich, Marguerite C., Schumm, Jeanne S. *How to Help Your Child with Homework.* Free Spirit Publishing, Inc., 1997.

Record Student Debt Spurring Employers to Offer Student Loan Repayment Benefits. Consumer Financial Protection Bureau, August 2017.

Resnick, Michael et. al. *Protecting adolescents from harm: Findings from the National Longitudinal Study on Adolescent Health.* Journal of the American Medical Association, Scientific Research 1997..scirp.org/reference/ReferencesPapers.aspx? ReferenceID=788343

Restak, Richard. *The New Brain: How the Modern Age is Rewiring Your Brain.* Rodale, 2004.

Rettew, Bill Jr., *Keystone Exams Get a Failing Grade.* Avon Grove Sun, Southern Chester County News, June 2017.

Roberts, Dexter. Bloomburg Business. *China Exam System Drives Student Suicides,* May 2014.

Rose, Charlie of CBS News "60 Minutes," interview of Tim Cook, CEO of Apple. 2015.

Ruder, Debra B. *The Teen Brain.* Harvard Magazine, Sept/Oct 2008.

Russell, Christopher. *The Battle of Turkey Thicket: A True Story.* Baritone Books, 2017.

Sagan, Carl. *The Demon-Haunted World: Science as a Candle in the Dark.* Ballantine Books, 1995, 1997

Sahlberg, Pasi. *Finnish Lessons. 2.0.* Teacher's College Press., November 2014.

Scheele, Paul R. *Natural Brilliance: Overcome any challenge...at will.* 2nd Ed. Learning Strategies Corp., 2000.

Schliecher, Andreas. Organisation for Economic Co-operation and Development(OECD). Accessed May 2016. qz.com/1074113/ oecd-2017-report-america-is-slowly-sucking-the-life-out-of-education-starting-with-its-teachers/. Accessed May 2018.

Schwartz, Eugene. *How to Double Your Child's Grades in School.* Barnes and Noble, 1997.

Sears, William and Martha. *The Discipline Book.* Little Brown and Co., 1995.

Sheffield, Betty. *Handwriting: A neglected cornerstone of literacy.* Published in Annals of Dyslexia, January 1996, Volume 48, Issue 1. https://link.springer.com/article/10.1007/BF02648169.

Sifferlin, Alexandra. *The Healing Power of Nature.* Time Magazine, July 2017.

Silk, Danny. *Loving Our Kids on Purpose.* Destiny Imaging Publishers, 2008. www.lovingonpurpose.com. Accessed Oct. 2018.

Stanley, Charles. *Finding Peace: God's Promise of a Life Free from Regret, Anxiety, and Fear.*

Thomas Nelson, 2003.

Stephenson, Sean. *How You Can Succeed: Transforming Dreams Into Reality for Young Adults.* S C S Publishing, 2000.

-----with Robbins, Tony. *Get Off Your Buts-How to End Self-Sabotage and Stand Up For Yourself.* Jossey-Bass: 2009.

Strauss, Valorie. *Five reasons why standardized testing isn't likely to be let up.* Washington Post. March 2015. www.washingtonpost.com/news/answer-sheet/wp/2015/03/11/five-reasons-standardized-testing-isnt-likely-to-let-up/. Accessed May 2018.

-----*Race to the Top isn't delivering big results.* Washington Post,12 September 2013.

Surgeon General. National Institute of Drug Abuse Surgeon General report: *E-Cigarette Use Among Youth and Young Adults.* 2016. Accessed June 2017.

Teen Mobile Report Calling Yestewrsdy, Testing Today, Using Apps Tomorrow. Nielson Corp. Nielson.Com/U.S. /En/Insights/ News/2010/U-S-Teen-Mobile-Report-Calling-Yesterday-Texting-Today-Using-App-Tomorrow. Oct 2010. Accessed July 2017

Testimony on the Federal Response to the Opioid Crises, Witnesses from the Department of Health and Human Services (HHS) appearing before Senate Health, Education, Labor and Pensions (HELP) Committee. October 2015.

The American Gap Association (AGA). Portland, Oregon nonprofitlocator.org/organizations/or/portland/455138030-american-gap-association. Accessed February 2018.

The Conversation.*Crisis in American education as teacher morale hits an all-time low. 7 April 2015.*

Thompson, Bradley. *Razor Sharp Focus.* Self Help Street.com *www. selfhelpstreet.com/selfhelp/*

Titmuss, Christopher. *Mindfulness for Everyday Living.* Bridgewater Book, Co., 2003.

Tolle, Eckart. *The Power of Now, a Guide to Spiritual Enlightenment.* Namaste Publishing, 1999.

Turkington, Carol and Harris, Joseph R. *The A to Z of Learning Disabilities.* Checkmark Books, 2006.

Tymon Cy. *Sneaky Math: A Graphics Primer with Projects.* Andrews McMeel Publishing, LL, Dec 2014.

U.S. CensusBureau. *Early Childhood Longitudinal Study - Kindergarten Class of 1998-99.* Statistical Analysis Report Center on Education Statistics, Fall 1998. February 2000, https://nces.ed.gov/pubs2000/2000070. pdf.

-----*Language Use in the United States.* **Report Number ACS-22. August 2013.**

U. S. Department of Education. Office of Federal Student Aid. *Student Financial Aid Handbook* https://ifap.ed.gov/ifap/index.jsp.

U.S. Department of Health and Human Services. Centers for Disease Control and Prevention, Office on Smoking. *The Health Consequences of Smoking—50 Years of Progress: A Report of the Surgeon General.* 2012. www.surgeongeneral.gov/library/reports/50-years-of-progress/full-report.pdf - PDF. Accessed June 3, 2017.

U.S. Department of Health and Human Services, National Institutes of Health. *Autism Spectrum Disorders*, 2007.

-----*Dietary Guidelines for Americans.* 2015-2020.

Van der Kolk, Bessel A.*The Body Keeps the Score: Brain, Mind, and Body in the Healing of Trauma.* Viking, September 2014.

Vasterling, Jennifer, et al. *Can Videogames Be Good for Your Health?* Journal of Health Psychology. SAGE Publications, *2004.*

Waber D. et al. *The NIH MRI Study of Normal Brain Development: Performance of a Population Based Sample of Healthy Children Aged 6 to 18 Years on a Neuropsychological Battery.* Journal of the International Neuropsychological Society. Vol. pp. 1-18. 2007.

Wagner, Tony and Dintersmith, Ted. *Most Likely to Succeed, Preparing Your Kids for the Innovative Era.* SCRIBNER. 2015.

Wait, Marianne. *Recreational Drugs: 3 New Threats to Know About.* www.webmd.com/parenting/features/recreational-drugs-threats_#1. Accessed May 2018.

Warren, Rick. *The Purpose Driven Life.* Zondervan, 2002.

WebMD. *Know the Facts and Risks.* www.webmd.com/ mental-health/addiction/street-drugs-risks#1. Accessed July 2018.

Wenger, Win. and Scheele, Paul R. *GeniusCode: Guiding You Into the Realm of Genius*2002. See also "Learning Strategies" by Paul R. Scheele.

Why China is Beating the U.S. at Innovation. U.S.A. Today. Boston Consulting Group report. April 17, 2017 edition.

Wikipedia. Nobel Laureates by Country. wikipedia.org/wihi/list of Nobel Laureates by country. Accessed May 2019.

Wikipedia. Race to the Top. May 13, 2019. Accessed May 2019. https://en.wikipedia.org/wiki/Race_to_the_Top.

Wilde, Jerry. *Treating Anger, Anxiety, and Depression in Children and Adolescents.* Accelerated Development. 1996

World Health Organization (W.H.O.). *Gaming Disorder.* Geneva, Switzerland. Accessed Sept. 2018. www.who.int/features/qa/ gaming-disorder/en/

Wright, Norman H. *How to Speak Spouse's Language.* Hachette Book Group, 2006.

Xie, Yu; Zhang, Chunni; Lai, Qing. *Chinas Rise as a Major Contributor to Science and Technology.* Proceedings of the National Academy of Sciences, Vol. 111, No. 26. July 2014.

Yefu, Zheng. *The Pathology of Chinese Education.* Accessed April 2017. www.chinaisgood.com/wn/638/gxaemhvg.html

Zhao, Yong. *Who's Afraid of the Big Bad Dragon? Why China Has the Best (and Worst) Education System in the World.* John Wiley and Sons, 2014.

Zong, Jie and Batalova, Jeanne. *International Students in the United States.* Migration Policy Institute, citing the Institute of International Education, May 2018.

Printed in the United States
By Bookmasters